new decorating book

Meredith® Books
Des Moines, Iowa

Better Homes and Gardens® new decorating book

Editor: Paula Marshall
Associate Design Director: Erin Burns
Contributing Project Manager: Jean Schissel Norman
Contributing Researcher: Cathy Long
Contributing Graphic Designer: Brad Ruppert
Copy Chief: Terri Fredrickson
Copy Editor: Kevin Cox
Publishing Operations Manager: Karen Schirm
Senior Editor, Asset & Information Management: Phillip Morgan
Edit and Design Production Coordinator: Mary Lee Gavin
Editorial Assistant: Kaye Chabot
Book Production Managers: Pam Kvitne, Marjorie J. Schenkelberg, Rick von Holdt, Mark Weaver
Imaging Center Operator: Trena J Rickels
Contributing Copy Editor: Jane A. Woychick
Contributing Proofreaders: Julie Cahalan, Sue Fetters, Nancy Ruhlin, Lida Stitchfield
Cover Photographers: front, upper row: Michael Garland (left), Kim Cornelison (right); lower row: Greg Scheidemann (left) Kim Cornelison (right); back cover: Jay Wilde
Contributing Photographers: Gordon Beall, Kim Cornelison, Jay Wilde
Contributing Indexer: Stephanie Rymann, Indexing Solutions, Inc.
Contributing Illustrator: Lori Gould

Meredith® Books
Editor in Chief: Gregory H. Kayko
Executive Director, Design: Matt Strelecki
Managing Editor: Amy Tincher-Durik
Executive Editor: Benjamin W. Allen
Senior Editor/Group Manager: Vicki Leigh Ingham
Senior Associate Design Director: Mick Schnepf
Marketing Product Manager: Brent Wiersma

Editorial Director: Linda Raglan Cunningham
Executive Director, Marketing: Kevin Kacere
Executive Director, New Business Development: Todd M. Davis
Executive Director, Sales: Ken Zagor
Director, Operations: George A. Susral
Director, Production: Douglas M. Johnston
Director, Marketing & Publicity: Amy Nichols
Business Director: Jim Leonard

Vice President and General Manager: Douglas J. Guendel

***Better Homes and Gardens®* Magazine**
Editor in Chief: Gayle Goodson Butler
Deputy Editor, Home Design: Oma Blaise Ford

Meredith Publishing Group
President: Jack Griffin
Senior Vice President: Karla Jeffries

Meredith Corporation
Chairman of the Board: William T. Kerr
President and Chief Executive Officer: Stephen M. Lacy

In Memoriam: E.T. Meredith III (1933–2003)

Ninth Edition.

Printed in the United States of America.
Library of Congress Control Number: 2007921762
Tradepaper ISBN: 978-0-696-23299-2
Hardcover ISBN: 978-0-696-23847-5

All of us at Meredith® Books are dedicated to providing you with information and ideas to enhance your home. We welcome your comments and suggestions. Write to us at: Meredith Books, Home Decorating and Design Editorial Department, 1716 Locust St., Des Moines, IA 50309-3023.

It's a popular word today and we at Meredith Books made it the watchword behind the 9th edition of *Better Homes and Gardens® New Decorating Book*. We streamlined the presentation of home decorating so you can get straight to what you want to know. Then we organized information in a way you can easily access whether you have just a few minutes to peruse a topic or an hour to go indepth to learn a design principle. All through the book you'll find as many photos and illustrations as the pages could hold because in home decorating nothing is more inspirational and teaches more effectively than good images.

Begin with the design basics that will guide your decorating experiences—and help you make smart choices when you begin creating rooms of your own. Explore ideas for every room and learn to design spaces that will function well for you and your family. Take house tours to see how good design works best with a cohesive plan for every room in a home. And finally find savvy solutions to some of the tricky problems every home designer encounters.

Throughout the book, these features make decorating information easy to grasp at a glance—design simplified!

Before-and-After Makeovers: From pieces of furniture to rooms to whole houses, see transformations from the mundane to the magnificent.

Quick Palettes: Ideas for creating personalized color schemes from the hues that appeal most to you for every room in the house.

Worth Noting: Key points and finer details of creating a great room design are called out in these "circles of knowledge" scattered throughout the chapters. Think of them as 30-second decorating lessons.

Tip Columns: Hit lists of decorating how-tos, these columns take you point by point through such things as mixing patterns, using white in a room, and taking into account certain features when buying upholstered furniture.

1 Room 2 Ways: Tweak your rooms and satisfy your need for change with these ideas for swapping out a few pieces to create a whole new look without a major redo.

Floor Plans: These bird's-eye views of a room show you how, when furniture pieces play well together, a room makes for pleasant conversation, a good night's sleep, or meals to remember.

Quick Projects: At the end of most chapters, we've included a fast-and-easy creative outlet to help you add personal style. Learn to make simple slipcovers, sumptuous pillows, and snappy office gear.

Discover Your Style

Design Basics

Room by Room

House Tours

Style Solutions

Discover Your Style

Uncover your inner decorator, analyze your home.

Learn the secrets that will unlock your personal style and help you incorporate what you love into a house that suits you perfectly.

TOP

Your style

for a perfect beginning

You might feel lost when you try to plan your home decor. Look around—your style clues are everywhere. Which colors and styles do you love to wear? Look in your jewelry box, purse, or closet. Do you dress for casual comfort or love to dress up in elegant style? What colors make you happy, content, serene, or energized? Do you love bold patterns and strong color contrast or are you drawn to classic patterns and time-tested color schemes? Notice which stores inspire your style. True personal style reflects your changing life experience: What you like now is based on past experiences. What you'll like in the future is based on the look you're building now. The only caveat: Be honest about what you really love.

in this section

To discover what you really like,

start by gathering objects, colors, and patterns that draw you in or elicit a strong positive response. The objects you collect could include a leaf gathered on a walk, a photo pulled from a magazine, a paint chip or fabric sample, a vintage button, pages from decorating books or magazines, or a funny greeting card. Keep your options open and leave the editing for later. Right now you're in the business of uncovering the style that's personally yours.

As you gather the objects, pin them to a bulletin board. If you're short on space, consider the back of a closet door or a large piece of foam-core board that slips under your bed. Clip, pin, or tape the

brights

Lessons from this style board: Bright color reigns, white provides visual rest, and bold shapes invite notice. Home decor inspired by this style board is likely to be white and bright with pops of color introduced in graphic shapes and patterns. The overall look is streamlined, hip, and fun.

items; stand back and observe. As your style board develops, eliminate those objects that no longer feel quite right. Continue the process until you fill your bulletin board.

What does your style board say about you? Look for consistent elements such as colors, shapes, patterns, textures, and scale, that turn up again and again. Study the mood of the objects you collected. Are they romantic, playful, creative, classic, rich, simple, graphic, or serene? Ask a few friends to interpret your style board.

Turn the page for more exercises to help you discover your style.

neutrals

Lessons from this style board: Neutrals ground the look, rich reds inject color, and overscale pieces add drama. This style board suggests richly appointed interiors and classic style. Unexpected accents, such as a huge Chinese lantern, play against neutral colors and touch-me textures. Elements from nature complete the look.

What's your answer?

Continue the process of discovering your style by answering these questions. There are no right or wrong answers. Also consider the questions that begin each chapter. Keep a list of your responses to help your style story unfold.

Displayed on your walls you have:
- several framed pictures of family and friends
- only one or two items
- items that follow a theme (chickens, apples, etc.)
- original art pieces by people you know

Your kitchen counter is usually:
- very clean—you can't stand to have anything out
- cluttered—a display of old cookie jars and cookbooks
- congested—full of random kitchen gadgets and a TV
- covered in dirty dishes

What item is most prevalent in your home?
- books and magazines
- baskets and candles
- photographs
- clutter

One item you would bring back from a trip is:
- a stack of pictures
- a good tan
- a souvenir sweatshirt
- a one-of-a-kind piece of local art

What's your favorite color scheme?
- neutral—beige, black, and white
- warm—reds and yellows
- cool—blues and greens
- a variety of color schemes

What trait do you value most in your home?
- creative influence
- aesthetic value and style
- physical comfort
- emotional sanctuary

When you shop for decorative objects for the house:
- anything goes—if you like it you buy it
- it's erratic—depends on timing and finances
- it's hectic—you would rather pick from only a few selections
- it's slow and deliberate—you search for the right thing

If you had a bit of extra money, you would:
- buy new expensive bedding just for you
- buy whatever strikes you in the first store you see
- treat yourself to a small cappuccino and put the rest away in a savings account
- go on a trip

1

2

1. Are you attracted to a variety of styles, finding something you like about each? Use this book to learn how to create an eclectic style that incorporates a range of looks without its feeling fractured.

2. Do you return from a shopping trip with a purse filled with swatches and paint chips? You're having trouble honing in on one look. Give each of the looks a name and group your swatches and paint colors under the look they match. Compare the elements collected to the style board you created. Which look most closely supports your decorating dreams?

3. No matter how hard you try to branch out, do you always return with a shopping bag full of one color, one pattern, or one look? Embrace it. If a single color or pattern exerts a strong emotional pull, it's sure to provide the foundation for a look that's right for you.

Your house

for style inside the box

chapter 2

You fell in love with a house and bought it or you put a down payment on a house that fit your budget rather than your dreams. Maybe you've lived in the house for a while and now it's hopelessly out of date. No matter; you have a universe of decorating styles and materials to select from and your real life house to redo. Consider these questions: How big is the house? Does it have a strong architectural style that might dictate the look, or is the style so plain that almost anything will work? Do you have small children, teenagers, or only adults at home? Are you ready to jump in and start decorating? All successful projects start with a plan. Here's how to create yours.

in this section

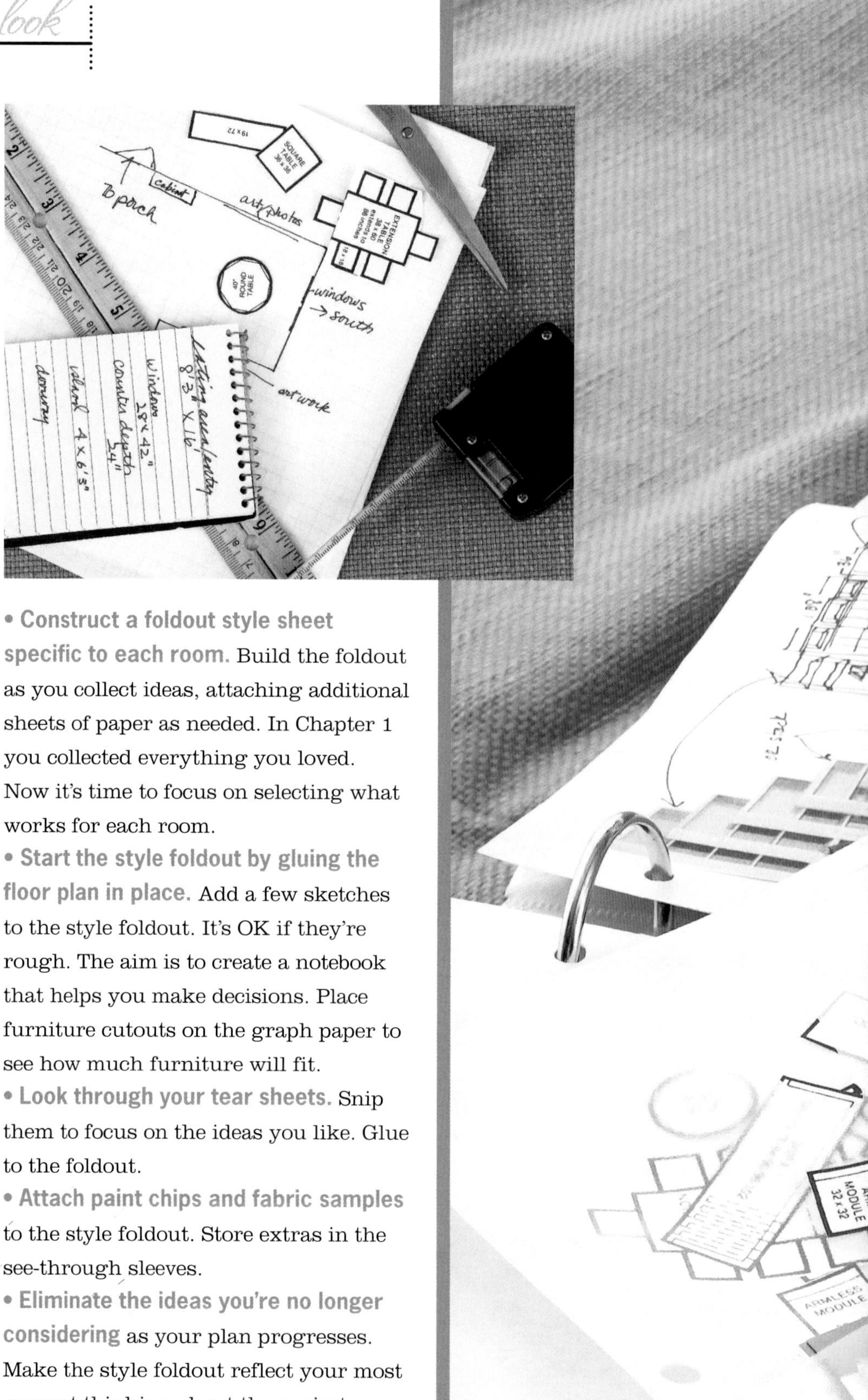

Now is the time

to work with restrictions—the size and style of your house, the ages of family members, your needs for space, and your budget. Start by creating a decorating notebook. It will keep you focused and on budget. Actual room sizes and real budget figures might necessitate a scaled-down version of your plan. That's OK. Stylish homes and rooms created on modest budgets appear throughout this book.

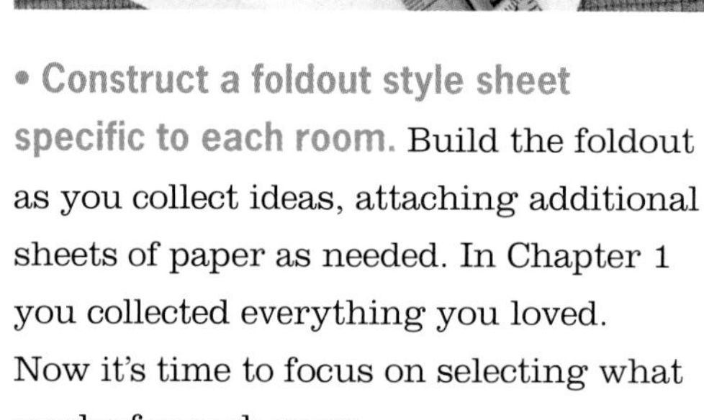

Begin a decorating notebook

- **Start by gathering these supplies:** three-ring binder, CD sleeves to hold paint chips and furniture templates, clear binder envelopes to hold fabric samples, graph paper, measuring tape, ruler, pencil, marking pen, and scissors.
- **Take snapshots of all rooms.** Store the snapshots in a plastic CD sleeve that attaches to a three-ring binder.
- **Measure each room.** Transfer the measurements to graph paper, noting the locations of doorways, windows, recessed lighting, electrical outlets, fixtures, and built-ins. Sketch a floor plan for each room.
- **Copy furniture templates.** See page 423 for the templates. Check that the scale of the copies fits the graph paper. Cut out the shapes; put them in a binder.

Build the notebook

- **Transfer copies or tear sheets from your style bulletin board.** Make a section for each room.
- **Construct a foldout style sheet specific to each room.** Build the foldout as you collect ideas, attaching additional sheets of paper as needed. In Chapter 1 you collected everything you loved. Now it's time to focus on selecting what works for each room.
- **Start the style foldout by gluing the floor plan in place.** Add a few sketches to the style foldout. It's OK if they're rough. The aim is to create a notebook that helps you make decisions. Place furniture cutouts on the graph paper to see how much furniture will fit.
- **Look through your tear sheets.** Snip them to focus on the ideas you like. Glue to the foldout.
- **Attach paint chips and fabric samples** to the style foldout. Store extras in the see-through sleeves.
- **Eliminate the ideas you're no longer considering** as your plan progresses. Make the style foldout reflect your most current thinking about the project.

LOVE SEAT
34 x 50-55-60
OTTOMAN
COLOR TV
20 x 42
PIANO
60 x 54
CKTAIL TABLE
32 x 66
louisburg green
b gray
TO ENTRY
throw or pillow
window seat
• add cushion pillows

Real life style foldouts

show various ways to address decorating decisions. Foldouts are valuable because they help mesh your style with the house you have. Learn how the decorating notebook works; then adopt the exercises and strategies that are most helpful to you. Here are 10 to consider.

1. Start sketching. Even if your sketch is rough, it can help you visualize what you want. It's also a good tool to use when trying to explain your ideas to someone else. If you prefer take a photo of the area, copy the photo onto paper, and sketch on top of the photo to help visualize how it will look.

2. Measure and plan. Floor plans drawn to scale on graph paper add a dose of reality. Measurements facilitate choices, leaving no doubt whether something will fit.

3. Cut templates. Furniture cutouts let you see how well furniture will fit in a room. They also let you move your furniture around without heavy lifting. Is there really room for an overstuffed sofa? Will that nightstand block the window? Will a wall of bookcases still leave room for traffic? Cutouts will answer these questions.

4. Gather color samples. Paint chips and fabric samples offer accurate color matching. Include them on the style foldout and carry a second set with you as you shop.

5. Clip tear sheets. Big-idea tear sheets (pages torn from magazines and catalogs) are another tool to use to explain your ideas to someone else. Write notes and sketch on the tear sheets.

6. Gather photos of details. It's important to keep in mind where you're starting and what you want for the finished

effect. Details fill rooms with personal style. They should be considered along with paint color and fabrics.

7. Make budget notes. In a few months it might be hard to remember a price when your head is swimming with details. Keep a budget sheet in your decorating notebook.

8. Brainstorm in writing. Add notes that serve as a to-do list for the project. Express questions and concerns. Unanswered questions should lead to more research and thought.

9. Cluster ideas to develop a look. For example, combine cabinet ideas, faucet models, paint chips, and appliance choices in the kitchen section of a style foldout.

10. Live with the style foldouts. Pin them to a bulletin board or keep them handy on a desk. Constantly referring to them will imprint your ideas and make it easy to spot the perfect elements when you're shopping.

Design Basics

Think like a decorator. Take this section's decorating short course complete with basic lessons and no-fail solutions. Discover how design professionals use color, texture, pattern, balance, and more.

Color for today's freshest style

Color has the power to rev up a decorating scheme or calm it down. The choice depends on the room and the hues you crave. Start with these questions: Which colors do you wear? If you piled favorite objects on a table, which tones would tumble out? Are your rooms predictably neutral? Do you want fabrics and furnishings to change with each season? Do you adore color everywhere—bold primaries, pastels, or one fabulous green? If the neighbors wouldn't question your sanity, which color would dominate your living room? Which hues make you happy, relaxed, at peace? You loved that new box of crayons as a kid. It's time to play with color again.

in this section

Color happens

when light falls on an object and reflects light waves of a certain length, say those of blue, and absorbs the rest. Red has the longest wavelength, and violet has the shortest. The progression of color from longest to shortest wavelengths appears on the traditional color wheel of 12 hues: three primary colors, three secondary colors, and six tertiary colors.

Color relationships built on these groups of hues form the basis of color theory. Any combo can work successfully. If you understand the color wheel and some theory, you'll have all the more fun playing with color.

primary colors

Red, blue, and yellow are the primary hues. These colors are pure, not blends made from other hues. All other colors are created from primary colors.

secondary colors

Orange, green, and violet are secondary hues. They are formed when equal parts of two primary colors are combined. Yellow and blue yield green; yellow and red make orange.

tertiary colors

Mixing a primary color with the secondary color next to it creates a tertiary color. With each blending, the resulting hues become less vivid. Yellow and green blend to make apple green.

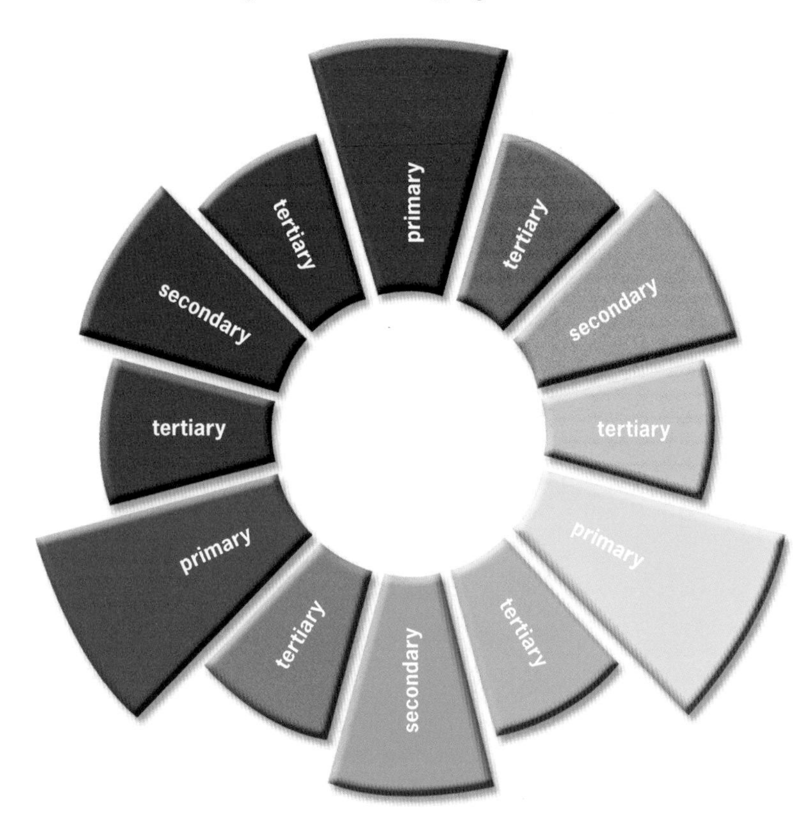

primary colors

secondary colors

tertiary colors

neutral colors

These "uncolors"—browns, beiges, grays, whites, black, and taupes—combine and cooperate, bridging different colors. Darker neutrals calm down other colors, while light neutrals intensify them.

color lingo

Learn these basic terms to help understand color conversations.

- **Hue** is another word for color. It's most often used to identify a specific color, such as apple green, robin's egg blue, or tangerine. Hues are affected by natural light, artificial light, reflections of trees and buildings, nearby colors, and even the paint sheen.
- **Value** is the lightness or darkness of color. Sky blue is a light value; cobalt is a dark value. Paint chip cards typically have light and dark variations of one color. For delineation, choose colors separated by at least one chip on a paint card.
- **Intensity** refers to color saturation and specifies clearness or brightness. Adding white, black, or a complementary color to a pure color diminishes its intensity.
- **Shade** is a color with black added to it. For example, navy is a shade of primary blue. Look for shades at both ends of paint cards. Pale gray blue is a light shade while deep olive green is a dark shade.
- **Tint** is a color that has white added to it. For example, pink is a tint of lipstick red. Look for tints at the top of a paint card or in a separate collection of whites.

warm/active

Warm colors seem to come closer while cool colors appear farther away. Designers use these color characteristics to balance rooms and pieces within rooms. Warm colors include yellow, orange, and red. Extroverts, these advancing hues inspire conversation, fuel appetite, wake up a space, and add heat to a north-facing room. Because of their energy they can make a small space or object seem larger. Beware: Active colors can be too energetic for bedrooms, where a restful mood is needed. Consider a shaded hue to balance energy while adding warmth.

Tropical tones of yellow and orange energize a bedroom and add visual tension. Warm hues might give a needed boost to early risers.

A fearless mix of reds and yellows brings drama to a daybed. Place the bed in a neutral space to add spice or surround the bed with even more color to make a color statement. Note that the mix depends upon using strong tones of all hues.

cool/passive

Cool colors—blue, green, and purple—stay quietly in the background, calming and soothing. They're ideal for bedrooms and private retreats. In a cold climate balance these cool hues with a shot of warm color in accessories. Every color has a warm and active side or a cool and passive side. Blending colors can add virtual heat or chill. Green, for instance, can be warmed with the addition of yellow or cooled down with a little blue. Neutrals also have warm and cool tones. Add blue to gray for a cool modern look; add red to gray to suit a classic room.

Soothe a bedroom by pairing sky blue with pristine white. The duo creates a relaxing getaway. In a bedroom always use colors that flatter skin tones.

Blues and greens make soothing cool companions. For energy and interest vary the tones and spread them around in a variety of patterns. For warmth mix in a shade of warm yellow-orange in a single picture mat.

White makes other colors even more vibrant. Here it adds energy to orange curtain panels and makes them the star of the room. To subdue the look select a shade of orange and soften the walls with taupe.

Shades of warm colors deliver richness and stimulation. Use deeper tones for smaller surfaces and as a color punch in accessories. Warm reds can be cooled down when mixed with blue or revved up with an additional shot of yellow.

Lavender and green, both cool hues, set a relaxing mood in a guest bedroom. Add temporary warmth with a bouquet of pink roses or permanent warmth with a pink pillow.

Bold green and aqua blue deliver a one-two punch of color. Mixing colors for a modern look works best when they're close in value. Create a noncompeting background by choosing white for floors, furniture, and accessories.

Every color elicits an emotional response that can be used in decorating. Here's what to know about colors.

- **Blue relaxes,** refreshes, cools, and produces tranquil moods.
- **Red empowers,** stimulates, competes, and dramatizes.
- **Pink soothes** and promotes affection.
- **Green balances,** refreshes, and encourages growth.
- **Purple comforts,** spiritualizes, and creates mystery.
- **Orange cheers,** commands, and stimulates appetites.
- **Yellow energizes,** expands, and brightens.
- **White purifies,** unifies, and enlivens all other colors.
- **Black strengthens** and stabilizes.

Complementary palettes,

noted for their maximum contrast and natural balance, are built using colors directly opposite each other on the color wheel. Complementary colors naturally allow warm and cool hues to play off each other, intensifying each color. Picture a violet flower with its green leaves as an example. For a safe scheme pair complementary colors in the same value: pale lavender and light green or rich orange and bold blue. Be cautious pairing colors of opposite intensities, such as pale blue and electric orange. Let one color star and create visual resting spots with neutrals.

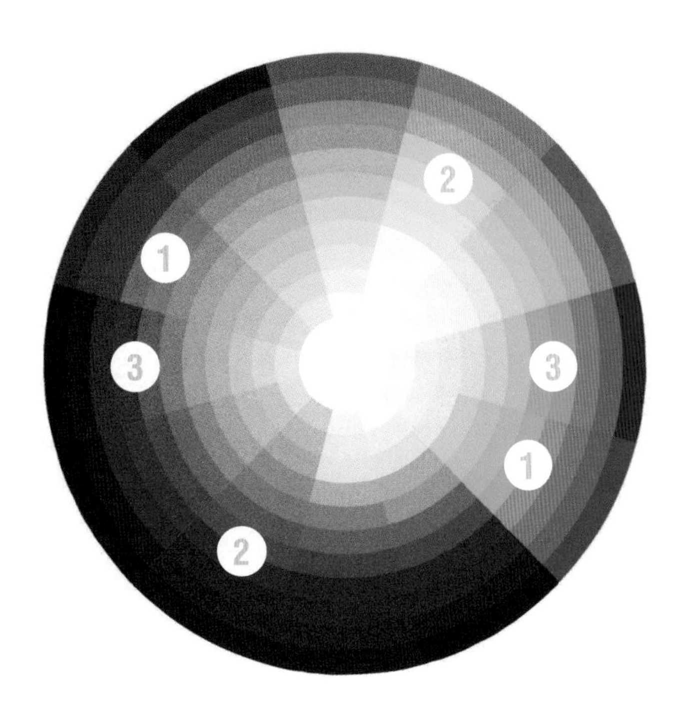

1. Blue-Green + Red-Orange

2. Lavender + Yellow

3. Pink + Green

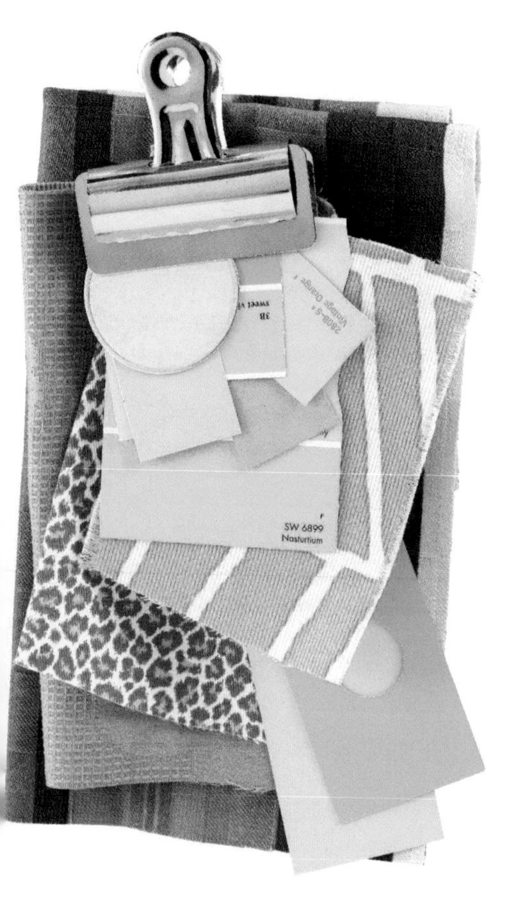

1. Yellow-Green to Orange

2. Yellow-Orange to Red-Orange

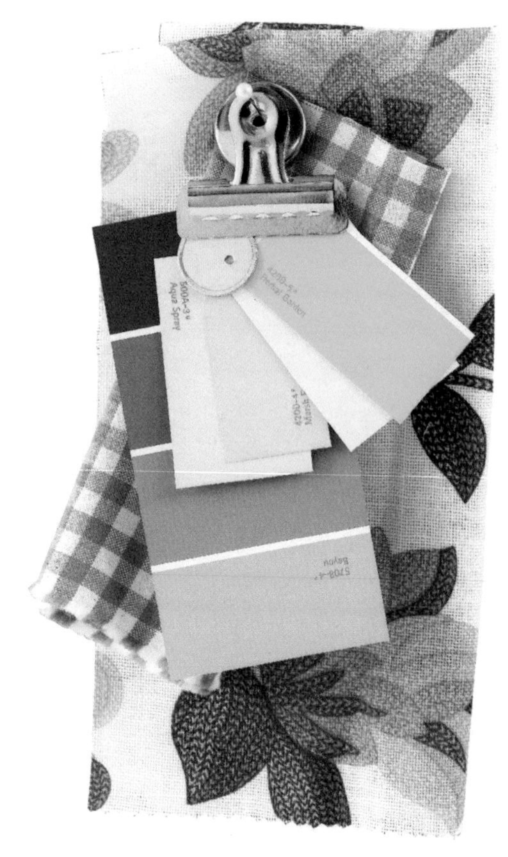

3. Yellow-Green to Blue

Analogous palettes, made from colors that are side by side on the color wheel, create a soothing look. Color wheel neighbors are closely related and easy to use together. Choose a favorite color for the main hue and add two hues; for a lively look, vary the intensities of the supporting colors. Consider, too, creating an analogous scheme that combines warm and cool neighbors, such as yellow, yellow-green, and green. The dominant color—warm or cool—will set the temperature for the palette.

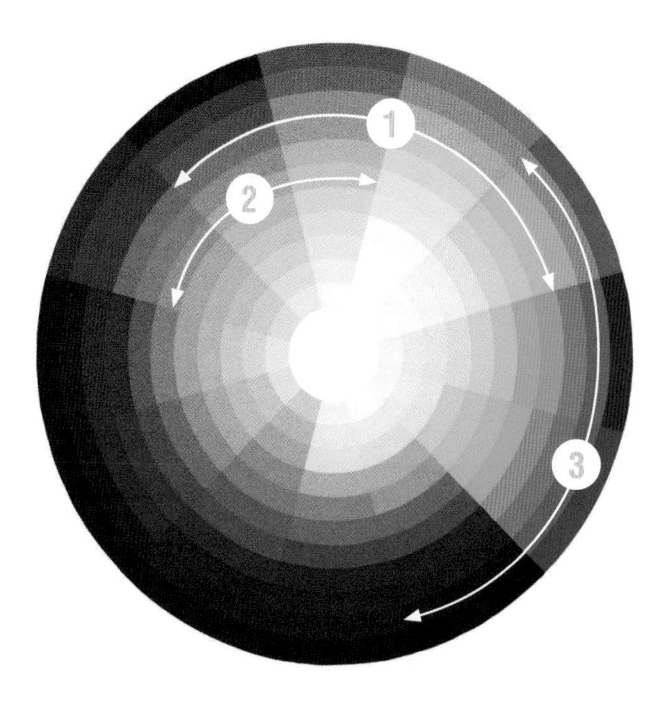

The easiest scheme for a decorating novice is white plus one color. The results are far from boring when you combine various shades of one color such as blue. Imagine a scheme built on white mixed with blues in every range, from tints to shades and warm blues to cool blues. Strong contrasts between lights and darks create energy; subtle variations subdue the mood. White becomes the great unifier.

Once you nail down your favorite color family (a primary print or pattern might lead the way), consider function and what you want the colors to do. Need to make a large space cozy? Choose a dark, saturated shade and apply it to the walls. Need to make a small space feel expansive? Go for lighter tints. Mix it up on furnishings as well using fabrics with dark and light backgrounds.

Opposite: As a rule, blue soothes. A bevy of blues is a different story, full of energy. Mix and match shades and tints to suit your taste.

Above: Cool colors recede and calm. A few tablespoons of apple-green paint give a gallon of white wall paint the look of lime sorbet. Refreshing!

Right: A small dose of hot color—fuchsia, orange, melon, and hot pink—perks up a room. Use bold colors to modernize a vintage chair or add stripes and squares of punchy color to the table and bed.

Here are six no-fail tips for a white-plus-one-color scheme.

- **Create a blank canvas** of white and off-whites for floors, walls, and furniture. It's a serene backdrop for collections and colors. When backgrounds are neutral, colors can change with the seasons.
- **Freely mix warm and cool** whites to ward off boredom and to stabilize visual temperature.
- **Add a little black** to white paint to ground the scheme. Spread the paint on a large surface such as a floor. Black will take some of the brightness out of the white.
- **Add some of the room's color** to white paint to create a tint that's perfectly in sync with the palette.
- **Use texture to warm whites** and make them livable: Think white Flokati rugs, wicker baskets painted white, white stone, white cable-knit throws, and shiny white paint.
- **Play shiny** against matte to add sophisticated style. Use white high-gloss paint on wood furniture and white matte paint on walls. New matte paints pair a stylish look with easy washability. Look, too, for latex paints in a high-gloss finish.

Brown + orange

create an urban mood in this handsome and welcoming sitting room. Brown is as hip as its uptown cousin, black, and it offers a softer sensibility as a backdrop for the brighter colors currently used in interiors. Burnt orange steps into the mix to enhance the natural warmth of brown and adds a pop of bright color. Cork wallpaper that looks neutral from afar reveals a colorful closeup view, thanks to retro orange and cinnamon woven into the paper. The 1940s chaise longue wears a rich orange velvet that's dressy and touchable. A drop-front bar in dark wood and a sleek leather chair repeat the warm brown hues. Accessories such as a pair of overscale burnt-orange vases on the mantel, a white bowl lined with orange on the coffee table, and an orange-infused rug support the palette.

Brown + blue

establish a soothing, sophisticated color partnership in this living room. Walls painted a deep, milk chocolate brown create a dramatic yet restful backdrop for cool blues in patterns and solids. The wall treatment, a four-step glazing process with a final coating of shellac, gives the paint a translucent, textural finish that stars in the space. Using warm brown with cool blues gives this room perfect color balance. Placing blue upholstery against brown walls makes the silhouettes of the chairs and sofa stand out. Horizontal stripes on the sofa enhance its long, low shape while the graphic designs on the pillows add a punch of pattern. Artwork also embraces the color palette by combining neutrals, browns, and gray-blues. The rug features a darker, cooler brown; the dark tone helps ground the seating area. Pops of white and olive green in accessories add energy.

Dresser rehab

Use color to turn a vintage dresser into a dining room buffet. It's the easiest, cheapest, and fastest way to revamp a dated piece of furniture that's also in bad shape. (If a piece of furniture is old and valuable, leave it "as is.") Here's how to get started.

- **Fill cracks** and hardware holes with wood filler; let dry.
- **Sand the piece,** starting with 200-grit sandpaper and progressing to 400-grit. Wipe sanding residue using a tack rag.
- **Apply a coat of primer** to all surfaces, including the edges and interiors of drawers; let dry. Rub candle wax on the drawer runners for a smooth slide.
- **Consider alkyd paint** for durability. Apply two coats of the finish coat, sanding lightly between coats.
- **Add vintage appeal** with mismatched pulls and metal casters.
- **Top the dresser** with a piece of marble cut to size. For a budget-friendly option, substitute marble tiles.

Chair redo

Color makeovers often start with a fun fabric. In this case, fabric delivers the color wow, while white paint plays a supporting role. Look for a chair that's in good shape but dated, then turn it into the best seat in the house.

- **Remove the chair seat.** Tip the chair over and unscrew the seat. Check to see if the chair back can be removed. If not, protect fabric edges with masking tape.
- **Paint the frame,** following the directions for sanding, priming, and painting. See "Dresser rehab" at left.
- **Place the seat** facedown on the wrong side of the fabric. On one side, pull the fabric to the back of the seat; staple. Pull the fabric to the opposite side; staple. Repeat for the other two sides. Flip the seat to check that the fabric is smooth.
- **Redo the fabric-covered parts** of the chair that can't be removed by pulling off the masking tape and stapling new fabric in place. Take care to staple as close to the edge as possible. Use a hot-glue gun to secure cording over the fabric edges and staples.

Color craving

Color exerts powerful effects—warming or cooling, calming or energizing, enlarging or reducing. Proof exists in a new house treated to two opposite color schemes. It's perfectly neutral most of the time and suited to a color explosion when the mood strikes. Study these rooms to learn the benefits of both options and how to incorporate them into your decorating schemes.

• **Build a background of support.** Whether you like neutrals or colors, expensive or difficult-to-change elements are best left neutral. Explore color trends using inexpensive accessories and paint. In this house sofas, carpet, and rugs in go-with-anything neutrals support both schemes. Color appears in accessories and paint that can be layered on to suit the season.

Colorful, **right,** or neutral, **opposite,** this living room proves that it's a decorating chameleon, able to change with a swap of accessories. Pillows, throws, and artwork offer quick-change options.

HALSTON An American Original

• **Mix it up.** Use variations of shades and tints for drama. This strategy suits any palette, bright or neutral. A variety of whites adds more interest than repeating the same white from woodwork to walls to ceiling. The same goes for a color such as hot pink. Vary the pinks, from bluish pink to coral pink and from pale to intense.

• **Add temporary/changeable color.** It lets you explore trends as well as experiment with the decor of your house. Accessories, such as throws and painted artist's canvases, pop into a room with ease and are equally easy to remove. Flowers and fresh fruit in bright colors can pump up the energy level even in a neutral space.

• **Embrace paint.** It's an affordable and quick-change decorating material. If you use a bit of colored paint on the walls, it takes only an hour or so to make a change. Consider painting one wall or an alcove around a window.

Consider this clever strategy for decorating the same dining room, **opposite** and **left,** with built-in changeability: Paint most of the walls in neutrals and add slivers of wall color that can be painted in an hour or two. Surfaces such as the dining room table, coffee table, and shelves offer perfect staging spots for color makeovers.

One dramatic decorating gesture—a stenciled black and white wall—works in the dining room, **right** and **opposite,** whether the palette is neutral or colorful. When using a bold decorating strategy like this, balance it with strong color, such as hot pink. The neutral version of the room works with the wall because of contrast between light and dark neutrals and the introduction of bold shapes and shimmery mirror and glass.

• Use a bright or contrasting color to create a focal point. Black can be as powerful as hot pink in creating contrast. In a neutral scheme make use of shades from black to white to add interest. In a colorful space use variations of one or two colors for a modern attitude.

• Create mood with color. Neutrals and pastels create a serene space while bright pops of color inject energy and attitude. Suit the color combinations to your goals for the room. Bright pink creates an energetic space while pale pink lends a restful quality.

• Add texture. Whether the scheme is black and white or bold and colorful, texture is a key ingredient in creating decorating interest. For whites, consider the variety supplied by a creamy wool rug, white linen slipcovers, shiny silk pillows, and a furry throw. Although bright hues require less texture than a neutral scheme, a quilted comforter, slubby silk pillows, and glossy lamp bases add variety to the bold colors. If everything is the same texture and hue, a room can feel boring.

• Support a color scheme with pattern. It can be a crucial element in a neutral palette. Pattern also can inspire a color palette, and it always creates visual interest.

The master bedroom can be energetic, opposite, **or restful,** this page. **It takes only a bit of color to change the attitude of a space or to flip the hues. For a softer look, use muted tones.**

Pattern

for style-friendly wow power

Pattern, like color, exerts an emotional pull that can jumpstart a decorating style. After all, even color schemes begin by matching hues in a well-loved pattern. So what's calling your name? Do you swoon over toile or are cottage roses a better fit? Look in your closet. Do you wear solid-color coordinates and accent them with a patterned scarf? Or is every other piece wildly designed? How many prints would you dare to combine in one room? Does one pattern—a stripe or floral—flow throughout your home? Loving a variety of patterns doesn't guarantee mix-and-match heaven, but these tips and techniques will help simplify your decorating experiments.

in this section

Combining patterns can be challenging,

even for an experienced decorator, so embark on this design journey with a sense of adventure and a few basic rules.

- **Consider the room size.** Small patterns can disappear in a large room while big patterns can overwhelm a small space. Some exceptions exist: A large pattern can rev up an entry or a bathroom and make the space look bigger. A tiny pattern might be the perfect foil for window treatments edged with exotic trims and ribbons.
- **Focus on the pattern repeat and how it will be used.** A large-scale print can be too big for a pillow or the back of a bookcase; a complicated pattern might disappear in the folds of drapery. Not sure? Buy a yard of fabric or one roll of wallpaper and test it out.
- **Vary patterns and scale for harmony.** The easiest way to start is with groupings of three. That might mean a narrow stripe, a midsize geometric, and a bold floral, or a mini geometric, a midsize floral, and a bold stripe.
- **Follow the 60/30/10 approach.** Use 60 percent of the favorite pattern, 30 percent of the second favorite, and 10 percent of the third as an accent.
- **Repeat patterns.** If you use one pattern, such as paisley, repeat it somewhere else in the room even if the scale and color change.
- **Combine by color.** Select patterns in a single color family for the easiest mix-and-match style. Color helps unexpected pattern combinations—a bold modern Swedish print and a classic damask, for example—work together.
- **Mix with white to simplify.** Large areas of white softly contain pattern and reduce visual clutter.
- **In general stay away from premixed fabric or wallpaper collections.** The mix might meet the criteria for three patterns in a combination of scales, but the finished look can be so predictable that it's boring.

Consider the size of the room.

Mix with white to simplify.

Here's how decorators use pattern to change perceptions.

- **Create a focal point.** Patterned curtains naturally call attention to windows, while a bold geometric pattern on a single wall can create architectural interest that's sorely missing from a room.
- **Change attitudes.** Gingham, for example, can make a Louis-something chair look relaxed while toile wallpaper can give a modern dresser a classic look. Similar patterns can deliver decidedly different results: Bold checks in a trendy color inject contemporary style; small checks in muted tones create country style.
- **Reshape awkward spaces.** A bold pattern in advancing colors can square up a long, narrow room. Bright accent pillows placed on a sofa in a long, narrow room can visually pull the sofa forward. Bold horizontal stripes lower too-high ceilings, while vertical stripes can visually raise a ceiling.
- **Reflect the seasons.** Light, airy patterns offer a summery attitude while dense patterns on bold or deep backgrounds warm a room for winter.

Patterns exist all around—

in nature and in man-made shapes, in colors and in black and white, and in every country around the globe. Patterns reflect the plants and animals of the region, the common landscapes and buildings, the historic colors developed from natural dyes, and even family ancestry in the form of Scottish plaids. No other decorating product delivers a specific look as easily. Here's a peek at some inspiring patterns and their countries of origin.

India/Block prints, ikat

England and Colonial America, Crewel botanical

France, Italy, Spain/Damask

West Indies/Tropical print

England/Paisley

France/Toile

Italy, Greece/Seaside fruits and flowers

Uzbekistan/Ikat

Mexico/Traditional patterns

Pick up the color thread. Repeating colors from pattern to pattern can help even disparate patterns seem like first cousins. In this room stripes, botanical prints, and overscale French cherub designs in yellow and red warm up a corner seating area. Even the 1930s Indian table adds pattern to the space. Introduce a strong color and spread it around in pattern from windows to furniture. Include a handful of solids as visual resting places.

Finding one

favorite pattern is the easy part. Now it's time to pick partners. Here are three strategies to use.

Left: Pair one-color patterns with white. White is a decorating magician. It pulls patterns together to create visual interest without taxing a space with too much of a good thing. Any soothing neutral—creamy white or grayed white—works in a similar fashion. The patterns can be inspired by a similar look, such as the Indiennes patterns used here, or they can be disparate patterns that work together through their color compatibility.

Below: Let architectural elements set the pattern tempo. Color can play up the architecture or play it down; pattern is the element that breathes life into a room. Lavished with ornate woodwork, this home is a surprising background for bold geometrics. To give the geometrics even more impact, one pattern is used on simple panels that hang like works of art over the bay window. Framed prints on the walls mimic the squares of the plush rug. Likewise, a linear house could be softened by modern botanical patterns or curvy contemporary designs. Overscale patterns are perfect companions to houses with strong architecture.

Pattern palettes

often start with a favorite design. Here's how to combine patterns and colors to create a look that's as individual as you.

1. Even the binding of a book and the design of a shell add pattern to a scheme. Start with the boldest print, such as the overscale damask fabric; add a second smaller print and a bold stripe. An interesting organic design on the tile works almost like a solid.

2. Color is the unifier in this bold plan that begins with oversize dahlias on a white background. Note that making ruffles from the fabric changes the pattern. Stripes pick up the tones and anchor the look. Accessories, such as woodgrain china and printed napkins, illustrate how patterns mix it up with style.

3. Let a collection of transferware plates inspire a pattern palette. Instead of matching the plates, pick patterns that play up one of the elements, such as flowers. Start with an oversize floral to give the look country attitude; then add a ticking stripe and a small check. A Greek key pattern in blue adds a surprise.

4. A pattern palette executed in neutrals can be classic or modern; either way, it's a sophisticated look. This classic pattern scheme illustrates that pieces such as a chair or metal urn add their own share of pattern. As with any pattern combination, mix large, medium, and small patterns into the scheme.

Skittish about using pattern?

Wade into design waters with a small project that confines the prints to a single piece of furniture.

Upholster an armless chair to enhance its shape. The trick? Pay particular attention to size and scale. For example, when selecting fabrics for three of the four chairs pictured here, the key was picking medium-scale prints with a central motif that could easily be centered on both the chair back and seat. Reserve looser, more overall prints, such as damask and paisley, for the shapelier frames. Update boxier chairs, such as the fourth chair here with tighter, more geometric prints.

Add a dash of excitement to a simple chest of drawers. A project like this might be just the focal point a room needs. But why stop at one pattern? For added fun, mix patterns on the same object. On this chest of drawers, two botanical-print papers are placed in an alternating fashion on the drawers. Use a decoupage medium as both an adhesive and a protective top coat.

Colorful stripe + bold florals

add up to a pattern scheme with a fresh, young attitude. The mix is easy to copy. Start by purchasing a large floral print with plenty of white background. This pattern immediately sets the direction of the partnership. Add colorful stripes with minimal white to help a smaller striped piece hold its own visual weight against the dramatic floral: Covering a bolster with horizontal stripes plays to the natural shape of this pillow style. Stripes can stretch diagonally as well for variety.

Classic stripe + vintage floral

toile set a traditional mood. Vary the scale so the look feels updated and right for today. In this case a medium-size stripe on the love seat pairs with an overscale print on the pillow. Stripes wrap the love seat from top to bottom, visually raising its height. If the stripes wrapped horizontally around the love seat instead, the piece would look much longer and lower. When using bold prints on a small piece, such as a pillow, take care to center the most important motif for a traditional look. To give a pillow a graphic yet traditional look, place a dramatic pattern off-center.

Plays well with pattern

A little pattern can be fairly easy to incorporate into a home—toss in a few pillows or hang a row of patterned plates on a wall. If you really love pattern, though, and want to use a lot of it, taking the print plunge requires a sure eye and a deft hand. The owners of this classic old house wanted it to be adult- and teenager-friendly and full of pattern. Mission impossible? Not at all. Learn how to create a similar pattern-happy house using these tips.

- **Create a unique reflection of the individuals** who live in a home. Spend some time uncovering the patterns and colors that compose your personal style story. Pull swatches you like, search the Internet for fun patterns in everything from rugs to lampshades, and begin building a swatchbook of pattern.
- **Use pattern to update** a classic house. Traditional designs in unexpected color combinations have instant impact. The yin/yang effect of pairing opposites balances design energy with style serenity.
- **Find a fabric company** or designer you love and stick with it. With clothing, you learn which designer's style you like the best, which patterns or colors suit you best, and what designs match your style. Select the ingredients for your home's interior the same way. "Try on" whatever looks appealing and see if it fits your home.

Despite its formal look the dining room is used for every meal and for homework. The striped Tibetan rug sets a playful tone and expertly camouflages stains.

Artwork also provides pattern in graphic black and white. Classic toile builds on the rug colors and holds its own visual weight as slipcovers for cameo-back chairs.

Worth noting

To build a color scheme around patterns, select a dominant hue, a secondary color, and an accent from the mix. Then purposely choose tones that are slightly different to create interest.

• **Create a room's "wardrobe"** in the same way you create an outfit to wear: Start with the larger pieces and add accessories as you find them. Leave behind pieces that strike you as merely OK. Keep searching for the perfect object.

• **Put less emphasis on** matching fabric colors and more on accentuating underplayed shared colors in the fabrics. Grayed-blue curtain panels work as a background for the dining room chairs' slipcovers with their grayed-blue shadows on the toile.

• **Use color repetition** to help patterns work together. For instance, the foyer walls are papered in black and white toile, so black and white repeats in each adjoining room. The Tibetan rug in the dining room grounds the color scheme and provides plenty of color choices. Blue-grays and rosy-reds make the jump from the rug to the chairs and draperies.

• **Create decorating drama** by pairing contrasting fabrics, such as damask draperies, an Asian rug, and French toile. In addition to their diverse graphic patterns, the fabrics vary in texture, from silky damask to velvety wool.

• **Start with patterned accessories.** Buying pillows, artwork, and lampshades is a fun way to add pattern without making a huge budget commitment.

• **Be smart about wear and care.** In a house populated by teenage boys, it makes sense to use a light-color fabric for slipcovers that can be removed easily for cleaning. Darker fabrics that hide stains work well for upholstery. Many patterns naturally hide stains and soil.

Opposite: A sofa in neutral wool serves in a supporting role to dramatic patterns on draperies and pillows. The scrollwork pillows and fuchsia-patterned draperies show the effect of combining color and garden designs in one vibrant space.

Above left: Traditional blooms on the draperies look modern, thanks to their size and spacing. Pairing them with a graphic-print pillow fabric adds to the effect. The pale chartreuse cotton velvet chairs offer a solid swath of color that plays well with pattern.

Below left: Black and white wallpaper in a large print creates a dramatic front entry and a design surprise: Used in quantity, bold prints can blend into the background. Here a series of framed art pieces dominates an overscale toile.

Texture

for comfort you can feel

Touch is a huge part of comfort, and that's where texture enters the decorating world. It might not be as dramatic as color and pattern, yet texture quietly adds tactile warmth and visual appeal. Your closet will prove you're a fan of texture—soft cashmere sweaters, a tooled-leather purse, silky pearl buttons, and corduroy slacks. So which textures are your favorites? Do you love the crisp feeling of leather seating or would you rather sink into a mohair-velvet sofa? Do you like matte surfaces or shiny glam? Are you drawn to the coolness of stone or the warmth of wood? Start making mental notes the next time you shop. Which textures beg to be touched? Go hands-on to gain an understanding of your own texture story.

in this section

Think texture

as you decorate a space. Texture can be part of the background, such as a stone wall or wood floor, or introduced in furnishings. Have a little fun with texture: Play rough against smooth and shiny against matte when planning floors and walls. A shaggy rug adds warmth to a smooth wood floor while walls coated in matte paint contrast subtly with shiny woodwork. Use texture in furnishings and accessories to reflect decorating trends.

Right: A low, round, woven abaca table stars in this Asian-inspired dining room. The walls and floor are plain, allowing textured elements to set the mood. The rustic weave of the table base contrasts with the smooth top, enhancing the textural effect of both. Other surfaces—velvet floor pillows, a woven metal basket, and a linen rug—create a space with touchable style.

Opposite: Stone walls and floor provide dramatic texture for this family room. A rustic coffee table and woven sisal rug add more. Although the style of the slipcovered sofa is sleek, the mix of textures makes this space feel warm and cozy. Imagine the room with glossy walls and smooth wood flooring. The same furnishings would feel dressy in that setting.

Diversity is the key to creating interest with texture.

- **Let opposites attract.** For design interest pair smooth and rough, sleek and nubby, coarse and fine. Encircle a rustic wicker table with slick laminate chairs. Toss silk pillows on a velvet sofa.
- **Create touchable style.** Rough textures work in casual and eclectic rooms while the smooth textures of lacquer, glass, mirrors, and polished woods convey a sleek, formal attitude.
- **Set the mood.** Textures can steer a room toward the feeling you want. Consider soft, fine fabrics for a feminine mood, rustic metals and woods for a more masculine bent, sleek and shiny surfaces for a modern attitude, and a mix of textures for eclectic appeal.
- **Add texture to the background.** Use woven sisal for rugs, wood or rough plaster for walls, shiny tile for floors, and brick for a fireplace front.
- **Repeat the feeling.** Textures need some repetition. Consider using wicker in baskets and in a piece of furniture. Combine leather on a sectional with stacks of leather-bound books.

Capitalize on texture to create a mood.

It's a smart strategy that lets the mood change with the seasons. It's easy to alter a bedroom with a change of linens—furry throw in winter and cotton throw in summer. The same trick can change a living room for company—silky pillows and velvet slipcovers for dress-up and corduroy pillows and denim slipcovers for every day. Imagine how great they'll feel!

Far left: Shiny fabrics and elegant finishes dress up this living room. Spread the shine around, from a softly glowing wall finish to shiny vases to pillows with woven sheen. Repeat textures for balance.
Left: High-style wovens naturally introduce brown into a decorating palette, where it joins many colors with ease. Note the natural partnership of brown and green. Other textures include a woven basket and a cozy chenille throw.

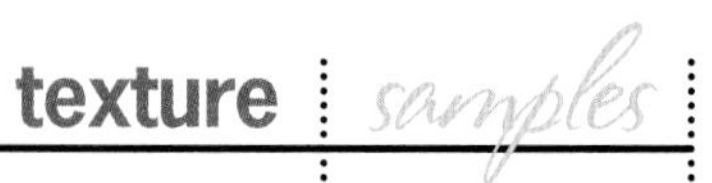

Opposite textures attract to give interiors a jolt of style while similar surfaces add a soothing note. Combine textures to create the attitude that's right for your home. The samples shown here offer some favorite combinations, but the options are endless. Which ones are right for your haven?

Textures suit any style. Here are a few to consider.
Traditional: Hand-tufted rugs, woven wools, tooled silver, cut crystal, gilded frames, silk, china, and polished wood.
Country: Braided rugs, worn wood, rusted metals, chenille spreads, ironstone pottery, blown glass, and ticking.
Romantic: Velvet, furry throws, crystal prisms, embroidered fabrics, lace, painted furniture, and hand-hooked rugs.
Modern: Laminated-plywood furniture, plastic, smooth leather, stainless steel, terrazzo flooring, and teak.

Natural fabric + bamboo flooring

Palmwood flooring + bamboo rug

Seed pods + vintage wood

Crisp ceramics + ornate mirror
Sisal-covered dresser + textural drapery
Woven footboard + cotton curtain
River rocks + smooth ceramic

Sensory Perceptions

A downtown loft in an old warehouse building offers many decorating possibilities, including the opportunity to enhance the rich interplay of textures already in place. After all, with exposed brick walls, concrete ceilings, wood flooring, and exposed pipes and heating ducts, this loft was a case study in industrial/modern texture. To create a soothing yet classic cocoon in the city, the homeowner added touchable textures—worn antique furniture, woven chairs, wool rugs, washed linen, and high-thread-count bedding. Use her strategies to comfortably settle into any home.

- **Let texture set the mood**—modern, country, or sophisticated and classic like this loft. A rustic loft need not be masculine or modern. Silken textures, such as antique Oushak rugs and billowing curtains, keep the look traditional but less formal. Curves on the sofa and elegant monogrammed pillows support a more feminine look. Sleek surfaces, such as stainless steel and glass, inject a livable modern attitude.
- **Find suitable companions.** Texture is the perfect decorating teammate for shape, color, and pattern. It enhances and contrasts with each of the elements. Consider a shiny green vase with a curvaceous silhouette. It offers texture, color, and

In this empty-nester loft, a white sofa adds a sophisticated element. One long pillow made from an antique tapestry adds a vintage note. A collection of throw pillows would detract from the simplicity and symmetry of this area. A triptych over the sofa serves as a focal point in the open living area.

EARTH FROM ABOVE
EARTH FROM ABOVE
THE SEA

shape all in one vessel. The same is true of a vintage Chinese cabinet or an iron chandelier.

- **Support texture with color.** Rustic texture plays well with deep colors and neutrals. White, off-white, brown, and gold flow throughout the apartment, creating a cohesive design scheme. If you use a bold color, such as hot pink, partner it with a refined texture, such as glass, honed marble, or velvet.
- **Go for variety.** Select furnishings that explore a range of texture. That might mean a smooth coffee table and a sofa upholstered in mohair, or a metal-wrapped mirror hung on a rustic brick wall.
- **Pair new with old.** Antiques instantly change the mood of a space. With their worn and paint-faded surfaces, they provide needed warmth in a room filled with glass and stainless steel. That's the strategy used to lend a homey feeling to this industrial loft.
- **Signal function with texture.** A bedroom might be cozy and calm with high-thread-count linens while the same fabrics

Opposite: Symmetry defines the living room, including these pairings opposite the sofa wall. The antique Chinese cabinet conceals electronics equipment. Blown-glass vases on top repeat the shiny texture of framed prints and coffee table pieces.

Above left: Furniture placement keeps pathways open, allows flexibility for entertaining, and defines the spaces. The brown, white, and gold color scheme flows throughout to visually connect the areas.

Above right: An antique Japanese screen in the dining room plays the patina of age against new upholstered seating.

Above right: An airy chandelier preserves the view in the open dining room. A vintage table makes a stylish companion for new upholstered chairs.
Below right: Crystal decanters provide shimmery texture. Placing the decanters in front of a mirror maximizes their effect.
Far right: Texture adds comfort to every bedroom surface. Consider the raised stitching of monograms on the shams, the smooth surface of glass lamp bases, and the nubby texture of the rug.

could lose their design punch in a living room. Textured objects such as nubby fabrics, sisal rugs, and rustic ceramics might be better options for a living or dining space.

• **Put texture within reach.** Color and pattern can produce dramatic effects from afar, but texture demands a closer look. Issue an invitation to touch by combining a variety of textures in pillows and upholstered fabric or setting the table with glass, china, silver, and linen.

• **Use texture in moderation.** Carefully select each accessory and piece of furniture. Too many objects clutter a space and dilute the effect of texture.

Ultimate Herb Gardener
REBECCA COLE PARADISE FOUND

Elements
for a designer's touch

Scale, balance, and rhythm are the underappreciated parts of most decorating schemes. So much focus is placed on color, pattern, and texture that it's easy to forget that these three other elements are at work in every decorating plan. When they are in sync, you'll feel more comfortable in the spaces. So consider how a space makes you feel. Do you like an energetic mix of big and small pieces? Do you feel more relaxed with symmetry, such as balanced nightstands and lamps by the bed? Are you tempted to duplicate a color around the room or to repeat textures? The lessons in this chapter will help you understand how scale, balance, and rhythm team up with style choices.

in this section

Scale refers to visual size—how furnishings look next to each other and how they fit in a room. Varying scale is key to creating interesting rooms. Rooms need big things, little things, tall things, and low things. Obvious choices—small objects in a small room—may not always work. In fact, a large chandelier can add style oomph to a small room. Study how size works in these rooms; then play with scale by trying objects of different dimensions in various combinations to see what feels right.

Left: Grouping many small items, such as a collection of blue-green pots, can make one big statement. That's the lesson of scale. Small objects can be combined with other like objects to create size. A disconnected grouping of small items on the mantel would look busy.

Above: Playing with scale involves creating some unexpected pairings, such as a beefy coffee table with a demure sofa and a large globe on a small table. Getting it right means working out relationships among furnishings and choosing and arranging pieces so they appear compatible and interesting.

Opposite: One large piece of art is all it takes to balance a room full of furniture. The painting is almost as big as the sofa. Because the art has a lot of light-colored background, it provides mass without dominating the sofa. A wall full of smaller prints would lack the drama of a big piece.

- **Create drama by varying scale.** If everything is the same size, nothing will stand out.
- **Group small items**—from accessories to furniture—to create scale in a large room.
- **Maximize a room's size.** A single oversize piece, such as a tall armoire, can make a small room feel more generous and less predictable.
- **Think beyond mirror images.** Objects on either side of the sofa or bed can be similar in scale rather than matching. Variety increases visual interest.
- **Consider visual weight.** It matters as much as height. Even if chairs are the same height, a reed-thin one looks awkward beside an upholstered one.
- **Start with the largest piece of furniture** in a room, such as a bed or a sofa. Then add other furnishings that visually fit. A table and lamp may be proportionate to each other, yet placed next to a bed or sofa, they may look too large or too small.

Balance works on the teeter-totter principle. If a large seating group at one end of a living room lacks a counterweight—built-ins, an armoire, or even a weighty painting—the room seems lopsided. It's not necessary to match a chunky sofa pound for pound with another hefty piece. Instead group a couple of chairs, a table, and an area rug; together they will match the visual weight of the sofa.

Below left: Formal symmetry offers mirror-image balance. Objects must match, such as the lamps, or be close enough in size, shape, or color to look like a perfect match, such as the chairs. Symmetry soothes the eye. It can lapse into boredom without off-center items, such as the flower, frame, and books on the table.

Below: Asymmetrical balance evenly distributes visual weight without creating a mirror image. A fat, short object can balance a tall object, as in the floral arrangement on the sideboard. A group of objects on one side of a mantel can match the visual weight of a single massive piece on the other side.

Opposite: Radial balance works like the dial on a clock. Chairs around a table and round plates around a sconce illustrate the concept. Note that the objects in radial balance can be similar in shape without being exact matches. Like objects create more visual interest than identical pieces.

Formal symmetry

Asymmetry

Radial symmetry

- **Balance using scale.** The scale of individual pieces contributes to the overall balance of a room. A large piece of art or a grid of small framed pieces both can balance a large sofa. A fireplace opposite a bay window also can deliver balance.
- **Count on color.** Dark upholstery grants importance to seating and can also make the piece seem larger. Covering a sofa to match the wall color helps the sofa blend into the background. To balance a space filled with strong, dark colors or bold patterns, scatter colorful accessories around the room.
- **Balance wall colors.** When using two paint colors on one wall, anchor the lower part with the warmer or brighter hue and apply the lighter, receding color on top. Otherwise the space will look top-heavy.
- **Balance windows and walls.** High ceilings and tall windows require at least one other tall object in the room to achieve balance. Consider a tall cupboard or artwork that stretches up the wall.

Rhythm, the way colors, patterns, and shapes fill a room, keeps a space interesting because it requires constant eye movement. The tempo can be lively and playful or slow and graceful. A rapid repeat of a big pattern can keep the eye hopping while a soft color palette can slow it down. Learning how to set a style tempo starts here.

Below: A little corner of a room can create its own visual energy. That's the case with this round mirror hung above a circular stool seat. Even the glass bottle repeats the circle theme. Repeating colors also adds to the tempo.

Below right: Rhythm works in predictable ways. The pillows on the sofa and the prints above it march the eye toward the focal point of the room, the fireplace. Gray dominates the space; red livens it up.

Right: The honey tones of wood and wicker showcase one way to create rhythm that's restful. Instead of demanding visual time, these textured pieces encourage the eye to move around the room but at a leisurely pace.

• **Play with shapes.** Consider the natural rhythm of rectangular windows and doors, round tables, and curvaceous vases to grab attention. Vary the scale of the elements to create even more movement.

• **Incorporate patterns.** Repeating florals or stripes around a room sets the tempo. A small floral on curtains can be reflected in an oversize flower painting; a bold wall stripe works with ribbon trim on a shade.

• **Scatter a dominant hue** throughout the room. Color repetition keeps the eye moving and weaves the space together. Bold colors rev up the speed while shaded colors slow it down.

• **Partner with texture.** A rough texture in a sea of smooth surfaces adds interest and keeps the eye moving. Shiny surfaces, such as glass and metal, have the same effect when combined with nubby fabrics.

• **Group for impact.** Small objects scattered around a room can be overlooked. For more impact create several groupings of small objects.

• **Apply the brakes.** Subtract patterns, colors, or objects to slow the tempo and calm a space.

Shape can add rhythm. Here the key shape is curvy, from the lampshade to the coffee table to the modern vases. Spreading like objects around the room keeps the eye moving.

seeking Balance

The elements of style—scale, balance, and rhythm—should be any decorator's constant companions. Whether the house is small like this one or big, these basic guidelines will help create a home that looks good and feels right. Take a walk through this classic bungalow to see how the elements work together.

- **Stick with the basics you love.** This house is a case study in fresh yet timeless design. It makes use of a white and khaki color scheme and mixes it with functional items with simple lines. That strategy plays in every room of the house, keeping the look cohesive and amplifying the rhythm of the design.
- **Design for continuity.** This living room once featured a tiny gas fireplace, small built-in bookcases, and double-hung windows opposite beautiful Gothic arch windows. The room was in need of continuity, so the owners removed the bookcases, converted the double-hung windows to casements, and replaced the fireplace surround with limestone carved in a Gothic arch.

An oversize bouquet of flowers adds importance to a simple framed print, showing one strategy for using balance and scale.

A pair of comfortable leather chairs flanks the new limestone fireplace, whose Gothic arch mirrors the arches found in the front windows and doorway of the home.

• **Think big.** In a small house too much small furniture can make rooms feel cluttered and full. Instead buy larger pieces to make spaces feel roomier. That's a savvy trick designers use when working with scale.
• **Play with balance.** Symmetry, asymmetry, and radial symmetry are all strategies that help when arranging furniture and objects. Follow the rules to achieve stylish results. Once you learn the rules, you'll gain the confidence to break them when it delivers a better solution for your home.
• **Create symmetry with similar yet different objects.** The fireplace wall provides a perfect example of this technique. Side tables, one in wood and the other skirted in linen, hold matching lamps and varied collections. The overall effect is balanced and symmetrical.
• **Group small objects to minimize clutter and build scale.** That's the

Left: Slipcovers that stretch almost to the floor visually enlarge the dining room chairs. A round table in a square room ensures that traffic lanes stay open.
Right: A banquette works for two or a crowd. Crisp linen contrasts with brown faux suede. A pair of small tables provides easy access to seating.

design outcome of a wall of bookcases or a kitchen or bathroom island.

• **Slim down and beef up.** In a small home it's easy to gain storage with built-ins. At 12 inches deep, a bookcase provides storage without gobbling up square footage, and the piece stretches from wall to wall to inject scale. An upholstered headboard uses only about 4 inches of depth, yet it creates a grand backdrop that stretches high up a draped wall.

• **Buy for shape.** It's the one thing you can't change. Granted, you might be able to skirt something to the floor to change the apparent size, yet the basic shape remains. Replay those shapes from room to room to achieve cohesive design.

• **Move the eye around the room with color.** When rooms are decorated with neutrals, use contrast from dark brown to pale ivory to energize the color scheme.

Below: Symmetry and asymmetry join forces near the guest bathroom sink. The small table to one side of the sink offers a surprise that adds visual interest.

Below right: Wraparound counters slip below the windowsills in this former porch. The matching vessel sinks sit on the countertop. A centered island introduces order and function into the master bathroom.

Rhythm adds a restful note to the bedroom. Matching lamps sit on similar nightstands. A wicker trunk repeats the tones of the bamboo window shade. A soft oatmeal color repeats on walls, ceiling, rug, and draperies.

Surfaces

for walls, floors, and ceilings

chapter **7**

Based on sheer size alone, walls, ceilings, and floors make a huge impact on the style of your home. Your options for decorating these spaces are unlimited, and that can be overwhelming. Minimize the possibilities by answering these questions. Do you like calm, neutral backgrounds or vibrant, colorful spaces? Would you rather have pattern on furniture and keep the walls plain, or the opposite? Do you like to change backgrounds often or rarely? What are the surface treatments in the rooms you love most? Whether you plan to create a new background for a well-loved sofa or start from scratch, it's time to sample products in the home design marketplace.

in this section

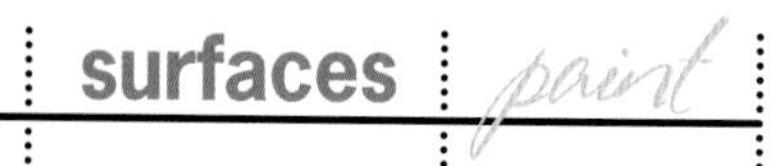

Paint tames any surface,

thanks to the large variety of products on the market. Pair that with endless options for colors and finishes—and an affordable price—and it's easy to see why paint remains the number one makeover product. Test one of these ideas, or pick your favorites from the hundreds of options shown throughout this book.

Left: Stripes run around a room to make a graphic statement. This technique also can lower too-high ceilings. To strike lines on the wall, use a 4-foot carpenter's level and a colored pencil that matches the darkest paint. For crisp edges apply painter's tape to the penciled lines before painting. Paint freehand for a softer look.

Above: Add drama to a wall with a rectangle of painted color. It's a surprising way to call attention to a piece of furniture, add architecture to a room, or break up an expanse of neutral wall.

Opposite: Delicately painted botanical motifs stretch across the painted floor in this porch. Planks painted on an old vinyl floor create the illusion of wood. The floor was stripped of wax and dirt, rolled with a coat of primer and two coats of floor paint, detailed with acrylic paints, and protected with two coats of polyurethane.

Use these tips to simplify painting jobs.

• **Test paint colors or techniques** by painting large samples on foam-core boards.

• **Never coat latex paint with alkyd or oil-base paint.** The flexible latex paint will cause the hard oil-base topcoat to crack and peel.

• **Choose the surface finish** to suit your style: flat, eggshell, semigloss, or high gloss. Gloss finishes reflect light and enlarge space, while flat paints do a better job of hiding wall damage. Gloss finishes may be easier to clean, but some new flat paints also are scrubbable.

• **Tint primer to the top-coat paint color.** It's the secret behind painting a light surface dark or a dark surface light. Primers contain more resins so they provide better coverage.

• **For surfaces painted with a gloss finish** or smooth ceramic tile, use a primer made specifically for slick surfaces. Follow the manufacturer's instructions.

• **Buy the paintbrush to suit the job:** synthetic bristles for water-base or alkyd paints and natural bristles for alkyd paints only.

• **When painting a high-moisture or damp area,** use mildewcide, a chemical additive that prevents mildew from growing on paint.

• **Remove painter's tape** (and check manufacturer's instructions) to prevent the paint film from bonding with the surface and the tape. If the paint dries it will tear when the tape is removed. If the paint has dried and the tape is still in place, run a crafts knife along the seam before removing the tape.

Get started hanging wallpaper with these tips.

- **Consider prepasted, scrubbable vinyl** coverings for kitchens, bathrooms, and children's rooms.
- **Use smooth wallpapers** only on smooth walls. If the walls are rough, hang liner paper first.
- **Have a little fun with faux papers** that look like log walls or even a library of classic books.
- **Accentuate architectural features,** such as doors and alcoves, by outlining them with borders.
- **Apply the same creativity** to wallpaper placement as you do to paint techniques. Consider these ideas: Tip the pattern on its side, paper a small section, cut the paper into squares to create a patchwork effect, or use it to line bookcases or cabinets.
- **Substitute wallpaper borders for molding** at the ceiling or at chair-rail height. Experiment with making a frame from a border; use it to accent a wall.
- **Build a color palette using wallpaper.** Find colors that complement rather than match.
- **Using only one roll of wallpaper?** Consider buying a luscious, handprinted paper to elevate your interior.

Wallpaper adds pattern and texture, a sure way to inject character into even a brand-new home. Wallpaper can work its magic on ceilings and furniture too. If you're worried about removing the paper later, carefully follow the manufacturer's instructions for sizing surfaces before applying wallpaper.

Opposite: Wallpapered panels can create the same effect as painted panels. Select a pattern that complements the wall color, then paper a section of wall. It's a sure-fire way to call attention to a seating area or to add pattern without the expense of papering an entire room.

Above: It's fun and unexpected to paper a ceiling. In this bedroom the ceiling becomes a worthwhile view when covered with an eye-popping print. Note that a dark or colorful ceiling can visually lower the height of a room.

Right: Think of this project as wallpaper without commitment. Covering a sheet of MDF with wallpaper lets you move the pattern where you want it and move it out when you tire of it. This project requires only one roll of paper, so even pricey paper will fit almost any budget.

Exercise your creativity with a variety of affordable and common materials, such as ribbon, molding, and paint. Some of the same techniques also can be used on ceilings.

Below: Thin strips of molding applied in parallel lines create beautiful rhythm and added detail without being fussy. Soft pumpkin paint spices it up. Use a 4-foot carpenter's or laser level. Measure carefully.

Right: Crisscrossed lengths of orange silk ribbon create a memory headboard in this sunny bedroom. Fabric-covered buttons hide the staples that secure the ribbons where they cross.

Opposite: Linen applied to the bedroom walls adds texture and warmth. Fanciful designs stenciled in white create a playful and unexpected finish. Use paint mixed with a textile medium to complete this project.

eco chic

Every single choice, from flooring to fabric treatments, affects the world and your home environment. Consider a few of these green yet stylish options.

Safer products

Consider these air-safe products.

- Paint with zero VOCs in any color.
- Low- or no-formaldehyde building and decorating products with minimal toxic chemicals.
- Dye-free, glue-free carpeting that's 100% wool with natural padding.
- Organic, chemical-free fabrics for bedding, bath, and more.
- Nontoxic printing processes for fabric yardage and rugs.

Renewable/recyclable resources

Use it again and again.

- Wood from sustainably harvested forests for floors and furniture.
- Renewable products, such as bamboo or cork for flooring.
- Products made from recycled materials: polyester fabrics, glass tableware formed from recycled glass, floor tiles made from crushed lightbulbs, accessories created from recycled aluminum, and more.
- Salvaged materials, including bathroom fixtures, windows, and flooring; also used furniture, revamped or not.

Splurge on the real things: wood and stone flooring.

If the budget is tight, check out the new look-alike flooring products that leave you guessing whether they're real or fake.

Left: Trendy yet timeless, natural stone cut in tiles provides upscale flooring that's beautiful and practical. Consider these products an investment in your home. With prices ranging from $5 to $40 per square foot, it's wise to shop the market before making a commitment. For a more affordable option, check out ceramic tile.

Right: Real wood flooring comes in a variety of woods and finishes. Traditional woods include maple, ash, and oak. Strip flooring comes in boards less than 2¼ inches wide. It's usually less expensive than wider plank flooring. Extra-wide planks, 7 inches or more, are the most expensive. Wide planks show off the woodgrain and look like antique wood floors.

Wood flooring looks gently aged when it's stained to let the grain show through. The same process works with paint. This graphic painted floor makes use of a diagonal pattern to repeat the backsplash design. The gray and white motif lightens the room.

real or fake?

Here's what to consider.

Wood

• Invest in real wood in your forever home. Real wood and engineered wood (hardwood bonded to plywood) last a house's lifetime. Except when used in wet areas, wood ages gracefully and is available prefinished in easy-care polyurethane.

• Add function with laminate and strip-vinyl wood look-alikes. Use them for a wood look in areas prone to water damage. These products resist scratching and staining. Despite an underlayment, laminate floors can be noisier than wood.

Stone

• Consider budget. Stone offers beauty, natural appeal, and easy care but is expensive. Stone floors are cold underfoot, unforgiving on dropped plates and slippery when wet. They provide little insulation against noise.

• Use stonelook products, such as laminate flooring and vinyl tiles, as an affordable alternative to real stone. Although these products mimic stone, they cannot reproduce its depth of color, organic textures, and durability. These look-alikes offer affordability, warmth, traction when wet, and easy installation.

Worth noting

Let the floor covering handle decorating dilemmas. Large pieces tame a large room and keep the eye moving. Using the same flooring from room to room can make a small house feel larger. Vintage styles can "age" a space.

Vinyl and ceramic tile

deliver durability that suits hardworking rooms, such as kitchens, bathrooms, back entries, and laundries. Look for products that mimic wood and stone or check out the endless variety of other designs.

Opposite: Real or faux? It's hard to tell. This stonelook ceramic tile offers the designer style of stone at a lower cost for materials and installation. Large tiles inject drama into a large kitchen.

Below: Tile floors add elegance and durability to a sunroom that's a direct link to the outdoors. With a multitude of colors and shapes, tile can create a variety of patterns. Look for new grouts that are stain-resistant.

Right: Merging two flooring materials demands design attention. Consider adding a thin layer of one material to bridge the gap. Here, quartzite stone tiles cut in narrow strips abut durable bamboo flooring. Make sure the floor heights create a no-trip seam.

Vinyl is the great impostor. Here's proof: These terrific faux looks include (from left to right): tortoiseshell, industrial-look treaded concrete, and Italian slate. These sheet-vinyl examples come in 6- and 12-foot widths.

Soft and comfortable, carpet and rugs anchor the style, define a space, and add warm color and texture. They're perfect companions for hard-surface flooring, such as wood, stone, and vinyl, especially during the cool months.

Above: A round or oval rug throws soft curves into a mix of angular furnishings. Put one under a rectangular table and chairs. This new rug duplicates the bands of color that wrap around a center section of a classic braided rug. Because it blends new and old, it's a likely choice for a modern space and a surprising twist in a home filled with antiques.

Right: A bold rug provides color inspiration for a living room, anchors the seating area, and softens the hardwood floor. Patterned rugs work well in plain rooms. They also can work with other designs to create a vibrant, pattern-filled space.

Floorcloths combine all the comfort of rugs with the easy care of vinyl floors. Most are made of canvas treated with gesso, hemmed on all edges, and painted in fun patterns. The look is perfect for any room; easy care makes floorcloths ideal for kitchens, entries, and bathrooms.

comfort cues

Consider how carpet and rugs can add character, style, and comfort. To shop wisely take along paint chips, fabric swatches, and room measurements. Consider care needs: Bathroom, back entry, and kitchen rugs need to be washable.

Carpet

- Express an attitude. The stronger the texture, the more casual its effect. Consider berber or sisal-look carpet for family rooms and a velvety texture for more formal rooms.
- Unify rooms. For continuity and a spacious feeling, install the same carpet throughout your home.
- Create divisions. Use a change of carpet color or texture to deliberately divide one room from another, such as a hallway from a master bedroom.

Rugs

- Pick a palette. Start redecorating when you fall in love with a rug. It can supply style and colors for a redo.
- Enhance an existing color scheme. Add punch to a boring room with a patterned rug, or calm a room by adding a solid-color rug.
- Make it a focal point. Choose a rug with bright colors, strong color contrast, or a vibrant pattern to draw the eye to a seating group or to slow the pace in an entry hall.

Lighting

for mood and function

chapter **8**

Well-designed lighting brightens the way and makes you feel good in a space. It adds style by highlighting the focal points of a room. So turn up the lights and ask a few questions. Do your rooms feel well-lit *and* stylish? Do you have enough lighting in the right places? Does light glare off surfaces or provide a soft glow? Can you read in your favorite chair or in bed, cut and paste at the kitchen table, or sew in the spare bedroom? Does the style of the fixture enhance your home's look? A change in lighting can make a powerful difference. New fixtures update a look and they can change the way you look at things. Isn't that worth the effort?

in this section

Suit your needs when determining the type of lighting and its location. The distance from the lamp to the person depends on the type of light and your lighting needs. Floor and wall lamps bring in light from above. Table lamps cast light from the side. Both types of lighting add function and style.

Right: For adequate lighting in a reading area, use either a wall lamp or floor lamp. Consider ones with shades 48 inches from the floor and about 26 inches from the center of the reading material. This flexible floor lamp bends to suit any reader. Select a desk lamp with a shade about 15 inches from the desk surface and centered 12 inches from the desk edge. Make sure it casts a glow at least 15 inches to one side of the base.
Above right: For reading in bed, opt for a swing-arm lamp that pulls close to the reading material and can be pushed out of the way as needed. Consider swing-arm lamps that adjust horizontally or vertically to suit your reading needs.

Use lighting to add drama over a fireplace by combining a picture lamp attached to a frame with a pair of candlestick lamps that fit on a narrow mantel. Use low-wattage bulbs for a cozy effect.

The type of lightbulb determines the color and quality of the light. Consider these options:

- **Incandescent.** The classic choice for warm, soft light anywhere. Look for it in standard and blue lightbulbs. This bulb is the least energy efficient.
- **Halogen.** Choose halogen bulbs for their clear white light and energy efficiency. The bulbs get hot so allow for ventilation and protection.
- **Compact fluorescent.** Designed as a replacement for standard light bulbs, these compact tubes come in sizes to fit any fixture. Choose them for pleasing light, little heat output, and energy efficiency. Recycle with care because they contain mercury.
- **Fluorescent.** Standard tubes are cool to the touch and provide cool light. Economical to buy and operate, use the bulbs in utility areas.
- **Xenon.** A newcomer to the market, it has a small amount of xenon gas enclosed in an incandescent bulb. It makes the light brighter and the bulb last longer, but energy efficiency is still low.

For more about lighting options, visit the American Lighting Association's website: www.americanlightingassoc.com.

Lighting types.

• **Ambient or overhead** lighting provides brightness to support the room's activities. Glare-free, indirect light bounces off walls and ceiling to create a general level of illumination without dark pockets. Before buying a new fixture, check the wattage of the existing fixture. If the light level works, purchase a new fixture that emits the same amount. If the room seems dark, opt for a higher-wattage light with a dimmer switch. Dark color rooms require more lighting than light color ones.

• **Task lighting** supplements ambient lighting by casting light for activities, such as reading or crafts. Table and floor lamps and undercabinet lighting support tasks. For comfort, place a table lamp so the bottom of the shade is at eye level. When the shade is higher, the resulting glare causes eyestrain.

• **Accent lighting** calls attention to a special feature, such as an architectural element or art piece. Recessed spotlights and track lights are the most common accent lights, but sconces, uplights, and some table and floor lamps also provide accent lighting. A spotlight draws attention to an object while wall washing can highlight a grouping of objects or an architectural feature.

From modern metallics to rustic carved wood, lamps fill a room with light and style. The trick is to match the style of lamps to the room, coordinate the size of the lamp with the table or stand where it sits, and decide whether it's a focal point in the room or simply a light source.

Give a room an instant facelift

by changing the lampshades. Think of these affordable accessories as jewelry for a room. If you're ready to try something new, take your lamp base to the store and experiment with the options. There's more than one perfect shade for each base.

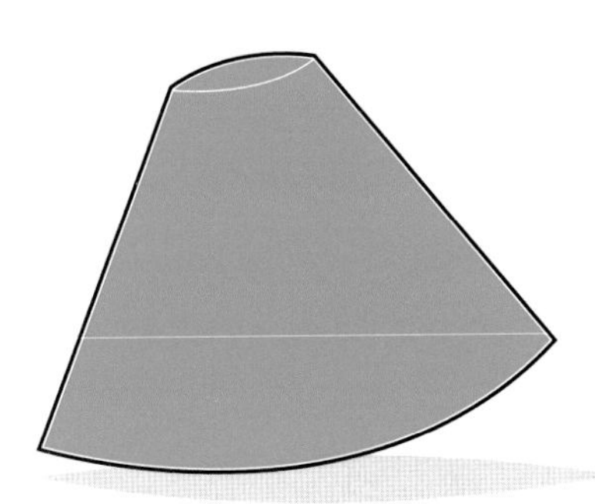

Coolie: A coolie lampshade, shaped like a coolie hat, provides balance for a wide lamp base. Perch one on a scrolling iron base or over a glass cylinder. Use a shallow shade on a short base.

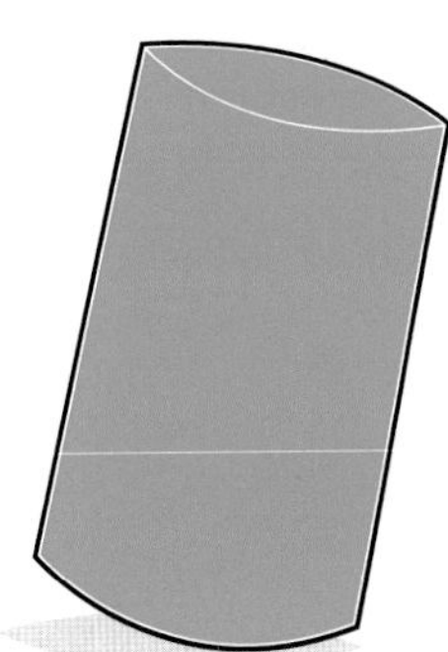

Drum: Drum lampshades are perfect cylinders. Use them to add drama as a pendent light, to highlight a column base, or to add a modern spin. For accent lighting, use opaque shades to cast light up and down.

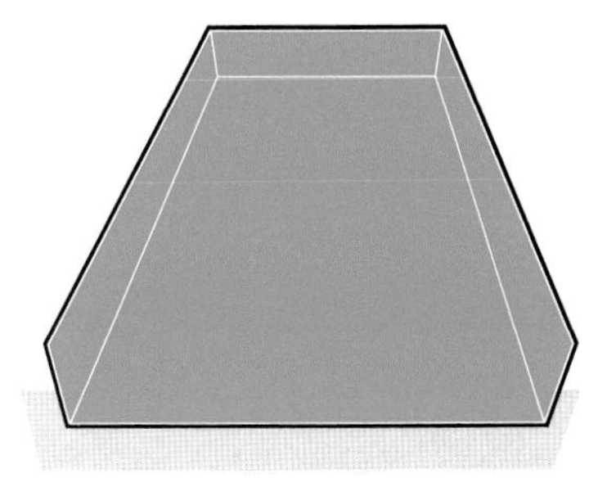

Square or rectangle: Match these lampshades to a square or rectangular base. Choose shades that extend at least 2 inches beyond the lamp base. Opt for light-color shades for maximum glow.

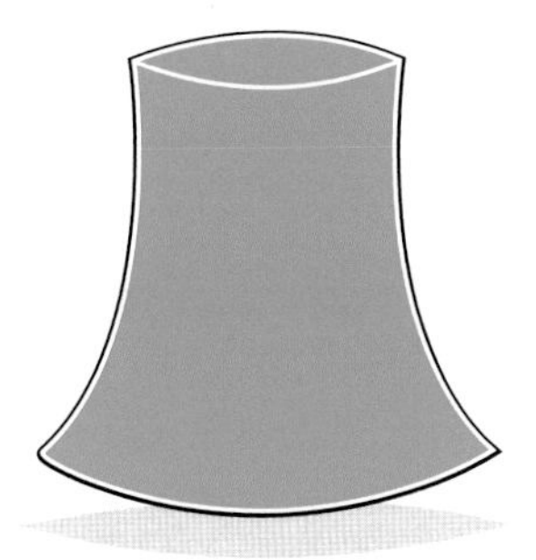

Bell: A gentle flare at the bottom of a bell-shape shade adds classic appeal. Choose a shade texture to complement the base, such as a silk shade on a crystal base or natural linen for metal or stone.

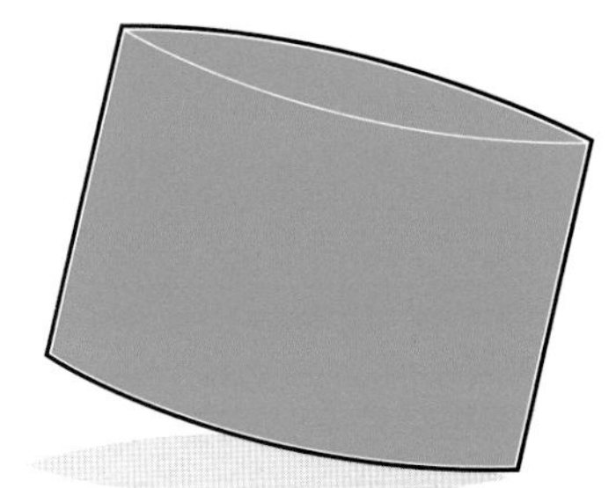

Oval: Long and narrow, an oval shade fits in smaller spaces without sacrificing light. Experiment with an oval shade to make sure it does not overpower the base. Add dimmer controls to adjust lighting to needs.

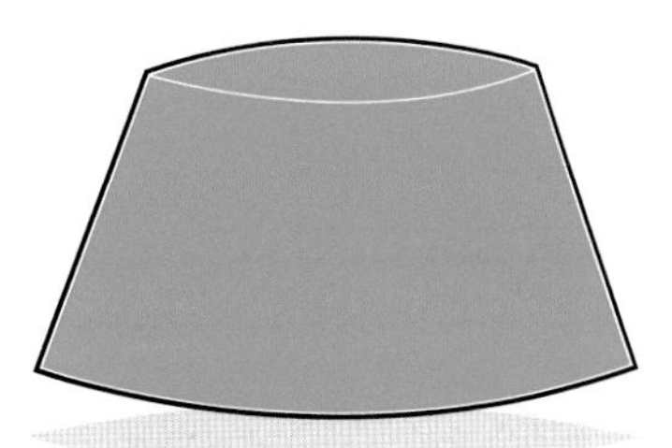

Empire: Round yet flared at the bottom, this popular shape sits well on top of almost any base. Size the lamp base to the size of the flare for the best match. Make sure the shade covers the lightbulb.

Put these lighting tips to work.

- **Hang a chandelier** so the shade bottom is 30 to 34 inches from the table. If the ceiling is higher than 8 feet, hang the fixture 3 inches higher per foot of added ceiling height.
- **Select a chandelier** that's 2 feet narrower than the table length.
- **A lampshade should be** two-thirds the base height, deep enough to reveal a portion of the neck, and 1½ times the width of the base.
- **Accent an object** by placing a light at a 30-degree angle and focus it on the object. The light should be three times brighter than room light.
- **Wash a wall with light** by installing one row of accent lights on the ceiling 2 to 3 feet from the wall.
- **Position short floor lamps** so they are even with your shoulder when seated; set tall floor lamps 15 inches to the side and 20 inches behind what you're reading.
- **Space recessed fixtures** at least 4 to 6 feet apart for general light, 15 to 18 inches apart for task lighting. Allow one recessed light fixture for every 20 to 25 square feet of space.
- **Install sconces** about 65 inches from the floor, above standing eye level.
- **Position the shade** of a desk lamp 15 inches above the work surface.

Think of fixtures

wired into place as permanent additions to your home. Look for options that include sconces, chandeliers, pendants, track lighting, and more.

1. For flair and function

Three drum-shaped fixtures add task lighting over a kitchen island. For the best lighting suspend the fixtures so the bottom of the shade is about 28 inches above the work surface. A lower position may obstruct the view across the room, but a higher position can visually disconnect the island from the fixture. Use crisp, white halogen bulbs to show off food colors.

2. For a modern attitude

Chandeliers don't have to be ornate. This handsome five-armed version offers a sleek alternative. Add a dimmer switch to set the mood for dining. For more about chandeliers, see pages 182–183.

3. For old-fashioned charm

Most experts agree that wired-in fixtures should reflect the architecture of the house rather than match the furniture. This reproduction schoolhouse fixture brings charm to any house built around 1900. The opal glass shade casts a soft glow.

4. For a hint of romance

Tiny olives and green leaves wrought in metal lend an elegant flair to this double-armed sconce. Use a fixture like this as is, or top the flame-shape bulbs with miniature shades.

Use lighting to add drama and function. It's the perfect combination in a kitchen where task lighting adds safety to food preparation and mood lighting creates a cozy eating space. Here's how it works.

1. Pendants. A pendent fixture over the sink and the multi-shade pendant over the island hang 22 to 28 inches above the surface to provide general illumination as well as task lighting. For lighting flexibility add dimmer switches. Note: Light quality gets warmer as it dims.

2. Undercabinet lighting. Whether fluorescent or halogen, undercabinet lighting provides glare-free, task-oriented lighting. Task lighting from above and in front eliminates the possibility of having to work in your own shadow.

3. Range-hood lighting. Most range hoods come equipped with task lighting that illuminates this crucial area.

4. Inside cabinet lighting. Add light fixtures inside glass-door cabinets to make it easy to find tableware. The soft lighting also adds a moody glow and highlights objects.

Balance lighting to create comfortable, well-lit living spaces. That means overhead fixtures for general lighting, lamps for task lighting, and sconces, picture lights, and downlights for accent lighting.

1. Pendants. These fixtures spread general lighting throughout rooms; wired with dimmers, they can be adjusted to suit any activity. In the dining room hang the fixture 30 to 34 inches above the table. Suspend the living room fixture so it provides a clear view of the television.

2. Table lamps. Master the art of flexible task lighting with table lamps that can be moved as needed. For soft mood lighting use lamps with low-wattage bulbs. Beef up the wattage for use as a reading lamp, or opt for in-line dimmers for flexibility.

3. Directional lighting. Use light as a decorating accent. A torchiere spreads light by bouncing it off the ceiling. Spotlights attached to bookcases highlight the contents and add drama. Spotlights also can accent works of art.

Windows
for style-setting views

Windows invite light inside and offer views of the outdoors, but the need for privacy and light control can require some cover-up. Take time to analyze your situation. Do you want window treatments to soften the room and add style, pattern, and color? Or do you need them for privacy, light control, and insulating value? Consider your style: casual or dressy, modern or classic? Do you like a layered effect, or would you rather have one layer that provides the function you need? Do you want to show off classic windows with beautiful detailing by leaving them unadorned? Each room will require a different solution so get started now by considering the options.

in this section

Build on this designer secret:

Window treatments can be problem solvers. Fabric treatments can soften angular walls, make windows look taller and wider, save space by tucking inside the window frame, and add visual inches to a low ceiling. Here are a few strategies to try.

Right: Window treatments can change the shape of a room. These curtains create continuity by repeating the stripes of wall color. It's a look that evokes the colors and clean lines of the 1930s. Fine Irish linen serves as the dark stripes; a linen sheer makes up the light panels. To create a crisp effect, the fabric was cut horizontally and finished with French seams. This way, no vertical seams disturb the soft folds. **Above right:** Stretching window treatments above the window can add height to a room. Two silk fabrics combine to make these panels. The topper, made of quilted fabric, folds over the rod. Decorative glass buttons add sparkle while securing the panels.

Suit the window covering to the sash style. Here are a few options.

Single windows

- Enlarge a window that looks too small for the space by surrounding it with gathered tiebacks or flowing curtains that hang outside the frame.
- Use a shade or top treatment if the window size is right for the room.
- Raise the apparent height of a ceiling by mounting the curtain rod above the frame top.

Multiple windows

- Decide to treat each window separately or the series as one.
- To get the architectural impact of joined windows, use a top treatment only or inside-mount curtain panels.
- For light control and privacy mount shades, blinds, and shutters inside each window molding.
- For a soft look use full-length draperies and mount them to hang over the window frame.

Bay and bow windows

- Dress them with a variety of treatments. For simplicity use shades, blinds, or shutters. Add sweeping curtains or a valance.
- For a formal effect hang draperies to frame the window alcove.

Above and right: Lacy curtains float in front of a bay window, adding depth and importance to the bay. The panels are suspended from a ceiling-mounted hanger and doubled lengths of silver cord threaded through silver eyelets inserted along the top edge of the curtain. Hanging light-amplifying white curtains can brighten even a dull room.

Left: Wide panels on both sides of a single window can add scale to a boxy room. To create a look like this, tie curtain panels to hooks evenly spaced above the curtain. Rows of black ribbon accentuate the curtain's width and height.

Left below: Matching treatments unify windows that vary slightly in size. The trick is to hang the panels to create the illusion of matching windows. A single panel of fabric separates joined windows. Hanging the panels above the top of the windows adds height to an 8-foot ceiling.

Below: Large windows on the front of a house or windows without a view call for a treatment that brings in light but eliminates the problem views. Three coordinating fabrics—a plaid, a small floral, and a large floral—come together in panels that flip back at the bottom. Covered buttons hold the revealing look in place.

Worth noting

Fabrics for draperies include lightly glazed chintz, light- to medium-weight cotton, lightweight corduroy, damask, dotted swiss, faille, flannel, homespun tweed, linen, silk, taffeta, and toile de Jouy.

Ready-made panels and shades are inexpensive and widely available. Here's how to turn them into your own one-of-a-kind creations.

- **Check for flaws.** Inspect for crooked seams and fabric flaws before buying. These little imperfections will make embellishing more difficult and the results less professional-looking.
- **Take time to prep.** Before adding embellishments, first prep the draperies to remove all wrinkles and creases. Accurate positioning of ribbons and trims will be easier on a pressed surface.
- **Use the right glue.** A washable fabric glue will be strong enough to withstand the agitation of the washing machine and will remain clear and flexible. Snip the smallest possible opening in the top of the glue tube to keep the thickness of the glue line under control; poke the opening with a pin if necessary to keep it clean during the project. Run a thin bead of glue along the ribbon edges rather than squeezing dollops here and there.
- **Wash with care.** Many ready-made window treatments can be washed, either by hand or in the machine on the gentle cycle, and machine-dried. If you add delicate beads or fragile buttons, or are in doubt about the care, opt for hand-washing with a gentle detergent and hanging to dry.

Above and right: Add drama to a boxy room by hanging tab-top panels embellished with a grid of ribbon and rickrack. Natural colors and textures keep the boldness of the pattern in check. For a no-sew project, use fabric glue to attach the ribbon to the curtain panels, and the rickrack and buttons to the ribbon.

Spare the window

treatment to keep the window in view. That's the trick used in these simple window coverings. They provide privacy as needed, while celebrating the architectural beauty of a window and its frame. Give the coverings your own style by adapting these ideas.

Above: Roman shades can be the perfect choice for kitchen windows. They pull up to show the view and fit within the window frame. That keeps them out of contact with splashing water. Consider a colorful print to create a view when the shades are drawn.

Right: Bold gingham dresses corner kitchen windows in style and simplifies construction of the Roman shade. It's easy to follow the lines of the fabric to create a crisp, clean look. Mount them on the outside of the frame to make the window appear larger.

Ribbon edging gives a ready-made Roman shade a fresh new look. One row of ribbon might be nice; layering ribbons adds an extra dose of style. Ribbon wrapping all four sides of the shade creates a box of color.

Below: Large-scale toile creates a dramatic window treatment in this kitchen. The flouncy edges introduce a little romance. Before using a large-scale print, hang a yard of fabric in the window to see if you like the look. Bold prints add impact whether they're gathered or hung flat.

Below right: Layering a vintage window over a double-hung window is a perfect treatment when there's no worry about privacy and light control. Use eye hooks and wire sized for the weight of the vintage window to suspend it from the window frame.

Right: Fancy ribbon adds personality to a ready-made Roman shade. Stretch the Roman shade flat on a table; then tack or glue the ribbon to each fold of the shade.

Simple Roman shades in plaid provide light control and privacy without cluttering the view. Tucking the shades inside the window frame preserves the architectural impact. Line the shades to prevent sun damage.

Selecting a style

- For easy operation opt for window treatments that stay clear of window or door hardware. Check that curtains slide easily on rods and that cords are sturdy and safe.
- To set a mood use draperies and classic swags for a formal look, curtains and shades for an informal look, and simple blinds for contemporary appeal.

Measuring

- Measure the size of the window and how far the treatment extends.
- For fullness multiply the width where the panel will hang by 2½. Allow for seams and hems.
- Divide this measurement by the fabric width to calculate yardage.
- Determine panel lengths plus hems and casings. Allow for matching.
- Multiply the number of widths by the total length to determine how many yards you'll need to buy.

Lining

- Select lining—room-darkening or insulating—that suits the treatment.
- Use interlining for extra body.

Hardware

- Consider options, such as clip-on rings, track systems, grommets, tab-tops, pressure-installed curtain rods, wire systems, and more.

Beauty exists

in the details. Consider the added impact of ribbon, grommets, fabric inserts, lining, and curtain hardware on long panels of fabric. These ideas are sure to inspire.

1. For a casual topping

Tab-top headings give curtains a fresh, casual look. The secret is to make tabs that call attention to the curtain top and rod. These tabs, sewn in place, look like they're buttoned on.

2. For a flirty finish

Ribbons create a romantic finish and are a quick way to make ties. Choose two coordinating ribbon colors for each tie, thread them through 1-inch-long copper couplings attached to the curtain top, then tie them to a decorative curtain rod.

3. For a sweet drape

Wrap a single length of voile or lace around decorative rosette holders to create a romantic swag. Allow extra fabric so the swag can drape in the middle. The middle of the fabric strip acts as a valance; the ends softly frame the sides of the window. The beauty of the swag style is simplicity, so it's best used alone on windows where privacy is not an issue.

4. For a modern edge

Bold grommets add an industrial look to this kitchen cafe curtain. A grommet kit simplifies the process. The curtain hangs over the lower part of a window, offering privacy while letting in light.

5. For a loft look

Metal grommets and a wire curtain system lend an urban look to these striped curtains. The grommets are easy to add using a grommet kit and a hammer. No sewing is needed. Use this hardware only if children won't be tugging on the curtains.

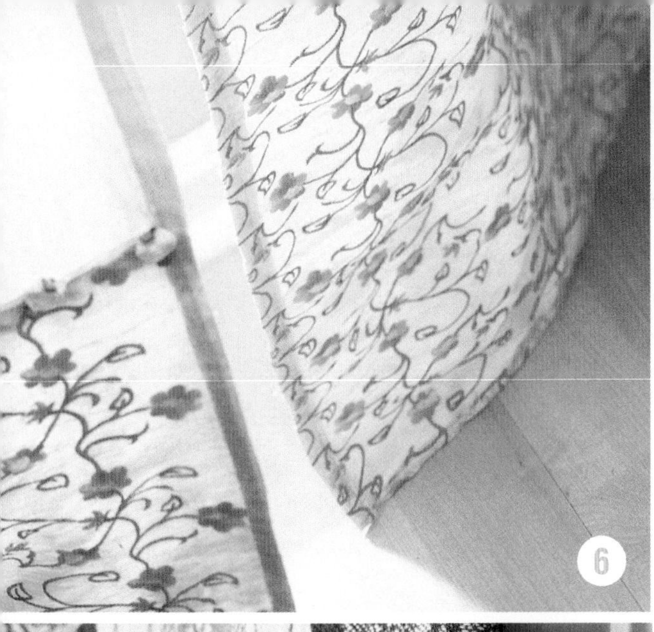

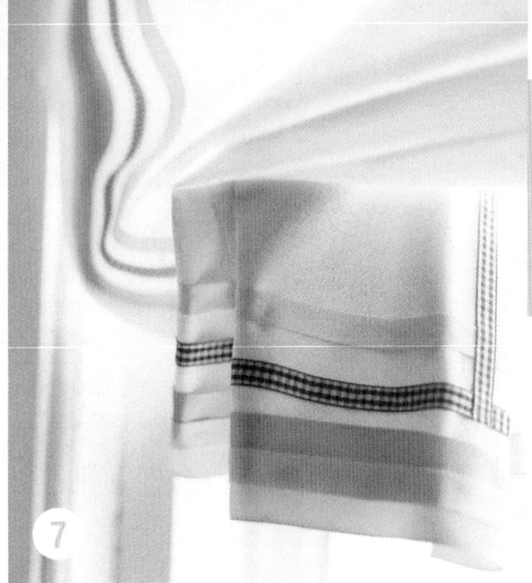

6

7

8

6. For a classic finish
Basic tie-top panels get a simple dress-up with a quick fabric accent near the hem. The coordinating fabric is added to the bottom of the panel, while ribbon rosettes glued to the seam add a feminine touch.

7. For colorful impact
Ribbons add a sweet edge to a Roman shade. The effect is magnified when the shade is pulled open. Select a variety of ribbon sizes, patterns, and colors to create interest. Use fabric glue to attach the ribbons.

8. For a tight roll
Tie-up shades use fabric in its most unstructured form. It hangs flat from a rod or mounting board; then the bottom edge is rolled into position and held in place with a cord. A reversible shade doubles design impact.

Worth noting

As you select hardware consider how often the window treatment will be opened or closed. Check that rings slide easily over rods and that cords are sturdy for daily use and safe around children and pets.

head of the class

Many types of fabrics work with various curtain headings. Evaluate the options.

- **Weight.** Is the fabric heavy enough to fall into the crisp folds created by a pleated heading and still hold its shape? Or is it lightweight enough to hang loosely beneath a rod-pocket heading? Gather a couple yards of fabric in one hand to observe how it drapes as it hangs to the floor. Choose fabric weight carefully according to the look and style you want to achieve.
- **Pattern.** Consider how the pattern will look on the heading you select. Some patterns may be too busy for the intricate design of smocking or will hide in the folds of pencil pleats.
- **Lining.** Whether you line or underline your curtains will depend partially on the look you want to achieve and the amount of light you want to block. Keep in mind that linings help draperies look and hang full and tailored, especially those with pleated and formal headings.

Redo a plain

ready-made curtain panel and Roman shade using these fun, doable ideas. By eliminating the cost of a seamstress, you'll be hanging creative new window coverings that pamper your budget and invite compliments.

Velvet ribbon in three sherbet shades turns plain white tab-top curtains into a fresh and flirty treatment. The design makes use of 1-inch-wide ribbons at the top and for ties, and 1½-inch-wide ribbons at the bottom. Use fabric glue to attach the ribbons. To add the ties cut off the tabs; then cut six evenly spaced 1-inch horizontal slits across each panel, 1 inch below the top. Thread a 22-inch length of 1-inch-wide ribbon through each slit, alternating colors, and tie the ribbon in a bow around the rod. Cut V-notches at the ends of each tie.

Custom-fit a Roman shade to your window by adding fabric strips at both sides. Or buy a shade that's wider than the window and mount it on the frame. To create the graphic design on the center of the shade, print out the letters (one per page) using a favorite font on your computer. For the silverware check the Internet or clip art books for a noncopyrighted image; enlarge the design on a photocopier. Tape the patterns in place under the shade and trace the outline using a black fabric marker. Shade the designs as needed.

Worth noting

For a perfectly centered and spaced word, start with the center letter; then add the next one to the right; then add one to the left, and so on. Use high-quality ribbon for stripes that stand out and bows with body.

Furnishings

for a home sweet home

chapter

10

The furniture and accessories you select for a room define your style. After all, the same sage green living room can look modern with a clean-lined sofa and glass-top table, and casual with an oversize chenille sofa and a wood-and-iron table. Take the time to get it right. Have you made a list of the items you need? Take photos of furniture pieces and accessories you like. If you find the right piece, are you prepared to judge its quality? Sit on the sofa you love to see whether it is comfortable. Do you already own accessories you want to place in the room? Your decisions on these issues will impact your budget and cement your style direction as well.

in this section

Buy smart when furnishing a living room, and you'll be rewarded with years of style and function. Consider these eight tips.

1. Do your homework. Magazines and catalogs are great sources to help define your look before you shop. Pull out pages that illustrate pieces you like and pin them up.

2. Mix it up. Coordinate styles that complement rather than match. Look for ways to combine curves and rectangles to add interest to a room. Consider pairing a modern boxy sofa with a side table that has curvy legs, for example.

3. Do the unexpected. Furniture is versatile. Use a bedroom dresser instead of a console table behind a sofa, a trunk as a coffee table, and an armoire for a kitchen pantry.

4. Focus on furniture scaled to the room size. Does this mean small pieces for small spaces? Not necessarily. In fact one large piece can make a small room feel bigger, opposite. Oversize pieces can sometimes overwhelm a large space. Confused? Study photos of rooms to spy a look you like; then copy the scale of the pieces for a similar effect.

5. Shop around. Look for bargains at outlet stores, used-furniture shops, and close-out sections in furniture stores.

6. Buy in multiples. A pair of ottomans, below left, can have the visual weight of a chaise longue while four small tables can mass together to create a supersize coffee table.

7. Go neutral with big, expensive items. That's the best way to ensure long-term appeal and versatility.

8. Splurge a little. A few good pieces, like this black marble and silver table, below, put a fresh face on everything.

soft seating

Here's what to consider.

• **Construction.** The telling clue about the quality of a sofa or chair is the construction of the seating system. There are two kinds: eight-way hand tied, and zigzag or sinuous springs. Judge quality by sitting. Be wary of a seat that caves. Over time, the springs will weaken, leaving an upholstered sinkhole.

• **Frame.** Look for a hardwood frame, such as oak, for maximum durability. Semihardwoods in 1¼- to 1½-inch dimensions are good too. Low-quality frames use softwoods or plywood. Good sofas use dowels at the joints; cheap ones don't. All frames should use glue, screws or staples, and corner blocks.

• **Fabric.** Keep in mind that fabric grades indicate different price levels and may or may not reflect the fabric durability (a lower-grade cotton twill may wear better than a higher-priced velvet). Most upholstery fabrics are made from a combination of fibers, including synthetics, that are durable and stain-resistant. The stain-resistant fabric coating touted by manufacturers is better at repelling spills than preventing dirt from becoming ground-in spots.

Buy for versatility when

selecting pieces for a dining room or dining area. The same space that's home to a family party might do double duty as a space for crafts or homework. Consider these eight points.

1. List your needs. A dining room that's used only for special meals is wasted space. Make every inch count by furnishing the room to suit a variety of needs, such as crafts and sewing, homework, and library.

2. Plan for storage. A dining room generates a lot of extra gear: tableware, table linens, wineglasses, and large serving pieces. Make a space for everything right where it's used. It could be in a buffet, china cabinet, or armoire, above right.

3. Buy smart. Suit the table to the space. In a small room, a pedestal base on a round table provides flexibility for pulling in extra chairs without being hampered by table legs, opposite. A drop-leaf table works well when space is tight.

4. Make size count. Stretch out in a spacious room by expanding the table size rather than filling the space with more pieces of furniture, below right. A roomy table can balance a ceiling fan, a pair of pendants, or a chandelier.

5. Serve with style. For buffet-style meals introduce a serving piece, such as a console or sideboard. Look for a top surface that's resistant to heat, such as stone.

6. Get set for comfort. Upholstered chairs can extend the time spent dining and can slip into the living room as well. Arms on chairs also make them more comfortable.

7. Plan for change. Consider parsons or folding chairs that can be dressed up with ready-made slipcovers. Change the slipcovers with the seasons.

8. Plan for expansion. A hallway bench or kitchen chairs, purchased to coordinate with the dining room, make good design sense and fit right in when company is coming.

Here's how to choose a table that handles what your life dishes out.

• **Measure up.** Know your room dimensions before you shop. A too-big table in a small room can put the squeeze on entertaining while a too-small table in a grand room can seem out of place. Check whether the table will fit through the doorway.

• **Make it work for you.** If you have children skip glass tops in favor of pine that hides scratches. In a little space buy a convertible coffee table that rises to dining height or a drop-leaf table that expands for company.

• **Check the finish.** Glossy sheens and dark stains or paints show nicks faster, while light woods and distressed finishes disguise blemishes. Ask about watertight coatings to avoid water rings.

• **Take a seat at every table.** Test for comfort and stability. Check that the table has enough elbowroom (ideally about 30 inches between chair centers) but not so much that passing dishes is impossible. Lean on the table to check for wobbling.

• **Pair up the table and chairs.** Test whether you can sit at the table and cross your legs. Check that the chairs, including arms, fit under the table edge.

Comfort and serenity reign in the bedroom, so select furniture that helps achieve these goals. Start with these six tips.

1. Invest in the bed first. It's the focal point of the bedroom and a sure way to anchor the design scheme, above. Check that the bed fits, with room left over for the other pieces of furniture you'll need. A king-size bed can overwhelm even a medium-size bedroom, but it's wise to make room for at least a queen-size bed.

2. Opt for stylish storage. Consider pieces that store clutter out of view, such as built-ins that surround a bed, opposite above. It also might mean finding space for the television so its presence is visible only when it's in use.

3. Slip in seating. Size seating for the space, such as a long narrow ottoman for the foot of the bed, opposite below.

4. Add table space. Bookend the bed with look-alike nightstands. It's wise to search for pieces with similar heights and finishes. Follow the same strategy when selecting lamps. Choose tables that will let you store all your necessities.

5. Play matchmaker or not. In a personal space put together furnishings that reflect your style. In a master bedroom, which is separated from the rest of the house, it's OK to introduce colors or styles that don't appear in other rooms.

6. Customize a closet. A walk-in closet with customized storage can eliminate the need for room-cluttering dressers.

Consider these tips when shopping for bedroom storage pieces.

- **Check tall pieces for stability.** If a unit is top-heavy, it's more likely to topple over when filled with heavy objects, such as a television and books. It's wise to secure a top-heavy unit to a wall.
- **Look for adjustable feet** for uneven floors and hidden casters for moving heavy pieces.
- **Test movable shelves** to be sure they're tight and secure. Check to see if they slide in and out with ease.
- **Opt for a stable storage unit,** one that has a back that is securely attached and does not bow.
- **Test drawers.** They should slide in and out evenly and easily. Drawers with rollers and glides on each side are best; one center bottom roller and glide is OK if the drawer won't get heavy use. See if the drawers have stops so they cannot be accidentally pulled all the way out.
- **Help drawers slide evenly** with a pull on each side of the drawer front (as opposed to a single center pull).
- **Protect clothes.** Consider a dresser with dust liners that form a divider between each drawer. They are found in high-quality furniture.

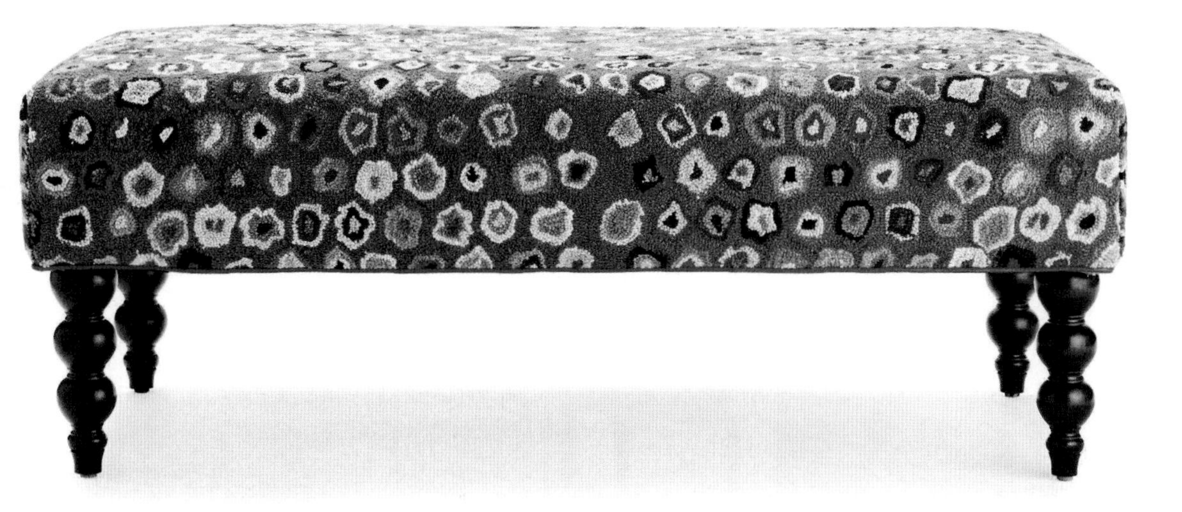

Dress a wall with objects you love. It's one way to surround yourself with memories. How you put them together defines your style.

1. For the collector
A collection of Vera scarves adds a punch of pattern to a living room wall. Elevating designer clothing to art status is smart and affordable.

2. For double-duty display
Frame favorite pieces of jewelry to hang above the dresser. Attach the pieces so they can removed for daily use. It's a fun way to keep organized and rotate a jewelry collection.

3. For a true blue lover
Symmetry gives this collection of blue and white platters and plates a sophisticated look. Skirt a table to provide balance for the collection. Use coated hangers to safeguard the plates.

4. For the nature lover
A bold sepia-tone leaf delivers a graphic statement in this bedroom corner. One oversize framed image adds stylish simplicity for a modern look.

2

1

3

Whip a blank wall into shape using collections. Here's how.

- **Pick your subjects.** Figure out what you'd like to hang, and the hardware you'll need to secure the pieces to the wall. Specialty hangers work on everything, including platters and heavy mirrors. Buy hardware rated for weight.
- **Experiment on paper.** Test out various configurations for your artwork by cutting shapes from kraft paper and taping them on the wall.
- **Consider the grid.** As a rule, a precise grid gives a graphic, formal look. An arrangement that's hung within the confines of a square or rectangle but aligned along only one axis (center, top, or bottom) also will appear orderly—yet a little relaxed.
- **Add a surprise.** Combine an interesting grouping of objects, such as round plates over a square sofa or thin vertical objects for a hallway.
- **Frame valuable pieces** following an archival process with materials such as acid-free matting and UV-protective glass.
- **Protect art in high-traffic areas.** Add hook-and-loop tape to hold frame corners to the wall.

Hard surfaces such as silver, marble, and porcelain contrast with the textures of silk lampshades, a rich wood sideboard, and a modern painting to add interest.

Arranging an eye-pleasing tabletop starts with your collections. Then find the table with a personality to match.

- **Find a focus.** Gather similar items instead of a mishmash of things. Play with the shapes, colors, and composition until your eye dances along the display.
- **Tell your story.** The quickest way to put a stamp on any space is to surround yourself with family photos you love.
- **Please your senses.** When you decorate a side table, toy with texture opposites, such as a smooth, polished silver tray filled with wild, woodsy twigs. Bring in garden flowers or healthy, green plants for aroma.
- **Go for the glow.** Use candles to add sparkle and scent.
- **Consider the impact.** The design elements of scale, rhythm, and balance join forces to create a focal-point arrangement on any surface. Use symmetry for a classic look and asymmetry to add surprise. Vary the scale for drama. Use repetition to move the eye across the objects.

Above left: Reduce the feeling of clutter by grounding a collection of objects in a large tray or shallow basket.
Above right: Vary scale and textures to add interest to a tabletop.

Below left: Surround beautiful objects with white space to elevate them to art status.
Below right: Create a cohesive look with a theme, such as these orbs placed on stands of various heights.

Room by Room

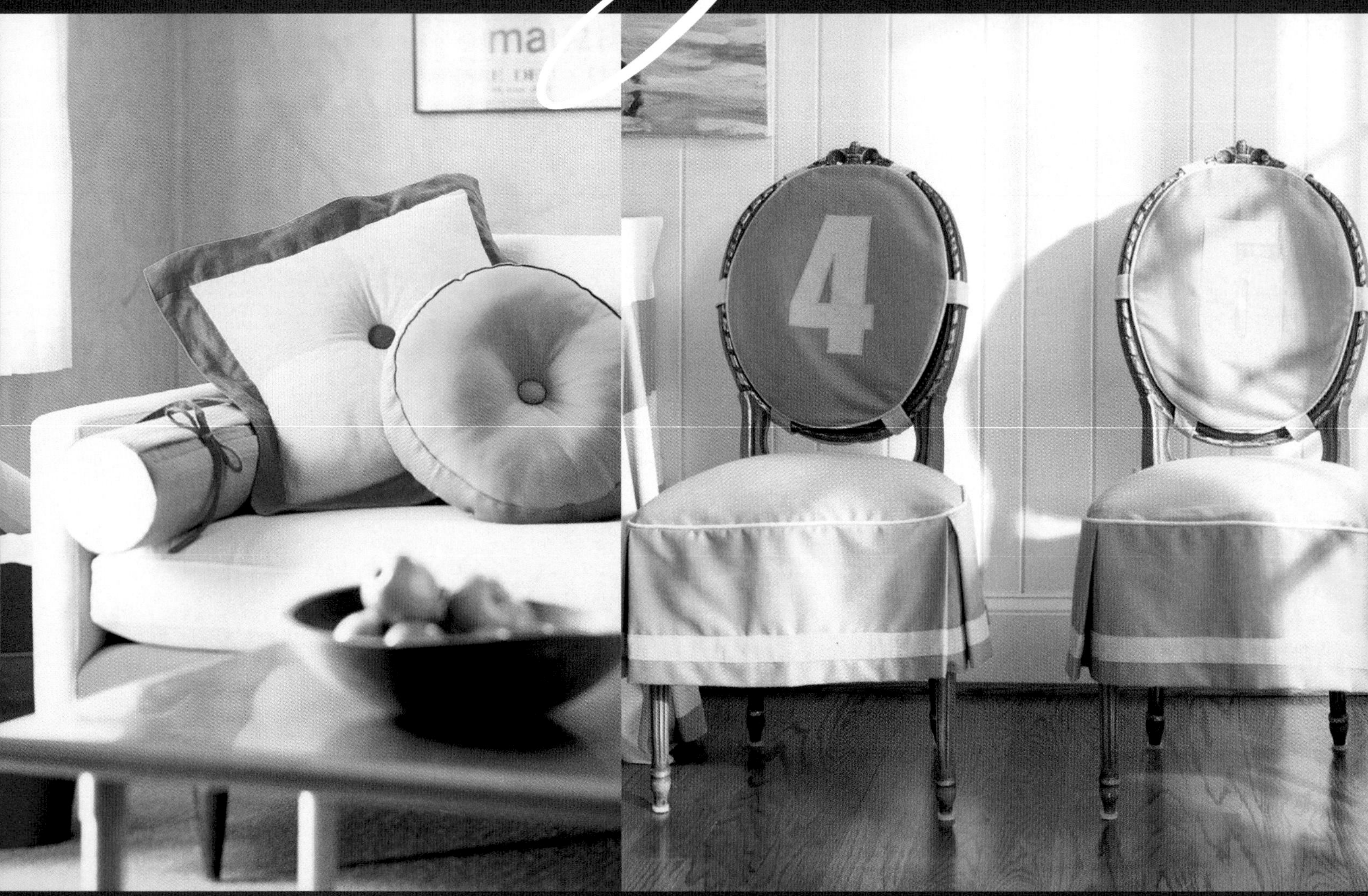

Smart solutions, fun palettes, easy makeovers:

Here's what you need to know to tackle a redecorating project, from master bedroom, family room, kids' rooms, and kitchen to bathrooms, working spaces, and outdoor rooms.

Living rooms for real living

chapter

11

Whether your living room is a quiet zone or an anything-goes space, it's time to make it work for living your way. In most homes it's the most public area in the house. Is it too visible and in full view of the front door? Think about how you use the room. Is it where you entertain or is it a cocoon just for you? Do you like to put up your feet and zone out? Listen to music or read a good book? Do you relax best in a circle of friends and family or by yourself? Consider built-in focal points, such as a great view or a fireplace. How can you use these features? Answering these questions will help you choose furnishings and features that will inject life into your living room.

in this chapter

Make small look big.

In a compact living room, adopt a neutral color palette and select unfussy furnishings, such as crisp-lined sofas and glass-top tables. The neutral yet roomy sofas blend into the background, preserve an open feeling, and provide plenty of seating space. Opt for a wall of storage to minimize clutter without banishing media gear and other living room essentials to storage in another room. Inject personality with pops of color in accessories and original artwork. The decorating plan works by keeping space-smart basics in place and embracing trends with a change of accessories.

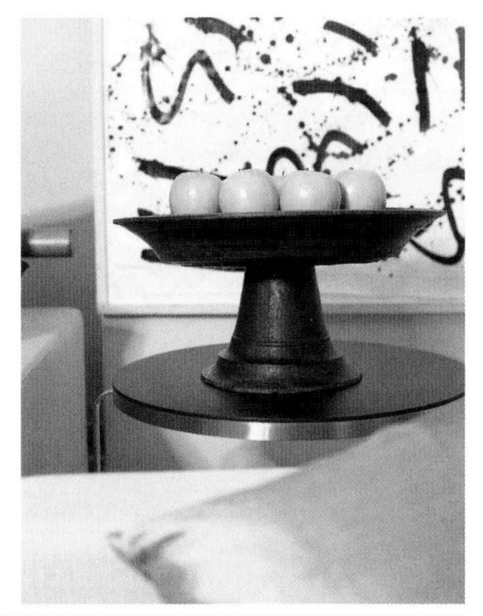

Left: Dramatic accessories give this room design attitude. For a cohesive look pair similar colors and shapes. Black tones and curvy lines unify the table, compote, and painting. **Below left:** Boxy sofas and a rectangular coffee table add a crisp outline to the living room. Curvy compotes and vases relax the mood, while red and orange accessories add visual energy.

Worth noting

Casters make furniture easy to move. Use oversize casters to make a design statement and small ones for a classic look. Opt for lockable casters to keep furniture stationary until moving time.

Savvy steps to a changeable haven

1. Choose one soothing neutral and use it for walls, carpeting, and upholstered furniture.

2. Add bold, changeable color with pillows and throws. A folded throw placed down the center of cushions can serve as a mini-slipcover.

3. Use original artwork to create a focal point.

4. Purchase glass-top coffee or end tables to minimize their visual weight.

5. Select storage units that offer open and hidden storage.

Stay flexible when

designing a living room that will look good now and into the future. First select go-with-anything basics that can change with your style and classic elements that can look casual for every day or be dressed up for company. Then add a signature color, pattern, or collection to give the room a little style punch. If you want a change in a few months, swap out the accessories.

Above: Bold wall color provides a sunny backdrop for neutral furnishings. The yellow mixes well with orange in draperies and pillows. Black-framed prints on the wall illustrate how to group small pieces to make a large focal point. Two small tables offer more flexibility than one large coffee table.

Right: A cohesive color palette and bold scale unite eclectic choices including farmhouse-style rafters, modern upholstered pieces, contemporary art, and a classic rug. Yellow rafters and a red ceiling fan repeat the muted tones of the rug in brighter hues.

In a home without a family room, the living room works hard day in and day out. A soft palette of blues and greens provides a soothing look for family-time weekend cartoons or for Saturday evening dinner parties. New built-ins surround the fireplace with storage. One cabinet holds the television set behind pocket doors and includes drawers for DVDs and videos. The other cabinet has adjustable shelves and drawers for electronic gear and games.

Select fabrics using these tips.

- **What's the mood?** A lustrous silk sets a formal tone, while a cotton check feels casual.
- **How will it be used?** Heavy canvas doesn't drape well so use it for a tailored roll-up shade rather than for pleated curtains. Upholstery fabric, unlike curtains, has to endure lots of wear, so purchase for durability and stain resistance.
- **What are the care needs?** Fabrics treated for soil- and stain-resistance are smart choices for use around children and pets.
- **What's the climate?** Natural fibers such as wool trap heat and work well in a cool climate. Light linens and cotton reflect sunlight, promote evaporation, and suit hot climates. If humidity is a factor, look for fibers with less absorbency.
- **Consider these guidelines.**

For slipcovers: chintz, linen, and cotton.

For medium-weight upholstery: chenille, corduroy, twill, flannel, Jacquard, tapestry, ticking, velvet, and wool.

For draperies: chintz, light- to medium-weight cotton, damask, flannel, linen, silk, and taffeta.

A welcoming red sofa invites readers to sit down and spend a little time with a good book. If a sofa or chair presents its back to the doorway, visitors won't feel welcome; in this room, an angled rattan chair helps direct traffic around the coffee table and to the sofa. A palette of reds and neutrals gives the space cozy warmth.

Left: This classic living room pairs modern furniture and artwork with traditional pieces to create a space that's dressed up without feeling stuffy. Colorful silk draperies billow from the windows, while a red-patterned fabric screen makes a vibrant backdrop for a neutral sofa. Opt for traditional fabrics used in tailored designs to get a good mix of classic and modern pieces.

Above: Washable slipcovers and a tapestry-covered "coffee table" offer put-up-your-feet comfort. That's an easy way to make sure a living room is well used. For an even more inviting mood, add favorite collections, soft pillows, and a throw for warmth on chilly nights. The color palette of warm reds, yellows, and neutrals also adds to the cozy feeling.

For an eclectic look, start here.

- **Pick an interesting backdrop,** one that suits the major theme. For a rich background use Venetian plaster or textured wood. For a modern look select glossy or metallic paint.
- **Combine by shape.** Consider a modern piece and a classic piece that share the same curves or variations of similar details. A fluted classic column might be mimicked by a grooved piece of molding on the edge of a modern cabinet.
- **Watch for balance.** Too much of one element can throw off a room; a mixture makes a space interesting. Before you start, decide which style will be most prominent.
- **Group for impact.** Collections have a way of spreading out and turning into clutter. Group small objects to create a focal point.
- **Edit, edit, edit.** Most people buy what they like, then try to make it work. If you buy like this, be prepared to edit or you'll end up with a cluttered room full of stuff.
- **Ask for help.** A fondness for an item can cloud your thinking. Ask a friend whose style you like to help sort your possessions down to a chosen few.

Soothe your living style with hues that cast a relaxing spell. For the appeal of a seaside vacation, marry the soft blues and greens of water, surf, and sky.

1. Start a soft and serene color palette by selecting fabric samples in analogous tones. Choose either from the cool side of the color wheel or toned-down hues from the warm side. Test fabric samples in the room, checking them throughout the day and evening to see how they look in changing light.

2. Let fabric colors determine paint choices, because paint can be mixed to match. Instead of exactly matching paint and fabric colors, choose a slightly lighter or darker hue to add interest.

3. If color commitment is a problem, start slowly with accessories. Paint woodwork and built-ins white to balance the colors you plan to introduce.

4. When using a pale palette, introduce a little black to ground the color scheme.

Wake up boring walls

with a color statement. For a sleek, sophisticated palette, consider using a primary color, such as sunshine yellow, in a grown-up room.

1. If you're shy about commitment but want a quick shot of color, paint one wall. It can provide a color fix and create a dramatic focal point.

2. Spread color around the room to keep the look cohesive. For example, the sunny yellow of the walls reappears in a toned-down version on the chair upholstery, pile rug, and fireplace accessories.

3. In a scheme of one color plus neutrals, such as gray or taupe, add style by varying the size and use of patterns.

4. Mix bright colors and bold patterns. They're both a little brave, a little cutting-edge, and together they strike a sophisticated balance.

5. For even more color fun and energy, introduce a few accessories that complement the main hue.

6. To enliven a north-facing room, use a bright color such as yellow. In a south-facing room, opt for bold aqua blue to cool the space.

Adapt the rules. Arrange your living room to reflect you and your family, how you like to live, the location of the room, and its traffic patterns. If the room is designed for conversation, gather furniture around a central point and keep it cozy. If the room is used as a serene getaway without a television, a chaise longue would be a nice complement to a sofa. Is reading the main activity? Plan for book storage, easy chairs, and adaptable lighting. Make sure to allow for access to furniture and a pathway through the space. Here are two plans to consider.

Living room 1

1. **Face sofas** for easy conversation.
2. **Allow room so people** can walk in, sit on the sofas or chairs, and leave without asking someone else to get up.
3. **Create a wall** of storage for books and a flat-panel TV.
4. **Install in-floor** electrical outlets for furniture-placement flexibility.
5. **Check that furniture backs** look presentable before floating pieces in the center of the room.
6. **Provide double-duty function** with an upholstered ottoman that serves as a coffee table and footstool.
7. **Use end tables** as landing spaces on both ends of long sofas.

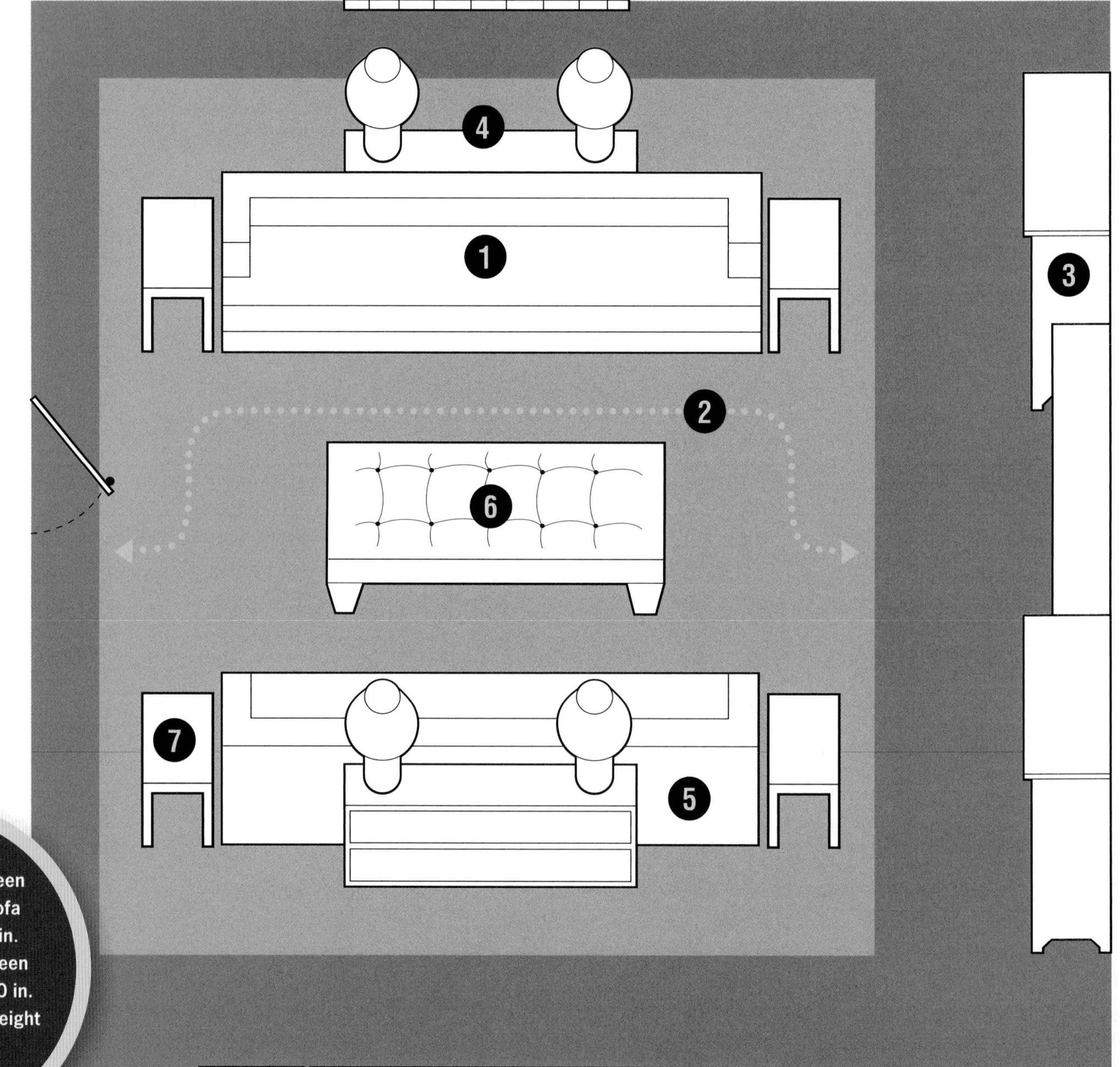

Basics

- **Knee space between coffee table and sofa or chairs = 14–18 in.**
- **Traffic lanes between furniture pieces = 30 in.**
- **Comfortable seat height for a sofa or chair = 16–18 in.**

- **Face the view.** Position the chairs and sofa so they take advantage of the view whether it's the fireplace, a television, or a window.
- **Cozy up for conversation.** For face-to-face chats, place chairs no more than 8 feet apart. If the room is large, use furniture to create comfort islands. Consider facing sofas in the center of a room and a chair, side table, and lamp at one end as a reading nook. Placing a rug and furniture on an angle can solve the problem of a living room that is also a corridor.
- **Create easy pathways.** Create traffic lanes that are several feet wide to allow easy passage around furniture. Leave 14 to 18 inches of space between a coffee table and seating pieces for passage and legroom. Keep the table close enough to the seating so the table feels anchored in the open space.
- **Maximize table space.** Use round pedestal tables as side tables between chairs and sofas. The central leg makes them easier to maneuver around. When space is tight, bring in nesting tables.
- **Plan for fine dining.** If your living room is also your dining room, consider using a library table with two upholstered chairs for daily use and adding movable benches along both sides for a dinner party.

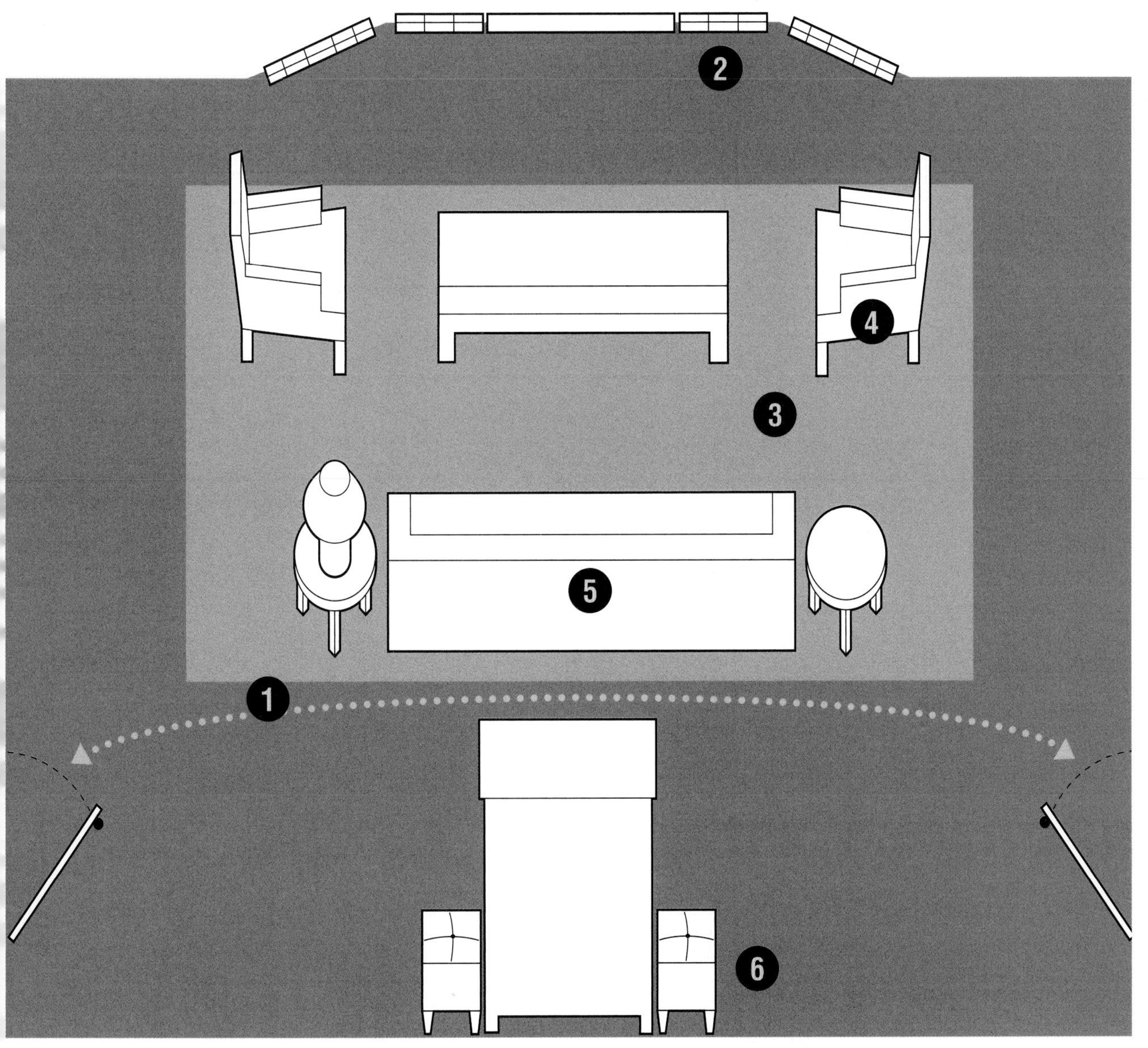

Living room 2

1. Leave walking space of 3 feet if the living room also serves as a corridor.
2. Take advantage of the view using furniture placement. In this case that means the grouping faces the bay window.
3. Anchor furniture in the middle of a room by using a rug. Choose a rug that's large enough for all the furniture to fit, or small enough so the rug edges just touch the furniture legs.
4. Narrow arms on chairs preserve sitting space in a narrow room.
5. A longer sofa provides more seating without adding multiple pieces of furniture.
6. Movable ottomans offer additional seating for a party but hang out near a cabinet most of the time.

Playing favorites

with color delivers a living room that's perfectly tuned to your personality. Starting with a neutral sofa and flooring ensures these costly items will last through several color changes.

Before: Beige and brown gave this living room a boring, dated attitude, below.

After: Now the room, opposite, is a colorful getaway in a house that also includes a family room filled with neutrals. Flowery fabrics, sweet ruffles, and a mix of furniture add style to this space suited for conversation and crafts projects. Here's how to get started.

- **Brighten the walls.** A bold color works in the living room when it's balanced with white woodwork and other bright colors. When using accent hues spread them around for balance. Here orange shows up on pillows, bench, framed flower prints, and Roman shades.
- **Update flooring.** Replace boring carpet with hardwood flooring, which will last for years and support any color scheme or style.
- **Build a focal point.** What looks like expensive custom built-ins are actually two ready-made bookcases and an armoire joined with additional wood and moldings. Window seats stretch between bookcases to add seating and storage, below right.
- **Purchase a basic sofa in a solid neutral fabric.** Choose a sofa that comfortably fits the space. A too-big sofa can hog square footage and still only seat two adults.
- **Add a drop-leaf table and chairs.** The combination provides a perfect spot for crafting.
- **Play with fabrics.** This energetic mix includes at least a dozen prints for pillows, cushions, and draperies. The mix works because the fabrics share at least one common color.
- **Create art.** Flower prints framed in crisp white add bold hues and patterns, below left. To make similar flower prints, use a digital camera and have the images blown up and printed on canvas.

Before

Center attention on the coffee table to make it the hub of utility in a living room. For a round table compose tabletop displays that span at least one-third of the table diameter. For impact make groupings a few inches taller than half the table height.

Right: Adding accessories to a round table can be challenging because it has to look good from all angles. Grouping tall objects adds scale and balance that makes the rest of the table arrangement visually comfortable. Look for design objects that share similar features to create a grouping. In this case rustic textures in natural wicker and wood provide cohesion, and roses add spots of color. Use an odd number of objects to create balance.
Far right: The same round table offers a simpler look. Five vases in clear glass echo the shape of the table without distracting. The table offers a solid background for pretty blossoms. To maintain a similar minimalist look on a coffee table, provide nearby storage or a covered basket for remote controls, magazines, and other living room clutter.

When shopping for a coffee table, start with these guidelines.

- **Select a coffee table** that's one-half to two-thirds the length of the sofa. That allows people seated on the sofa to have access to the table and provides room for accessories. A table that's too big leaves little room for traffic flow.
- **Check out the surface.** If you want a put-up-your-feet table, select a surface that can withstand the wear, or have a piece of glass cut to fit your tabletop to protect the underlying surface. Consider ottomans that do double duty as footrests and tables.
- **Watch the height.** Choose the height that works for how you plan to use the table. A lower table of 16 to 18 inches makes sense for display, while a slightly taller table may work for dinner and a movie.
- **Use shape to suit the space.** A round table can add flexibility to a small space with two chairs facing a sofa. It also opens up walking space. A rectangular table or a pair of small square tables may work better near a long sofa.

Cool retro

Think of a classic sofa and coordinating chairs as the little black dresses of decorating. Paired with the right accessories, they can adapt to suit almost any style.

- **Pick the palette.** What's better than blue? More blue! In shades from turquoise to midnight, periwinkle to aqua, this monochromatic living room takes on a fresh retro vibe. Blend light and dark shades to keep the color palette interesting.
- **Build on basics.** The sofa, in a white matelasse slipcover, and the slipper chair, in cream, stay put. The white cover on the armchair is swapped for one in chambray blue. White paint neutralizes the unfinished coffee table.
- **Add graphic style.** The modern look is built on the use of bold graphic elements: pillows in stripes and squares, an outsize checkerboard rug made from carpet tiles, a striped lampshade, and modern vases.
- **Finish with accessories.** Circle strings, a takeoff on '60s hippie beads, look grown-up when hung in front of sheer curtains. Narrow shelves provide space for dog portraits, computer-generated from photos and ordered online.

Warm urban

Pare this room down to its blue walls and basic furniture before transforming the style from retro to warm urban.

- **Add warm tones.** What could be more soul-satisfying than a generous serving of chocolate brown? Espresso brown. Cocoa brown. Toffee brown. After all, these warm tones provide the perfect counterpoint to cool blue walls.
- **Play with the basics.** Basic pieces stay the same except the blue chambray slipcover is replaced by one in crisp white denim. Brown paint remakes the coffee table.
- **Add style wow.** New pillows and cushions in mix-and-match shades of brown are piled on the white sofa. Underfoot a brown and blue rug grounds the color scheme and introduces a field of waves. A vase and lamp repeat the curves and contrast beautifully with the boxy brown side tables. Clear plastic nesting tables serve as a visual counterpoint to brown, which can be a heavy color.
- **Hang the finishing touches.** Rattan Roman shades add texture and pattern at the window. Artist's canvases, painted in brown stripes, become dramatic wall art.

A library of books always warms up a room and promises vicarious adventure. Whether you start with a purchased bookshelf or add built-in bookcases, the net effect is one of comfort, character, and style.

1. For the fashionista

A stately yellow-glazed bookcase provides the perfect setting for books and Chinese jars. A Provençal animal-pattern fabric updates the interior of the antique bookcase and adds the appeal of designer fashion.

2. For the collector

Bookcases that hug the wall require little square footage, but they deliver tons of storage. The upper section features long shelves that hold books, CDs, and collectibles. The lower part of the bookcase steals a little more floor space to make room for baskets filled to the brim.

3. For the decorator

Bookshelves built along two walls create a reading nook that harbors a creamy sofa. The walls and shelves are painted in rich burgundy, a regal backdrop for books and fine collections. Swing-arm lamps ensure comfortable light for reading.

4. For the mover

Metal restaurant shelving provides support for even the beefiest of book collections and a trendy look for loftlike living spaces. Casters make the shelves easy to move if the mood strikes.

5. For the nester

Bookcase cubes add a sense of geometry and architecture to this wraparound unit and help the Louis XVI daybed snuggle into place.

6. For the reader

Mismatched bookcases create an instant library in one corner of the living room. The combination of three bookcase towers in two styles and finishes adds a relaxed and confident mood to the space. Sink-in seating and two ottomans invite readers to settle in.

Good bones (sturdy, well-supported shelves that don't bow under the weight of books) are the key to attractive bookcases. Keep these tips in mind whether buying off-the-rack or custom bookcases.

- **Shelf and fitting construction.** Fixed dadoed joints and adjustable steps with pins are common construction methods for shelves. Both systems provide a finished look with the option of varying shelf heights. Such permanent shelving is designed and crafted as fine woodwork and often built from quality hardwoods. For less permanent construction a fixed-bracket technique can turn a wall into a library.
- **Measurements.** Start with these basics when designing book storage. Typically, shelves need to be built from ¾-inch plywood to avoid unsightly sagging. Bracket supports should be 30 to 36 inches apart, or 24 inches apart if ½-inch plywood is used. For the most versatility shelves should be at least 18 inches apart and 10 to 12 inches deep.
- **Stability.** If a bookcase unit is top-heavy, it is more likely to topple over when filled with books and other heavy objects. To secure it in place, screw through the back of the bookcase and into the wall. Use wall anchors suited for masonry or drywall.

Plump spots

of color and comfort, pillows work their magic on sofas, chairs, and even the floor. Make these pillows from scratch or add trims to purchased pillows.

1. Tied and buttoned

A bolster made from a striped silk fabric showcases an easy way to make a pillow by overlapping the long edges and securing the ends with simple ties. Covered buttons (use a kit to make them) accent the scallops at the center of the pillow.

2. Symbols of fall

A leaf appliqué adds style to this front-and-center pillow. To create the look cut fabric and a layer of fusible webbing in the shape of a leaf. Fuse it to the pillow top.

3. Quilted envelopes

Small pillows are great for chairs, and these are ideal for the dining room. To make them, overlap the two ends of a scallop-edge place mat, and topstitch the sides together. Slip a pillow form inside and close the pillow with a jeweled brooch or decorative button.

4. Ready-mades made better

Purchased pillows take to trims with ease. For these fun sentiments glue trims in the shape of an X or an O to the pillow top.

5. Edge trimming

A stack of coordinating pillows illustrates how to mix fabrics and trims to create interest in a room. A color palette of red plus a neutral ensures that every pillow coordinates. Various shiny trims enhance the good looks of the pillow set.

6. Stylish rounds

A bolster looks dressed up with bands of shiny ribbon and fuzzy chenille. The round pillow features contrasting quarter panels of a zebra print and floral. Striped cording adds a third pattern to the pillow. A standard knife-edge pillow gains personality by combining two pieces of fabric and covering the seam with red trim.

7. Color plays

Cotton fabrics in bold colors pair with simple designs to give these fun sofa pillows graphic appeal. For design pop use a complementary color scheme of yellow and hot pink.

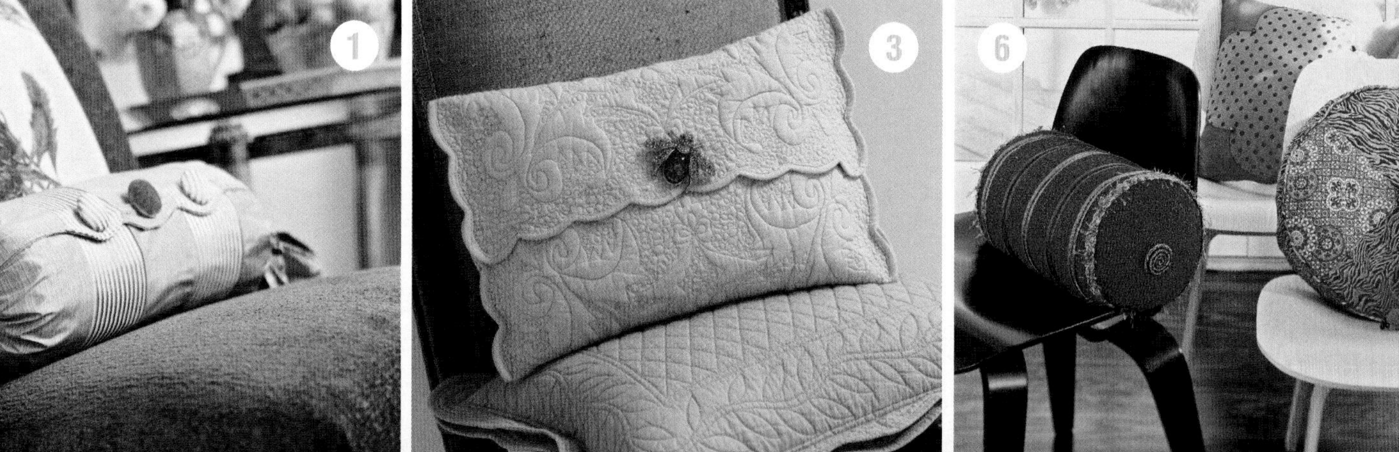

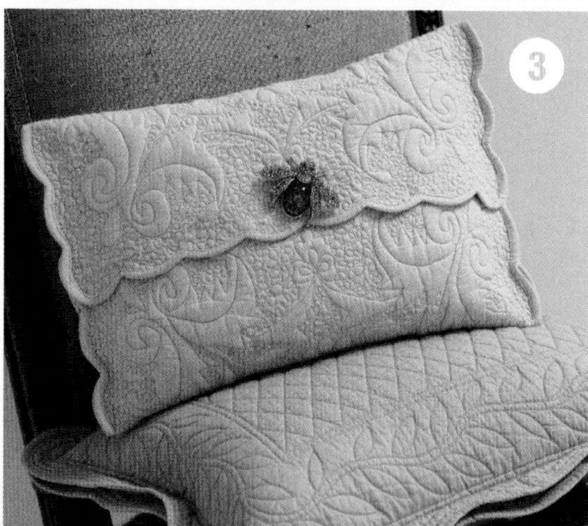

To get the most out of your pillows, follow these tips.

1. Assemble a group. Decorative pillows make more of a statement in a group. Combine them by color, pattern, or texture.

2. Create continuity. Reverse a pattern or use it in different colors to tie a group together. Do the same with texture, combining a silk pillow with a nubby pillow wrapped with a silk ribbon.

3. Diversify textures. Combine shiny fabrics with matte materials or smooth silk with textured wool.

4. Distinguish with details. Feather fringe, accent buttons, and welting add signature style. Search for trims, new and vintage, that can add a designer look.

5. Stick with basic forms. Choose square, round, oblong, and rectangle shapes. These shapes are very flexible and can be carried from room to room. Pillows in other shapes—stars and hearts, for example—may not suit every room.

Dining rooms

for gathering and sharing

chapter

12

Sharing food and conversation around a table speaks to the very heart of hospitality. Nourish that spirit with a dining room that's comfortable, welcoming, and easy to use. To achieve the look that's right for your entertaining style, ask these questions: How many people can comfortably eat in your dining room? Do you like casual meals or formal affairs? Is the dining room part of an open space or a room by itself? What changes could make your dining room better in a day, in a week, or in a month? Start making a list. It's sure to lead the way to a space that's perfectly suited to fine dining.

in this chapter

Dining rooms

share the same basic ingredients—a table and chairs and a centered light fixture—and that's where all similarities end. Here's proof. These two dining rooms flaunt one-of-a-kind style. One is sophisticated and modern; the other is dressy and glamorous. Pick your favorite and make it your own.

Clutter-free style

1. Create drama with dark walls and light woodwork. It's a classic recipe for adding importance to a room with minimal architectural detailing.

2. Opt for an anchoring table. A bold, simple table offers uncompromising simplicity and room to spare for family and friends.

3. Split up the suite. Metal chairs of different lineages look good together because they share the same material. The same is true for wood chairs.

4. Cast a warm glow. A cloth-covered lampshade provides ambient light and quiet good looks. Check out a home center for a kit to transform any lampshade into a hanging fixture.

5. Inject personality. A collection of old globes grouped into a permanent centerpiece pairs with clear glass votives for a surprising mix. A roomy table requires a large centerpiece or collection for balance.

Luxury details

1. Warm it up. Chicory brown grounds this elegant color scheme and provides a compatible background for the warm tones of red and yellow.

2. Marry a fabric-draped table and upholstered chairs. Use make-a-statement damask on the chairs. The style or condition of the table is unimportant when it's hidden under a beautiful cover.

3. Spread a little sparkle. Crystals attached to a candle chandelier reflect the light, and glass vases add extra gleam. Even the sheen of the silk fabric contributes to the soft glow in the room.

4. Slip in low storage. Use a buffet, rather than a tall hutch, to add storage and a serving counter without gobbling too much wall footage.

5. Create a focal point with prints. Pressed botanicals float in identical frames and make a dramatic grid on the wall. Custom frames maximize every inch of vertical space.

Round is right for this square, book-lined dining room. The Saarinen-look table, a classic from the mid-20th century, offers stark counterpoint to the walls of books. The table also makes a handy surface for projects and reading.

Round tables slip into dining rooms with ease.

Round tables slip into dining rooms with ease. The secret is the center pedestal that keeps table legs out of traffic lanes. Consider using a large table in a spacious dining room and a table for two or three where space is tight. When selecting a smaller table, look for one that can be used as a bedside table or living room table if future plans include a larger home.

Above left: Bold and beautiful, the pedestal base takes center stage while thin chair legs almost disappear. A grid of wall boxes contrasts with the table's curves. Note how the colors and shapes of the table and chairs repeat in the collections.

Below left: Rich and elegant, this claw-foot table is big enough for four and petite enough to fit in a small room. Opt for a dressy table so it can work in a living room and add armed chairs for comfort. For flexibility buy a table with leaves.

Below right: Dark and dramatic, this dining room table hosts chairs that are embroidered with a pithy saying. The Regency-style table, paired with upholstered chairs, offers comfortable seating for dinner and conversation.

Rectangular tables maximize space in most dining rooms. Long and narrow, they allow room for placing a buffet nearby. With added leaves they can expand into an adjoining living room or entry to seat a crowd. In tight quarters consider tables with drop leaves that fold into narrow rectangles.

Left: Scandinavian-inspired chairs add an elegant note of comfort in this classic dining room. Open to the living room, the space can expand to suit a party. Symmetry adds formal balance to the room. Built-in cabinets provide storage and display space.

Above: A glass top almost disappears to keep this dining table from overwhelming a small dining room. The simple table frame plays well against wood chairs while modern artwork adds style contrast. Allow at least 3 feet to pull out chairs and still maneuver around the table.

Opposite: Eclectic and refined, this dining room showcases how to mix it up. An abstract painting hangs over a classic sideboard, and an armillary sphere sits atop a pedestal. Classic chairs slipcovered in traditional English fabrics make stylish companions for the vintage table.

Set the table in a room filled with warm colors.

1. Play up the wood. This paneled room features warm wood tones. Enhance their appeal with the cool tones of blue and white dishware and the warmth of red leather-clad albums.

2. Layer on fabrics. Leaf-pattern fabric in a shimmery copper hue is a warm foil for blue and white dishes. A coordinating striped fabric covers the chair cushions. For a touch of color, use commercial-grade cotton dish towels as napkins.

3. Introduce color with a favorite collection of dinnerware. A neutral backdrop lets the blue dishes stand out. The blue shades found in antique dishware vary widely, yet they all look good together. Make sure to include several shades.

4. Bring flowers to the table to complement the food and the dishware. In this case only red will do. It plays up the warm tones of the wood and complements the blue of the dishes. A color such as apple green would add contrast to the dishes but feel jarring against the warm wood tones.

5. Use light to make the scheme moody or bright. A dark space can feel moody with low light and bright when lit up. To make a space like this feel even brighter, consider a white or light blue tablecloth.

Start collecting tableware, then build a color scheme that coordinates.

1. Embrace neutrals to create a relaxing dining retreat. This dressy floor-length skirt is made from hardworking all-weather fabric that resists spills. Nubby linen dresses the built-in banquette. Textured neutrals anchor the look.

2. Vary tones for interest. Check colors in daylight, candlelight, and lamplight. They'll take on a range of tones—warm, cool, grayed, and tinted—depending on the time dinner is served.

3. Build a collection of coordinating tableware. Select dinnerware first, then match colors to the pieces. Aim for a collection that mixes neutrals from several manufacturers to add interest. This dinnerware is in the Provençal style with embossed scalloped edges and pale glazes that vary in color from white to cream.

4. Add pattern in the same restful tones. It takes a deft hand to work with an all-neutral scheme. Two or three patterns can play small but important parts in the palette.

5. Inject a touch of glimmer to keep the palette interesting. In this case narrow gold frames add a dash of elegance.

Match a dining room's arrangement to your style of entertaining and the size and shape of the room.

A long, narrow room generally needs a long, narrow table while a square room can accommodate a round or square table. Drop-leaf tables offer options for seating more guests; when the leaves pop up, the setting becomes cozier. Benches can slip under the table for daily use and pull out to seat a crowd. If the dining room is too small for entertaining, outfit it with an oversize buffet and spread tables for two to four throughout the living room and dining room.

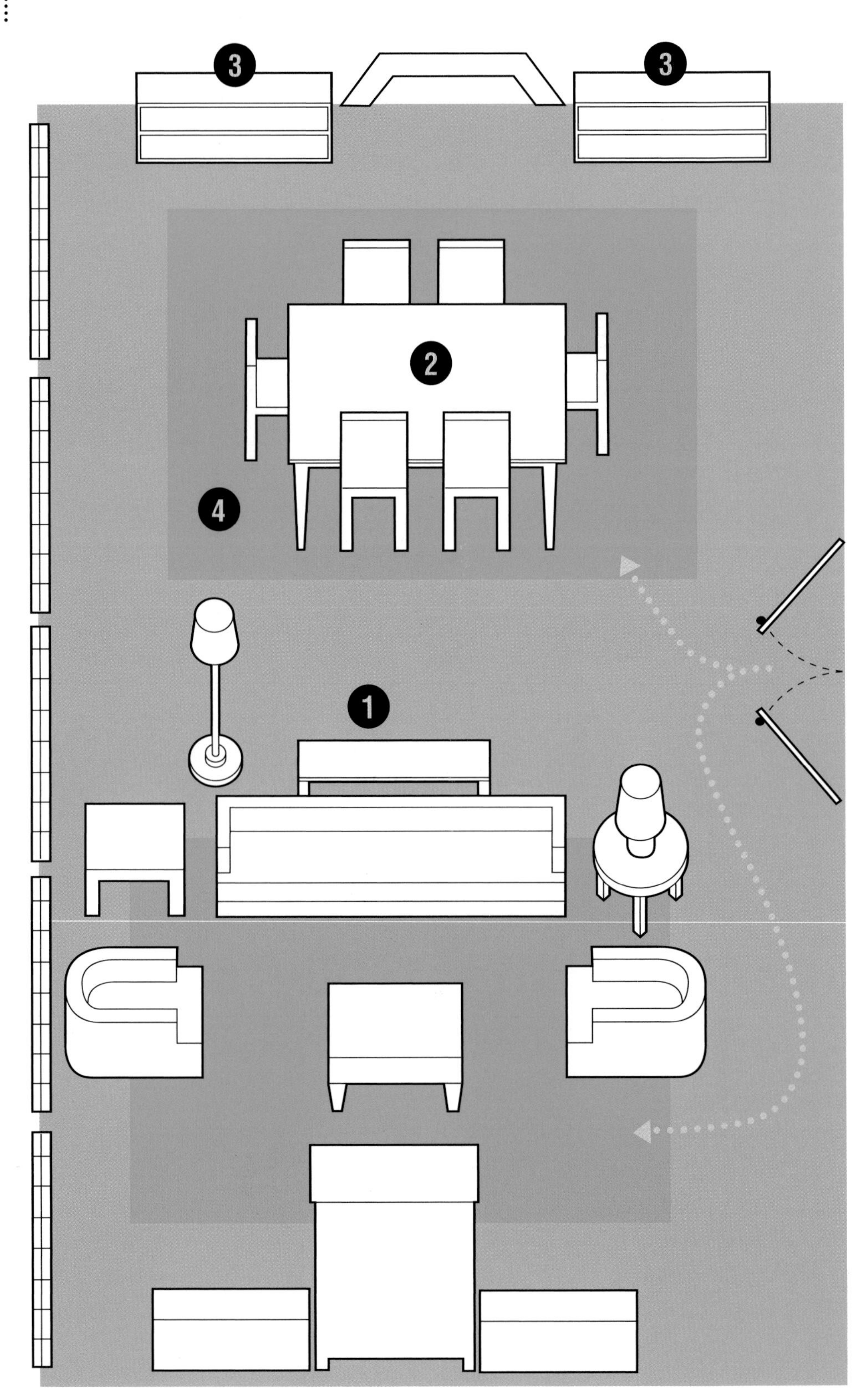

Rectangular room

1. Use one-third of the space for dining in a large rectangular living/dining room. Use a sofa or other piece of furniture to mark the dividing line between areas.

2. Choose a table to suit the room shape: Rectangles go with rectangular rooms; squares or circles with square rooms.

3. Flank a window with matching buffets for symmetry and to create a focal point. Low cupboards preserve views and space.

4. Pick a rug 4 feet wider on all sides than the table so chairs can be pulled out without snagging the rug edges.

L-shape room

1. Minimize furniture pieces, in size and number, when the living room and dining room share space.

2. Extend the dining room into the living room for company by using a table with leaves. Leaves that fold up from the sides would be too bulky for this narrow space.

3. Keep pathways clear, especially the doorway to the kitchen, so it's easy to navigate with plates and bowls.

4. Omit a buffet or china closet in a small dining room; opt for a narrow, well-supported shelf for serving space.

5. Suit the scale of chairs and dining table to the room. Open legs and backs keep dining chairs from visually gobbling extra square footage.

For more about furniture placement, see "Room Arranging" on page 422.

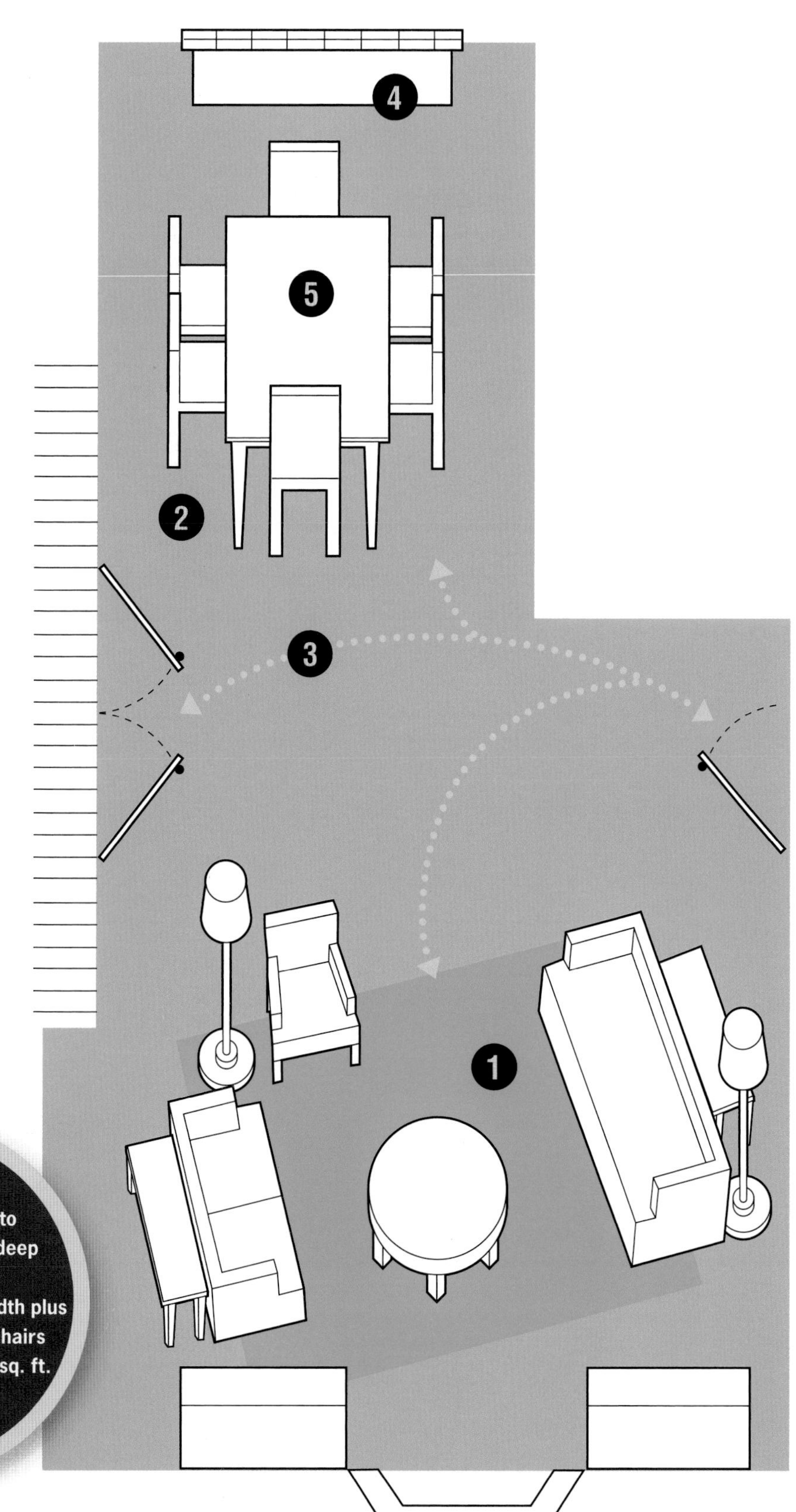

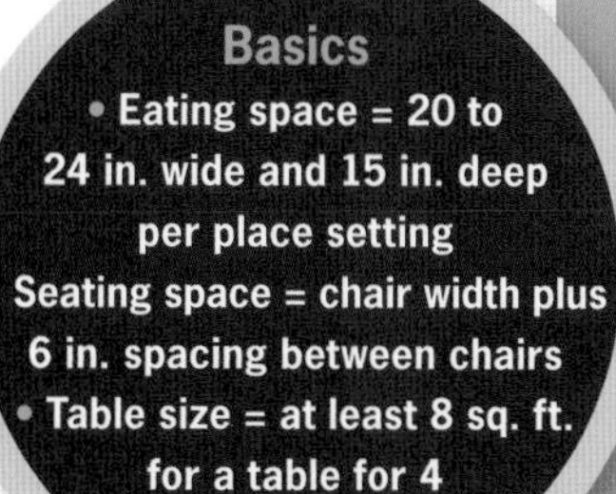

Basics

- **Eating space = 20 to 24 in. wide and 15 in. deep per place setting**
- **Seating space = chair width plus 6 in. spacing between chairs**
- **Table size = at least 8 sq. ft. for a table for 4**

- **Plan for company.** Measure the dining room and consider how many people will fit around the table. Circular tables, especially with pedestal bases, let folks crowd around, while rectangular tables limit the seating. Plan about 36 inches all around the table so chairs can be pulled out.
- **Get ready to move.** Before buying a new table, measure to see if it will fit through the door and up the stairs. Removable legs are a plus.
- **Maximize space.** To use a large table in a small room, consider a glass top to minimize the visual size. A drop-leaf table provides size flexibility. Replace a bulky sideboard with a narrow shelf that's just wide enough to hold dishes; anchor it to the wall to support weight.
- **Be a traffic cop.** Position the table so traffic flows smoothly around it. In most spaces the best spot for the table is near the center of the room. Make sure there's room to maneuver around a sideboard or china cabinet.
- **Provide flexible lighting.** If the table moves depending on the size of the crowd, hang the chandelier with extra lengths of cord so it can hang straight down or swag to the side.

Before: Dated, painted furniture and minimal accents give off a spare, chilly attitude, below.

After: Character-rich furniture, soft neutrals, and a punch of black pump up the style. Here's how to get the look.

- **Use favorite collections,** such as white ironstone and silver, to build a new look. They suit the country style of the space and establish a color scheme as well.
- **Collect new pieces,** such as this table, chairs, hutch, and chandelier, to give an old room fresh appeal. Search in antiques shops and furniture stores, and on the Internet.
- **Add a surprise,** such as a ceiling covered with tin panels. The reflection of the chandelier off the metal ceiling makes the room glow, right.
- **Soften the space with fabric.** A subtly striped rug, pretty table runners, and a skirted hutch add texture and character.
- **Dress walls with wallpaper,** wood wainscoting, and crown molding. The combination of materials adds texture and interest.

Before

Before: Plain walls and a basic table and chairs give this dining room a just-moved-in look, above.

After: Color, pattern, and lively accessories create a warm and welcoming dining space. Try these affordable ideas:

- **Layer on color** by painting the walls, woodwork, and ceiling. Use analogous colors for a soothing background.
- **Dress the window** with a store-bought Roman shade. Stitch on decorative trim for one-of-a-kind detailing.
- **Use plain white slipcovers** to give the folding chairs visual weight and softer lines. The white tablecloth also bulks up the table and balances the chairs.
- **Create your own chandelier** by painting a standard lampshade in bold stripes and combining it with a lighting kit from a home center. This focal point anchors the color scheme.
- **Layer the tabletop** with runners in solid and patterned fabrics. Or place a runner under a square of color.
- **Add a splash of color** in accessories. Patterned sushi plates hang on both sides of the window, left.

Classic

Play up this style with rich woods and traditional silhouettes. The mix of wood tones and leg profiles adds character.

• **Anchor the room** with an elegant wood table. It points the decor in a timeless direction. A new table is a smart way to launch any dining room makeover.

• **Give chairs a refined look** with crisp white slipcovers. Buttons and frogs offer inventive closures on the chair backs.

• **Nestle a sideboard** in the window as a home for voluminous floral displays or to serve as a buffet.

• **Hang a chandelier** to add light and personality.

• **Fill the tabletop** with favorite finds: pretty china and ornate silver. A cut-crystal vase and votive add sparkle.

Modern

Simplify to create a fresh mood in a room with classic lines.

- **Replace the wood table** with a rectangular glass-top table that maintains sight lines. The base adds a graphic touch.
- **Use the same chairs.** They're proof that the line between classic and modern design is easily blurred.
- **Slipcover the sideboard** to give it a contemporary profile. Lamps in tailored black and white offer soft lighting.
- **Keep the chandelier.** Surrounded by simple objects, it works like jewelry on a black dress and is easy to replace as well.
- **Edit accessories** to a few—framed photos and glass vases.

Dining rooms

offer valuable square footage that can be adapted to the way you live—a den most days and entertaining space when needed. Think of a dining room cabinet the same way. Changing the contents can change the attitude of a piece. It may take longer to gather up the objects than to make the switch.

Dining gear

Save your favorite pieces of tableware for display and stash the rest. Here's how to pick and choose.

- **Modernize it.** Sort through tableware, setting aside pieces that go together. Modern pieces offer a stylish contrast to the sculptural shapes and warm tones of the vintage cabinet.
- **Build a backdrop.** Use trays propped along the back of the shelves to add color and pattern. It's a quick way to change the look of a cabinet without making permanent alterations.
- **Pare down the collection.** Stuffed shelves can make a vintage cabinet look hopelessly out of date. Instead, select one bold piece for each shelf; then fill in with smaller items. Vary the height, shape, and color of objects to create a cohesive look.
- **Add small surprises.** A stack of dishes provides display space for a blue marble egg, colorful napkins peek out of bowls, and tall vases vertically stretch the cabinet.

Den gear

Transform visible storage space into a handsome bar. It's easy when you follow these mixing tricks.

• **Mix up the eras.** The cabinet is from the mid-1900s; the contents can represent any era. Gather new and vintage objects to achieve a collected-over-time look. Collect by color and shape to ensure cohesive groupings.

• **Add pattern.** Scraps of wallpaper and wrapping paper transform the back of the cabinet. To temporarily secure the paper in place, cut it to fit and use tacks in the corners. A tone-on-tone paper provides a subtle look.

• **Divide the cabinet** into display space and bar storage. Keep the bar equipment on the easiest shelf to reach. Use trays, old mirrors, or platters underneath a collection of glasses and bottles of liquor to protect surfaces from spills that might destroy the finish.

• **Display a collection.** Vintage barware and wicker-wrapped bottles support the theme and provide rich textures.

• **Add art.** The cabinet acts as an easel for an old portrait.

• **Stretch the height.** Baskets layered on top make the cabinet look taller, an easy way to change the proportions to suit a room. Use the baskets to store lightweight objects, such as table linens.

1

Dining rooms come to life after dark, so choose a fixture that adds style to the space and supplies the perfect glow.

1. For modern geometry
A felt-covered lampshade makes a dramatic contemporary statement. To create one, cut cream felt to fit the shade; stitch circles cut from dark felt to the cream. Spray-glue the back of the cream felt, and adhere it to the shade.

2. For candle power
Reproduction light fixtures take license with reality. They duplicate the look of candles but offer the modern convenience of electricity.

3. For a love of flowers
Skylights by day and an artisan-made light fixture by night are all the illumination a dining room needs. Add a dimmer switch for lighting perfect for any mood.

4. For double-duty style
Nested lampshades create an unusual look. Combine a smaller bell-shape shade with a larger shade, using a light fixture kit from a home center.

5. For star glamour
White paint turns a dated crystal chandelier into a focal point. A star painted on the ceiling calls even more attention to the light fixture.

6. For classic with a twist
Translucent amber pears and cut-glass crystals add elegance to this oversize chandelier. Hang it over a modern table for a surprising twist.

2

3

4

5

6

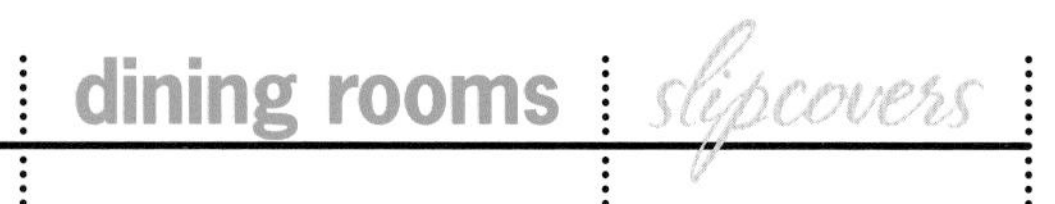

Transform dining room furniture—chairs, tables, and even buffets—with a slip of fabric. It's a temporary way to change the look of an heirloom without permanently altering it. If you're not handy with a sewing machine, a professional tailor or upholsterer (look for one who specializes in slipcovers) can make a slipcover to fit your dining room furniture. For maximum convenience choose a machine-washable fabric that stands up to spills.

1. Dressed for dinner

Every chair transformation should be so simple. Make some tucks in a purchased slipcover. Add a fabric belt to tie the new more-fitted slipcover in place. Shorten the skirt and add a flounce of ball fringe for a flirty detail.

2. Ready to party

Assigned another duty at the dining table, these sheer blue dinner napkins give side chairs a party-ready look. Tack the squares together with buttons, adding snaps across the back so the skirts are removable.

3. Outlined in style

Dress down party chairs with tailored slipcovers banded in white. The pleated skirts show just a little leg. For a fun flourish add painted or fabric numbers to the chair backs.

4. Table dressing

This custom slipcover softens the table and provides a tailored look. It comes only to the bottom edge of the tabletop, so laps and knees are free from overhanging fabric. It's also a fashionable way to show off beautiful table legs.

To dress up a chair without resorting to a slipcover, consider these ideas.

- **Fold and drape** an oversize napkin or scarf over the chair back.
- **Cut a length of ribbon** to wrap around the chair top and tie it in back. Twist a screw-end drapery pin through the ribbon in a hidden spot to keep the ribbon from slipping.
- **Cover the chair seat** with a napkin. Pleat napkin corners to form to the chair seat and stitch buttons to hold the pleats in place.
- **Add romance** by draping a chair with a layer of filmy tulle that puddles under the chair.
- **Tack two ribbons** to the underside of the chair seat near each leg. Wrap the ribbon pairs over and around each leg; secure to the bottom of the leg.
- **Fold a throw** into a long strip and drape over the chair seat and back.
- **Wrap a shawl** around the chair and tie it in back.
- **Tie a large bow,** attach a sprig of evergreen or rosemary, and pin the bow to the back of the chair.

CENTURY

Family rooms

for relaxing together

chapter 13

It's all about living, of course, but there's real heart in a room that begins with family. The busy hub of any home, a family room offers a spot for catching up and winding down. Consider the other functions it could handle. Can it hold a crowd for a movie, make room for dining, or provide display space for children's artwork? Does it need more storage, a built-in to hold electronics equipment, or a sectional with family-friendly fabric? Most family rooms are busy around the clock. What can you do to make yours more livable? Answer these questions and you'll be on your way to creating a living space that's filled with memories. Guaranteed.

in this chapter

Give a down-under family room

a bright new outlook with a soothing color scheme, clever lighting tricks, and smart storage. A basement provides lots of square footage for expansion without the expense and mess of adding on. Unfortunately, basements can be dark. The solution is easy: Duplicate daylight with lighting panels that look like windows, add sconces and recessed lighting to spread the glow even more, and opt for a color scheme based on light neutrals that reflect light.

Above: Limited space calls for special design solutions, like this pocket door that separates the hall from the family room. Arranging furniture is much easier with no swinging doors to interfere with traffic flow. The television is mounted on a space-saving panel that swivels for viewing.

Left: What looks like a frosted window above the gas-burning fireplace is a light box built using a window frame. The unit is lit from behind with fluorescent fixtures.

Opposite: Rectangles—wallpaper applied horizontally and a paneled wall behind the twin bed/sofa—create an energetic tempo. Diagonal lines add interest to the pillows.

1. In a low-light basement, use soft neutrals for most surfaces and add contrast and interest with dark cabinets and furnishings.

2. Select double-duty furnishings, such as the sofa/guest bed made from a twin bed backed with a long red bolster.

3. Create built-ins with stock cabinetry to make floor-to-ceiling storage units for games and media gear.

4. Seize lighting opportunities. Recessed lighting over the sofa and a sconce on the wall use no floor or table space.

5. Use colorful accents, such as bright yellow and red, to perk up and warm a basement family room.

Gather around the fireplace for warmth that can be seen and felt. Orient the furniture to the fire: It's the perfect strategy for drawing family and friends and a sure way to show off a natural focal point.

Above right: Casual and dressed-up may seem like opposite attitudes, yet they work together in this family room. Check out these combinations: a needlepoint pillow on a rush-top footstool, sink-in seating covered in elegant fabrics, and iron sconces paired with a gilt mirror. Look for inspiration for this type of style in English country homes, noted for their gentility and livability.
Below right: Focus seating on the fireplace. When the fireplace is centered on a wall, let the sofas float perpendicular to it. If the fireplace is in a corner, face the largest sofa or part of a sectional toward the fireplace. When the warm seasons arrive, move the furniture to capture a window view for a few months.

A long, low fireplace frames a vibrant floral painting. The juxtaposition of color with neutrals and organic shapes with linear ones adds energy. The coffee table lines up with the firebox to point the way to the view. Refacing a dated brick fireplace with stone modernized the setting to make way for sleek new furnishings.

smart tips

Consider these strategies for bringing style and function to the family room.

- **Choose focal point(s).** You may have more than one, perhaps a fireplace and a media center. If so, combine both on the same wall, or turn the furniture arrangement on the diagonal so it can face two walls at once.
- **Divide to conquer.** A family room or great-room is often large. Break it into two or more activity areas to increase versatility. A table and chairs at one end can be used for games or snacks. A sectional at the other end can gather friends around the fireplace. Choose furniture with wheels to make rearranging easy and fun.
- **Ease the care.** Opt for durable, easy-clean upholstery and rugs for this hard-used room. Consider wood or tile floors that are easy to clean, and finish wood furniture with scratch-resistant materials.
- **Make more storage.** Whether built-in or freestanding, storage units take the clutter out of even the busiest family rooms. Use open shelves for display, drawers and doors to keep stuff under wraps.

Built-in cabinetry, alone or paired with a fireplace, sets the style for a family room while providing much-needed storage for games and media gear. It's no wonder that built-ins rival fireplaces as the focal point.

Left: From floor to vaulted ceiling, bookcases set the style scene in this family room. Same-size rectangular cubbies keep the bookcases looking organized rather than chaotic. Stretching the bookcases to a vaulted ceiling makes the room look bigger. The furnishings include an inviting mix of classic and modern that feels warm but not stuffy.

Above: Built-ins that make space for the television are a smart solution in small family rooms. Be bold and embrace large units rather than small ones. The extra size minimizes the need for other furnishings in the space and increases clutter-hiding capabilities. The color of the built-in—a grayed green—is a soothing unifier that helps objects on the shelves blend in.

Opposite: The hearth has significance in this intimate family space. The large scale of the fireplace and the low iron sconces bring light and warmth close to the level of the seating area. Warm colors, soft fabrics, and earthy textures create cozy comfort. Bookcases extend the hearth and keep collections in view.

When the family room joins the kitchen or dining area, use these ideas to make them work together.

- **Lay the same flooring** all around. It's the best way to join rooms. If you do change flooring materials, stay in the same color family to avoid jarring contrast. Add rugs to define areas within the spaces.
- **Repeat colors, materials,** and fabrics. Consider these partners: stainless-steel appliances and chrome sconces, transferware plates and toile fabric, wood countertops and wood occasional tables.
- **Spread softness,** using pattern, fabric, and rugs. This step is especially important in the kitchen, which is full of hard surfaces.
- **Share collections.** The weave of natural baskets in the kitchen can reappear as woven chairs or ottomans in the family room. Blue and white dishes in the kitchen pair with blue and white lidded jars in the family room.

Create an energetic family room with a mix of bright hues—hot pink, orange, and red—backed up by refreshing white.

1. Create a bright white background. When used appropriately, white transforms rooms into crisp, airy spaces that reflect light and let other elements stand out.

2. Start shopping for accessories. Does this seem an odd way build a color scheme? Have faith: When the look you want is bright and young, accessories will lead the way. Think of them as eye candy for the room. White display cubes make the pieces look as if they're floating on the wall.

3. Search for a sofa or a fabric to use on the sofa. Choose a color that's strong and bold, such as this hot pink. Pair it with analogous shades of red and orange. Using a little of a complementary color makes the palette more vibrant.

4. Spread color for balance. If the colors are all on one side of the room, the space will feel lopsided. Play colors against white, even using a white shaggy rug.

5. Introduce noncolor pieces, such as glass-top side and coffee tables that sit on wood bases. These pieces add function without grabbing the color spotlight.

Worth noting

Repeat all the colors used in a room at least three times. Otherwise the single color will look like a decorating mistake. For the best effect balance the placement of the colorful objects.

Develop a look that lasts using nature's hues and materials.

1. Build the palette using samples. Consider fabrics, window shades, and furniture pieces. It's the easiest way to put together a scheme that's based on neutrals. Expand the palette by combining warm and cool shades, such as khaki and taupe, for example.

2. Select a warm neutral for the walls. Look to yellow to warm up a neutral shade and ground the room with character. Neutrals in the gray family can chill a room, something to take into account for north-facing spaces.

3. Introduce shaded hues in fabrics and accessories. The striped fabric on the chair includes a thin line of brick red. That same red can reappear as a subtle pattern for pillows, in a fine line around a framed print, or even in cut flowers.

4. Use plenty of texture. The window shades illustrate how texture can add interest to a neutral palette. Achieve a similar effect with a knit or fur throw, a collection of wicker-wrapped bottles, or a shag rug.

5. Add spots of bright color. In a nature-inspired room, consider fresh fruit and bouquets of flowers to bring in strong color that reflects the season.

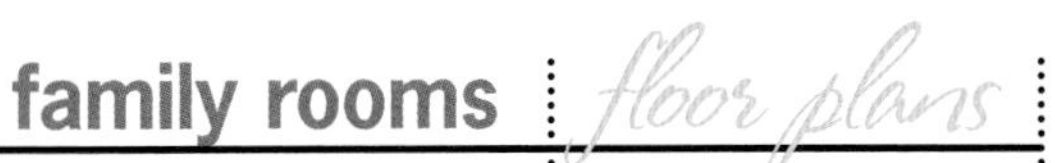

Start with the television when arranging furniture in the family room. After all, it's usually the main attraction. Position seating pieces for easy viewing. Consider a sectional to provide maximum seating in a small room, add a table and chairs for eating and playing games, and include plenty of storage to keep clutter out of sight. Choose smaller-scale pieces to allow room for a sofa and chairs as well as a table and chairs. Or use a larger table as a side table next to the sofa and move the table to make room for seating when it's needed for games and puzzles. Square ottomans on casters are easy to move where needed and can be used for seating or as footstools. If space is tight a wall-mounted television can alleviate traffic problems and deliver a good view to every spot in the room. Adaptable light is essential: low light during movies and strong light for crafts projects and games. Dimmer switches guarantee flexibility.

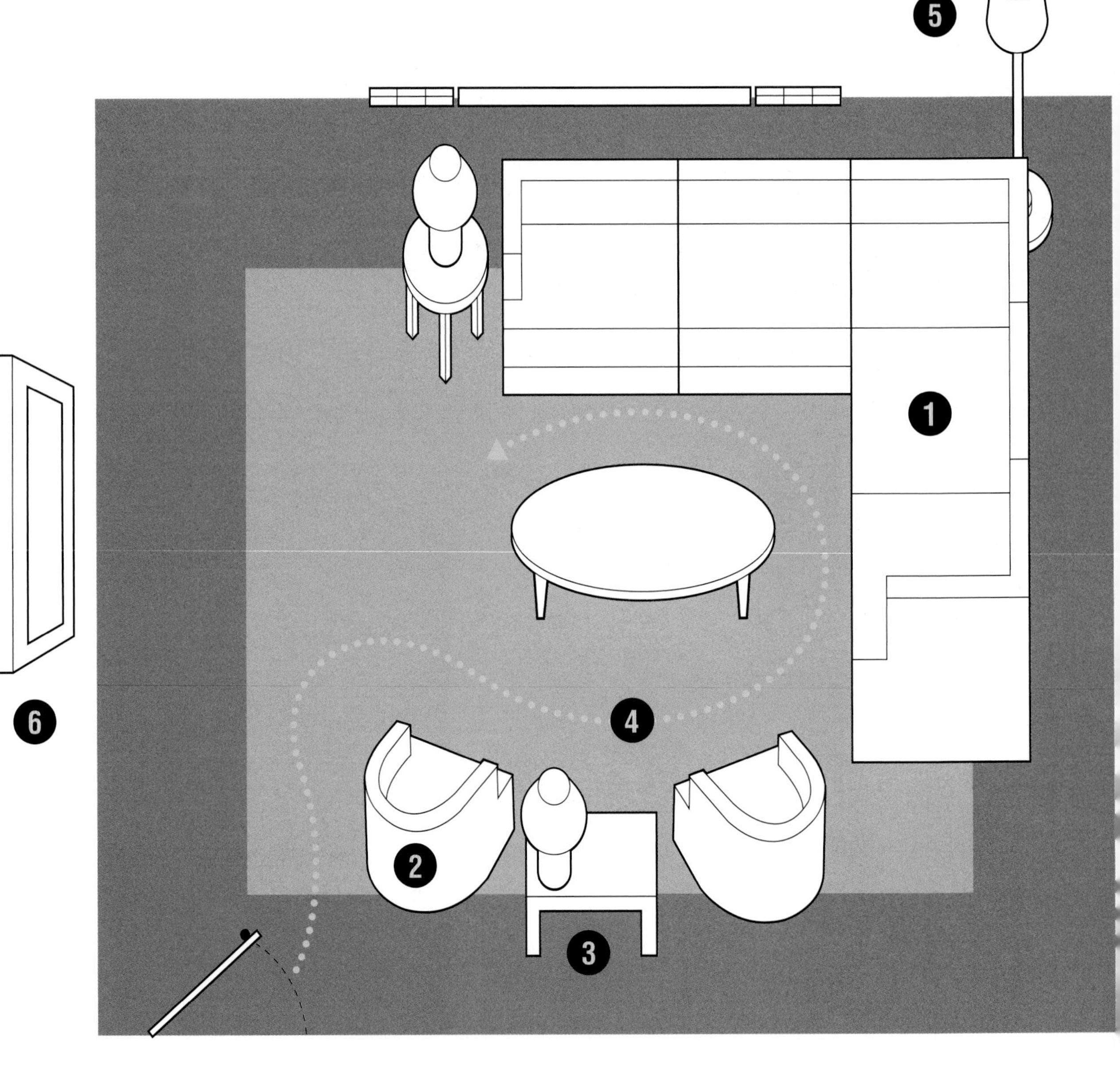

Family room 1

1. **Plan for a crowd** in a small room by using a sectional. The continuous seating allows room to squeeze in one more person.
2. **Chairs on swivels** turn to the conversation area or to the television.
3. **Provide table landings** by every seat. Use side tables and a coffee table.
4. **Keep traffic flowing** with an oval coffee table. The curvy lines allow guests to move easily.
5. **Use floor lamps** for portable lighting.
6. **Install the TV** at the right height for viewing. To check the height use painter's tape to create an outline on the wall. Temporarily support the TV at that height and check whether the viewing angle is comfortable.

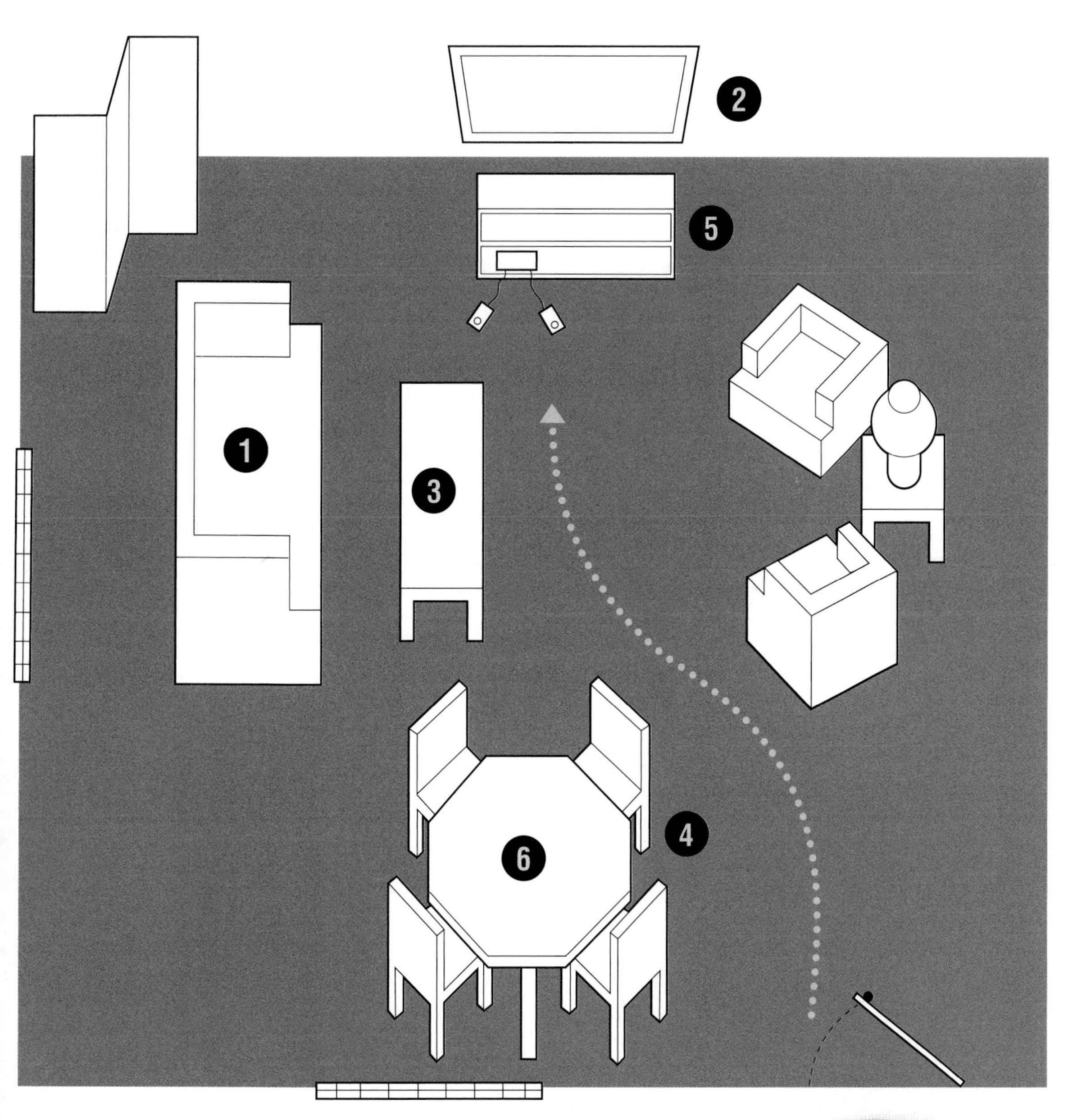

Family room 2

1. Circle the TV with seating, including a sofa, two chairs, and side chairs around a table. Using a number of small furniture pieces provides maximum flexibility.

2. Install the television to suit your style of watching. If you like to recline on the sofa while you watch, check the view from that angle before installation.

3. Add space with a roomy cocktail table that offers space below for storage baskets.

4. Include space for snacks and games. Provide at least four chairs. If your children are small, add a child-size table as well.

5. Plan for storage near the television to hold video equipment and board games.

6. Size the tabletop to suit family activities—crafts, puzzles, card games. A round or octagonal table suits activities better than a long narrow one.

Basics for standard TVs

- Min. viewing distance = 8 ft.
- Max. viewing distance = 12 ft.
- Best view = not more than a 30-degree angle from center of screen

what to put where

- **Focus on entertainment.** A television will probably be the focal point of a family room, so make plans around it. Place it so the screen faces away from sunlight, then arrange seating for the best view.
- **Direct traffic.** For family harmony create traffic lanes that flow behind viewers, not in front of the screen.
- **Incorporate storage.** Make use of floor-to-ceiling square footage by adding built-ins that hold CDs, DVDs, games, and books. Massing storage in one area makes better use of space than spreading freestanding pieces all around the room. Consider varying the depth of the storage to suit its use: 10 to 12 inches deep for books, 12 inches deep for games, 7 inches deep for CDs, and 24 inches deep for bulky toy storage. For efficient storage measure the items you want to store.
- **Update for size control.** Consider a flat-panel television to save space and enlarge the view. Remove a bulky entertainment unit and replace it with shallow or low storage units.

Transform a family room

from dreary to dreamy using a warm palette of green, red, and gold. Playful and classic patterns create a lively mix.

Before: Dark wood paneling and a brick fireplace add to the gloom of this hard-used and out-of-date room, below.

After: Warmed up with color and dressed in new fabrics, the freshened family room makeover proves that it's OK to keep what's working and change what's dull and dated.

- **Enhance the basics.** The wood paneling stayed; it's now painted warm, golden yellow, below left. The new color makes the wood ceiling beams and pine floor look even better since they're no longer competing with the walls.
- **Improve the proportions.** The fireplace overwhelmed the room. To bring it more in scale, the top half of the fireplace wall was drywalled and painted, and a new, simple mantel and surround were added, opposite.
- **Use color to create dimension.** Here it's sage paint inside the bookcases and cream on the fronts and sides. Because sage is analogous to the gold walls, it adds depth and dimension to the recessed spaces.
- **Add easy care.** Slipcovers on chairs, sofa, and ottoman make perfect wash-and-dry decorating.
- **Rearrange the focus.** Orient furniture around the fireplace, even if it's at one end of the room. Refocus the other end of the room with furniture that accommodates hobbies.
- **Repeat colors.** It's a sure way to make a room cohesive. Walls, built-ins, fabrics, and accessories all repeat the palette.

Before

A favorite mantel offers

multiple opportunities for style. Experiment with different arrangements on the floor, or tape up paper cutouts in the shapes of the objects you plan to hang. Start with the largest element and continue to add pieces in decreasing size.

1. Layered: Ideal for three-dimensional objects and easy changeability. The mantel rather than the wall above it becomes the focus of this arrangement. The technique allows you to show off a variety of objects without creating clutter. Begin by looking for continuity in your collections. Here pieces of white Italian pottery create a foundation. The variety of shapes and sizes creates interest but not dissonance. Other striking objects add height and contrast. Place taller objects—the mirror, candlesticks, and tray—against the back of the mantel. Vary the heights to create visual energy. Leave some gaps between items for breathing room. Study how small objects relate to each other and to the overall effect. Consider seasonal changes, such as ferns for summer or gourds for fall.

2. Asymmetrical: Ideal for small paintings and collections of plates in varying sizes. This look is sleek and sophisticated. The key to asymmetry is maintaining balance without placing everything in a straight line. Vertical elements are balanced with horizontal, and large prints are paired with small. Each object works on its own yet plays off the other elements as well. This creates a dramatic effect. To start unify the prints with proportional mats and matching frames. Paint the wall a saturated color that contrasts with the art. Hang the largest piece first, then add the other prints. Leaning one print casually on the mantel, slightly overlapping the largest print, tightens and centers the mantel grouping.

3. Minimal: Ideal for modern settings and graphic statements. Minimalism works best when it makes a graphic statement. If you can't afford an abstract painting or if you like the idea of a contemporary play on tradition, use a grid of white and pale blue plates against a rich brown wall color. The contrast between the round plates and the horizontal lines of the mantel turns utilitarian objects into art. The striking vases at the end of the mantel add depth to the composition and balance the grid. Keep in mind that a minimal mantel design in a room filled with large, overstuffed furniture would look empty and bare. In a room furnished in the same simple minimalist style, however, the mantel becomes a dramatic focal point.

4. Symmetrical: Ideal for classic homes and displays of collections. The time-tested symmetrical arrangement creates balance and avoids the potential sensory overload of disparate elements. A neatly ordered approach is ideal for those who have a "more is more" philosophy toward collecting and display. Start with your focal point object—usually the largest one or the one with the most visual weight—and work outward, creating mirror images on the left and right sides. Here antique china pieces complement footed urns, and a contemporary cork box adds a lively accent. Reproduction candle sconces reinforce the period feel and the symmetry of the grouping. If you don't have a set of matching dishes, combine ones that offer unity in size, visual weight, material, or color. The transferware used here is a classic example.

Houses have a front entry

—and the one by the back, garage, or side door that everyone uses. In most homes this space fills with piles of coats, shoes, backpacks, sports equipment, and briefcases. That's because most homes lack a convenient space to stash the stuff. Change habits by creating an everyday entry that tempts your family to stow things. Consider these ideas:

1. For the clothes horse

It takes only minutes to turn a long hallway into an efficient entry. Install peg racks at ceiling height for a hat collection and another rack by the door to hold jackets. If the floor surface is ceramic, line up boots and shoes along the wall. Slide a bench into place, and the entry is ready for action.

2. For sports fans

Storage wraps around a corner to suit a long narrow space. Open cubbies, one per family member, make it easy to put things away. The seat-height dividers provide handy perches, and open baskets corral small items that could otherwise become clutter.

2

1

3

3. For the organizer
Drawers and doors put storage under wraps. A long low bench provides seating as well as a handy landing for packages and backpacks. The surfaces, including a ceramic tile floor and slipcovered cushions, are easy to keep clean.

4. For the style purist
Here's an entry that's as handsome as any family room. This storage unit creates a functional island that separates an entry from an adjoining family room. The bench bumps out to create enough depth for seating.

5. For a big family
Open storage makes a good option in a back entry that's hidden away. It's more convenient to stash gear in open cubbies and on hooks, especially when there's enough room for every member of the family. Drawers provide space to store out-of-season gear while countertops make handy landing pads. Painted surfaces are a durable finish for this hard-use area.

Spend a few hours creating a focal-point project for a family room. These two playful ideas will get you started.

Add style from the inside out. A hint of color and pattern is an eye-catching touch, especially for hanging lampshades, right. Make a pattern by tracing the shape of the shade onto paper, allowing enough paper to overlap ends. Cut fabric using the pattern, coat the wrong side of the fabric with spray adhesive, and carefully adhere the fabric to the inside of the shade. If you have difficulty controlling the fabric as you work, fuse lightweight interfacing to the back of the fabric, then use adhesive to attach the interfacing side to the shade. Glue bias tape along the top and bottom edges to give the lining a finished look.

Make like a card shark. Playing card designs on the folding screen, opposite, rival stylish wallpaper prints. To duplicate the look, use a color copier to enlarge the backs of copyright-free playing cards to the desired size. It may take several attempts to get the size right. Insert the copies into a purchased floor screen that's made to hold photos. Use a one-color scheme like this or alternate colors for an even livelier look. For added fun copy some face cards to use in the mix. Other options for the screen openings include wrapping paper, wallpaper, and photos.

RABBIT, RUN
John Updike

Kitchens

for cooking and company

New homes with wide-open floor plans invite the kitchen into the rest of the house. It makes perfect sense to create this effect even in an older house with a traditional floor plan. Before you get started, ask these questions: Is your kitchen hidden at the back of the house or central to the action? Would you invite friends to join you there for cooking or chatting? Is the kitchen boring or out of date? Do you need more counterspace, more light, more character, more storage, or all of the above? It's time to start making some changes. The ingredients you use to redo your kitchen will add fresh style with a dash of spice.

in this chapter

Mix classic, modern, and country

Mix classic, modern, and country elements to fill a kitchen with down-home comfort and uptown style. It's a look that's easy to adapt to any kitchen, whether you're starting with contemporary or classic cabinetry. The challenge is getting the decorating mix right. Here a rough-hewn island adds country charm while sleek stainless-steel appliances crisply accent the classic cabinets. For rustic cabinetry consider adding an island with a modern edge. Fill in all around with fabrics, wallpaper, furniture, and accessories that complement rather than match the cabinetry. It's a sure way to perfectly relax this hardworking room.

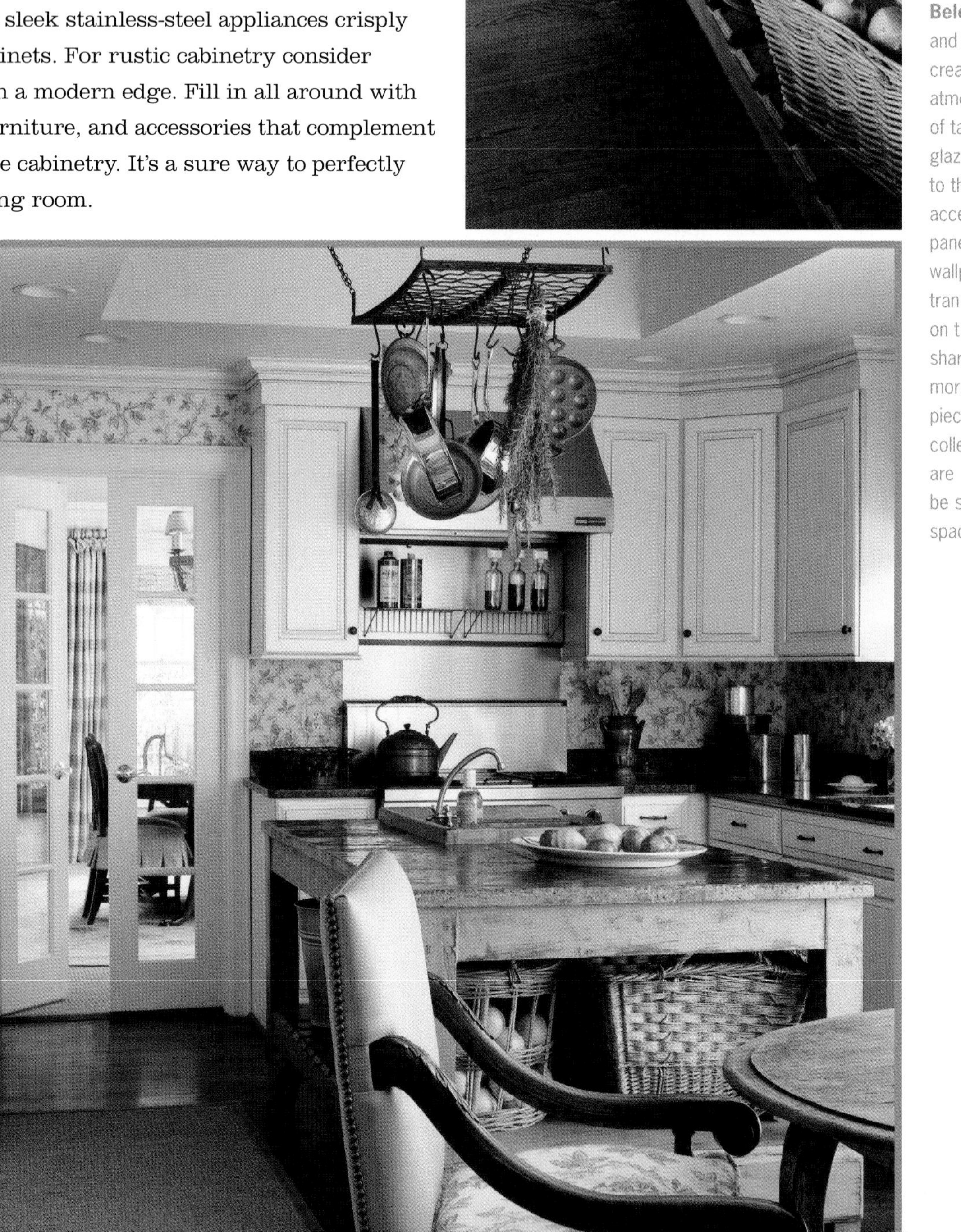

Left: A zinc-top antique farm table is the centerpiece of the room and a surprising companion to the dressy settee and chairs. Old bins and baskets add character and storage while an inset sink adds stylish charm and function to the tabletop. **Below left:** A coffee and cream color scheme creates a soothing atmosphere. A mixture of taupe paint and glazing liquid applied to the cream cabinets accents the raised panels. A Chinese-toile wallpaper complements transferware plates hung on the wall. Dressy chairs share floor space with more primitive country pieces. Cookware, collectibles, and foods are out where they can be seen, stamping the space with personality.

Recipe for kitchen decorating

1. Start with a warm scheme of coffee and cream to ground the French country space. Brown granite and vintage zinc countertops provide clever contrast.

2. Define the raised panels of the cabinetry by rubbing a darker taupe glaze over a base coat of cream paint.

3. Transform a vintage table into a centerpiece island. Add casters to keep it movable, or secure it to the floor if adding a sink.

4. Create character with antiques, such as the grate used as a pot rack and old baskets turned into stylish, convenient storage.

5. Soften the room with upholstered furniture. The fabric on the chair's cushion matches the wallpaper, a subtle way to add rhythm to the room.

Left: Diagonal squares make a galley kitchen look wider; large tiles stretch space more than small tiles. To create this look, use paint and stain in two coordinating hues. If you're looking for colors to use on a floor, search no further than a favorite piece of art. Here the artwork inspired buttery yellow walls and stainless-steel countertops.
Below: Honey-tone cabinetry anchors this kitchen with warmth. To enhance the look of the cabinets, top them with sleek black granite countertops. The warm tones of flooring and walls keep the cool stainless shelves from seeming too industrial for a country kitchen. Open shelves add storage in a small kitchen without gobbling visual space.

Banish those cookie-cutter kitchens with

their rows of cabinetry and predictable countertops. Instead cook up a kitchen that's sizzling with personal style. Consider how small dramatic changes, such as a painted floor finish, wall shelves, or an island adapted from a vintage piece of furniture, can power up any kitchen. The ingredients for your kitchen makeover are up to you.

Left: This kitchen owes its good looks to a mix of vintage finds and new industrial pieces. The top hutch of an old country store display piece fits perfectly over the new sink and stainless-steel cabinets. The work island, a 50-year-old bakery fixture, was cleaned, sanded, and put back into use. To master a mix of old and new, buy vintage pieces first, then purchase complementary new pieces.

Below: Bold rectangular shapes give this kitchen a modern edge. Oversize chunks of wall painted the color of graphite repeat the rectangles. The cabinets, countertops, and wall color merge, thanks to the use of similar tones, while artwork, stools, and pendent lamps stand out. This look works best when there's strong color and value contrast between neutrals, such as pale gray and graphite.

simple fix-ups

The kitchen may be the hardest-working room in the house—and runs the risk of looking overworked. Give it fresh appeal with these easy tricks.

- **Introduce pattern and color.** The same colors and patterns that work everywhere else in the house can add style to a kitchen. Use washable fabrics and scrubbable paints for easy upkeep.
- **Update the lighting.** Replace an overhead light fixture with a handsome hanging fixture. Hide task lighting with a piece of molding. Let the effect of task lighting—rather than the lighting fixture—show.
- **Add furniture details.** Remove a pair of upper cabinet doors and line the cabinet with wallpaper for dish display. Install chunky legs in the toe-kick area and dressy knobs on doors.
- **Minimize clutter.** Turn a back entry closet into a pantry to hold bulky items, such as rolls of paper towels and bakeware. Make space for appliances in cupboards rather than on countertops, keep cooking gear in drawers, and store staples, such as flour, in simple glass containers.
- **Accessorize.** Hang favorite pieces of art on the walls, drape the table with a beautiful piece of fabric, and unroll a dramatic rug.

Invite family back to the kitchen table by creating a special place for casual meals. Match the style of the furniture to the kitchen cabinetry, checking first to see if the furniture suits your family. Upholstered seating is comfortable but demands special care; slipcovers mimic the look and slip into the wash for easy stain removal. Expandable tables offer the option of adding room for guests. In small spaces consider a table on a center pedestal to avoid the obstacle of table legs. In general, allow 36 inches all around the table so chairs can be pulled out easily. Figure on a space 20 to 24 inches wide and 15 inches deep for each place setting.

Above left: Graphic elements add design power to this small eating nook. The X-base table pairs up with tropical pillows for dramatic style. The window view expands the small space, while sleek slipcovers, tucked-in bench seating, and the glass-top table keep visual clutter to a minimum. This bold and playful eating area proves that small spaces have room for both style and function.

Above: Elegant furnishings can feel right at home in a dressy kitchen. Design flexibility is part of the plan. A generous sofa mixes it up with three armless upholstered chairs. The thick glass tabletop is impervious to stains and easy to keep clean. Neutral fabrics and elegant finishes, such as nailhead trim, give this eating area the look of a fine salon. Accessories, including pillows and pottery, are easy to change with the seasons.

Framed by an arch and flanked by shelves, the built-in banquette provides seating at the breakfast table. Hexagonal tile on the floor complements the stenciled detailing on the chair backs. The homeowners' collection of white pottery stacks on shelves flanking the banquette. Double-door cabinets offer storage for kitchen gear and display space on top. The creamy walls and built-ins provide a dramatic backdrop for the vintage table and chairs.

Left: Thanks to the space-expanding ability of a generous round mirror, this breakfast area looks ready for full-scale entertaining. The table and banquette are made from the same wood as the cabinetry and finished in the same stain. The unusual shape of the table—like an oversize piece of pie—adds tabletop space without impeding traffic flow. The low back of the banquette lets outdoor light stream into the space while the only chair, a Philippe Starck design in clear plastic, is barely visible. **Below:** Elegant enough for a library, this sophisticated table and chairs are perfectly at home nestled up to a built-in banquette in the kitchen. Drawers in the

banquette offer storage while cushions add comfort. Pale lavender walls anchor a stylish color scheme that builds on the contrast between lights and darks.
Right: An L-shape banquette wraps around the corner to deliver family style and space to spare, both for diners on the cushioned seats and for kitchen supplies under the lift-top built-ins. Color energizes the space. A bold yellow-green on the walls repeats the colors on the vintage map and new striped cushions. Pillows in bright orange and yellow offer the boldest shots of color.

Build a color scheme inspired by trendy new appliances and favorite dishes.

1. Uncover your color scheme inside your cupboards. They're probably already filled with the hues you love: tangerine, lime, lemon, and blueberry. Bring those hues into view on a tile backsplash, painted cabinets, and walls. If you want a paint color to match an item, take it along to the paint store for computer matching.

2. Create a colorful focal point. In this kitchen tile in five spicy flavors paves the way. Wall and cabinet paint and even accessories build on the colorful palette.

3. Be bold with color. When only small chunks of wall show, choose colors from the brighter end of the spectrum for maximum oomph.

4. Create visual resting spots by using neutral surfaces, such as hardwood flooring and stainless-steel appliances and countertops.

5. Keep color in mind when selecting appliances. Because they present large planes of color, it's important that the colors match, or at least blend. If you buy all you appliances from the same manufacturer and at the same time, the colors will work together. Otherwise even white appliances can clash with each other, and stainless steel changes tone and sheen with each manufacturer.

Shop the market for natural stone, wood, and metal to use for remodeling materials, and build a color palette that complements.

1. Start with a quiet and consistent palette to create a space that's easy on the eyes. Save bright or primary hues for another project.

2. Choose paint colors that form a soft contrast with the wood of the cabinetry and pick up tones from other materials, such as tile, metal, or stone. Too much contrast will be jarring.

3. Ground lighter elements in the room with darker hues. Here a charcoal stain on the island base complements colors in the granite top. Use dark colors as lower elements; dark hues used on upper cabinetry can feel too heavy for a space.

4. Bridge the color gap between the darkest and lightest hues. Here, grayish-green tile covers the most prominent side of the island, tying together charcoal and sage hues.

5. Choose an accent color that's slightly brighter than the wall color and use it in a shiny material, such as the glass mosaic tiles on the backsplash. Their translucent properties make them shine.

6. Pull the color scheme together with artwork that adds drama to the space and repeats at least three or four of the color choices.

Here's a challenge faced in new subdivisions across the country: How do you add personality to a perfectly functional—and perfectly boring—new kitchen?

Before: White cabinets and walls plus neutral countertops—why maintain the ho-hum status quo?

After: Gingham wallpaper jump-starts this cottage-style makeover, while new glass cabinet doors, updated trim, and pretty fabrics keep the momentum going. Here's how to duplicate the look.

- **Add color.** Color provides the easiest, quickest way to change a space. Here coordinating check wallpaper and toile fabric in vibrant red add color drama and help the white cabinetry visually advance.
- **Update and upgrade the cabinets.** Replace a few upper cabinet doors with glass-front doors to give a custom look. Order doors like this at a home center, or hire a carpenter to cut holes in existing doors. Order glass to fit and install using clear silicone caulk.
- **Add new cabinetry hardware.** Instead of using all one style, mix and match handles, pulls, and knobs. Opt for new hardware that uses existing holes if you want to avoid repainting the cabinetry.
- **Install beaded board.** Sheathe the backsplash and island sides in beaded board. Look for this product in a ¼-inch-thick version that's perfect for nailing to a solid surface.
- **Collect vintage pieces.** Two large antique brackets found at a flea market add interest to the island. A ladder coated with whitewash now serves as a one-of-a-kind pot rack. The chains are anchored into bolts screwed to the joists.
- **Dress a window.** Give a window extra appeal with a matchstick Roman shade. In addition to diffusing the view, the shade adds a warm natural color. Crown molding purchased from a home center forms a wider window ledge.
- **Introduce fabric.** Soften a kitchen by adding a toile skirt below the sink. The skirt creates the illusion that this ordinary porcelain sink is an old-fashioned apron-front beauty. To copy this idea remove the cabinet doors under the sink and gather fabric on a tension rod that's suspended inside the cabinet frame.

Good decorating includes knowing when to stop, what to add, and what to take out, *above*. The white scheme in this modern kitchen was worth keeping; now it pairs with red to deliver surprising energy, *right* and *opposite*. With only a few cosmetic changes, the look is refreshed.

BREAD

Open and shut,

the right storage can set the style tone for a kitchen. Open storage shows off a collection, keeps supplies within view, gives the kitchen an airy look, and demands neatness. Hidden storage organizes everything without cluttering the view. Instead, all eyes are on beautiful wood doors or elegant glass inserts. Hidden storage is the perfect place to stash bulk supplies and oversize cooking gear.

Left: The same cabinet can be used for open or closed storage. The plate rack relies on a time-tested method of slipping plates between dowels to store them standing on end. The plates add a decorative element. Mini drawers provide spots for out-of-sight storage.

Above: These classic white cabinets offer open and closed storage in one coordinated package. The open corner unit is deep enough to hold a small microwave oven and roomy enough to handle a cookbook collection. The adjacent pantry cabinet has glass doors backed with fabric to hide clutter. The fabric on the pantry doors matches the fabric of the Roman shades. The window seat tops a radiator; similar seating in a nook could house storage underneath.

Above and left: Open and closed storage work together to fit every need. Frosted-glass doors hide the cupboard contents. Check visibility through frosted glass to see if the glass is opaque enough. At the other end of the kitchen, walnut shelves, stacked with sculpture-like supplies, stretch to the ceiling. The dramatic effect is achieved by stacking objects so they occupy the space instead of fill it. Stainless-steel shelves, only 12 inches deep, are roomy enough to hold dinnerware yet not so deep that they become cluttered.

The right storage in the right spot can add style as well.

- **Install small metal knobs** to hold kitchen towels near the sink.
- **Line lidded laundry baskets** with plastic bags to make handsome recycling bins.
- **Add hooks** under a window to create hanging space for totes.
- **Stack narrow shelves** or ledges along an open wall. Use the storage for mugs and soup bowls.
- **Fill matching glass containers,** large or small, with kitchen staples. Gathered in a row on the countertop, they provide subtle color and texture.
- **Show off copper pots** by hanging them along a wall. Use S hooks and towel bars for flexible display.
- **Add height to a vintage dresser** by adding casters, painting it a bright color, and rolling it into the kitchen.
- **Add narrow plate racks** to the side of a kitchen island and fill with colorful patterned plates.
- **Replace upper cabinets** with shelves that show off dinnerware, mixing bowls, and pitchers.
- **Add a chalkboard or bulletin** board and edge with hooks for keys.
- **Stretch glass shelves** across a window, and store colored glasses and bowls in the light.

Design a kitchen with flexibility

and you'll be able to make changes whenever the mood strikes. Display spaces are essential. Here a large island and a ledge that tops the wainscoting provide room for style statements. Bold black and white checkerboard flooring and soothing chocolate brown paint above the wainscoting underscore the other elements.

bold color

- **Collect with color in mind.** It's the easiest way to build a collection that can transform a kitchen in minutes.
- **Use paint to color basics,** such as the painted orange letters perched on the ledge, right. Suit the paint to its usage. Some paints work on china and are even dishwasher-safe.
- **Inject the unexpected** for serving food. A kitchen scale can hold fresh fruit. Glass canisters keep all sorts of foods handy. Bowls make perfect holders for colorful napkins.

soft neutrals

- **Shop for stylish basics.** They can be the cornerstone of the kitchen and accessories as well. Look for tableware, cutting boards, and napkins that are pretty enough to keep out.
- **Pick bold pieces.** Oversize bowls hold fresh produce or flowers. A large clear glass compote turns baguettes into kitchen art.
- **Be playful.** Food, drinks, and labels create a fun, artistic partnership. Note how bottled water decorates the kitchen ledge, opposite. Search grocery and specialty stores for other labels you love.

THE BREAD BIBLE
The Bread Baker's Apprentice

Ask a group of remodelers

what homeowners want most in a new kitchen, and a large working island is sure to make the list. That's understandable. Islands package form and function into one tidy feature, and they're easy to add to an existing kitchen. Here's how to suit the cook and the kitchen.

1. For the collector cook

A vintage cart on casters stands in as a perfect island for a kitchen with an old-fashioned look. Small islands like this one work well in a space-starved room. To use an island for food preparation, opt for one that's 18 to 24 inches across. Allow 3 feet of floor space around a centered island, more if appliances open into the area.

2. For the cottage lover

Install a double-decker island to create a space that's handy for storing gear or rolling out dough. For a standard 36-inch-tall counter, a seat height of 24 to 30 inches lets legs slide easily under the counter without knocking knees. For added comfort select a stool with a back or padded seat.

3. For the modern soul

Corrugated stainless steel on the island sides and a concrete countertop give this large island an industrial look. The island doubles as a computer center, thanks to a hookup installed and concealed in the toe-kick. Take care when selecting the material for the countertop. Some surfaces, such as concrete and marble, may require periodic sealing to retain their stylish good looks.

4. For the cook who loves an audience

Centered in a room, an island immediately becomes a style focal point. It can also become the center of work. A large island offers enough room for dropping in appliances or the kitchen sink. The extra storage space underneath can eliminate the need for upper kitchen cabinetry. Use caution when selecting a long island: One that stretches more than 8 feet can become an obstacle for traffic and workflow. Most experts suggest a minimum of 4 feet of floor space on each side of the island if appliances open into the space. A 3-foot-wide aisle may work; to check, block off the size of the island by sticking masking tape to the kitchen floor and see how it feels to work around the imaginary island.

4

1
Milk
Eggs
Cheddar
I ♡ NY
Sunday
Brunch
Kips Bay
Movie

Update any kitchen

with a cabinetry makeover. Cabinets generally dominate the view, setting the scene for the whole room. Consider these ideas:

1. Chalkboard paint

A pantry cabinet sports a new finish of chalkboard paint applied to the upper cabinets. This easy-to-apply paint changes any surface into a family message center. If you're not ready to commit to paint, use a peel-and-stick chalkboard product. Check online for these films.

2. Frosted film

Tired of too many glass-front cabinets? Hide the contents by applying a frosty film to the inside of the cabinet doors. Some films have an adhesive backing while others adhere using electrostatic technology.

3. Stainless steel

Stainless steel gives worn cabinet doors a modern face. Most metal fabrication shops will cut stainless-steel panels to fit the doors. Use contact cement to glue panels in place.

4. Molding framework

Molding dresses up any door. Purchase three or four styles of molding in various widths and layer it on the doors until you like the look. Glue molding to the doors and then paint.

5. Perforated metal

Long used in radiator covers, perforated metal withstands kitchen heat and humidity and is easy to clean. To use it, cut out the center panels of the doors and apply clear caulk to secure the metal in place.

6. & 7. Furniture finishes

Blah and boring, the "before" kitchen sports generic cabinets and a death-by-neutrals color palette. The "after" kitchen includes a backsplash of beaded-board paneling, an arched fascia and curved brackets on the upper cabinet, new glass doors, and bun feet. White paint and red accents complete the makeover.

Bathrooms

for easing daily routines

chapter 15

The best baths play dual roles: practical workstations at rush hour and pretty getaways after hours. Do yours measure up? Do you have put-away space for everything from towels to cleaning supplies? Are the surfaces pretty and easy to clean? Do you need to share the space with a partner and kids? Does the space work for grooming and bathing but lack style? Options range from a quick makeover to a full-scale redo. Consider your list of dream features: soaking tub or new shower curtain, new vanity or a paint job on the one you have. Small changes instantly update a bathroom, and big changes can turn it into a dream spa.

in this chapter

Give a ho-hum bathroom a color transfusion.

Most bathrooms start with crisp white fixtures, a perfect companion for bright hues, such as ocean blue and sunny yellow. A pretty floral fabric or graphic rug can establish the palette and cozy up the space. Selecting a paintable wallcovering and incorporating color via paint and accessories make it easy and affordable to change the look.

Left: Faucets designed for bar sinks add convenient height to the bathroom vanity and require less bending to wash face and hands. Pretty fabric inserted in the door panels adds color and pattern.

Above: Towel hooks, a sisal basket, and a small painted cabinet put storage where it's handy.

Smart strategies for a refreshing soak

1. Install a textured base for paint by papering the walls with embossed wallcovering.

2. Support the vintage theme with beaded-board wainscoting that rises about 38 inches above the tiled floor.

3. Replace wood panels in the cabinet doors with colorful fabric shirred on rods top and bottom.

4. Incorporate a sisal basket and hooks for handy towel storage.

5. Provide softness and warmth underfoot with a trio of striped washable rugs.

Erase those age spots

Erase those age spots with a top-to-bottom bathroom makeover. The materials can be as affordable as paint, as sophisticated as marble, as luxurious as a nickel faucet, or as hardworking as a bank of floor-to-ceiling cabinets.

Above: Prints from an antique English natural history portfolio inspired the silvery blue-green wall color of this vintage-inspired bathroom. The island vanity, topped with marble, takes center stage in this spare room-turned-luxurious spa.

Right: A dramatic cast-iron soaking tub, cradled in a maple frame, serves as the focal point in a roomy bathroom. Take a tub beyond mundane; hang an oversize graphic wall art above it.

Above: A classic toile pattern in both wallpaper and fabric illustrates the ease of using a two-hue color scheme. The muted tones of the pattern soften the look of the space. Simple Roman shades offer privacy when needed.

Opposite: Vintage pieces—a claw-foot tub and two oak dressers—add character to a brand-new bathroom. Look for similar pieces at an architectural salvage store or antiques store. Condition is important. Find out if the pieces can be refinished to stand up to daily use.

bathing style

Use these ideas for the splashiest room in the house.

- **If you have space,** pull in furniture pieces for comfort and style. Consider footstools or end tables by the tub and a comfortable chair.
- **Use warm textures,** such as wood floors, nubby rugs, and handmade tile, to add interest and character. Textures also add a calming effect.
- **Free up floor space** in a small bathroom by replacing a boxy vanity with a pedestal sink.
- **Add depth to walls** with paint finishes. Consider combing or sponging, and use semigloss or gloss paints instead of flat finishes.
- **Create a spacious feel** with mirrors. Encircle them in wood frames for a traditional look or metal frames for modern appeal. Place them so they reflect light.
- **Soften hard edges** with fabrics. Use fabrics on windows, to skirt a sink, or for a shower curtain paired with a vinyl liner.
- **Add favorite scents.** Incorporate candles, sachets, soaps, and just-picked flowers to freshen the air.

Worth noting

Give your bathtub star status with a little extra detailing. Surround a spa tub with a wall of beautiful tile, dress a claw-foot tub in a floor-to-ceiling shower curtain, or hang a candle chandelier over a soaking tub.

Opposite: Elegant blue and white tiles introduce color and pattern into the bathroom. The abundance of tiles makes the space look luxurious and rich. Simple curtains keep splashes contained. The tub surround provides a perching spot for bathers and a ledge for storing bath supplies.
Right: The vanity area is a study in symmetry as matching tablelike vanities with quartz-surfacing countertops and spun-glass vessel sinks stand beneath oval mirrors. The sconces and sink faucets feature nickel finishes. Get a similar effect by duplicating the symmetry.

Left: Color can be a basic white bathroom's best friend. An apple green shower curtain and towels show the dramatic effect color can have on a space. Change them tomorrow, and the bath has a new personality.

Above: Rustic and ready for action, this bathroom suits a couple of little cowpokes, with pullout step stools tucked in the vanity base, a nightlight behind a star hung above the mirrors, and wall pegs perfect for towel storage. The dark stain on the vanity cabinet repeats on peg racks. A honey-color stain highlights the cabinetry knobs and mirrored cabinets.

Relax in a getaway bathroom filled with colors that evoke memories of a favorite water vacation.

1. Gather vacation photographs for color inspiration. The colors of water, surf, and sky offer an analogous color scheme, a sure way to bring serenity into a space.

2. Search the market for products that fit this popular color scheme. The tile options are diverse: cement tiles in powdery blue, fused-glass tiles with bubble insets, glass mosaic tiles, tumbled-stone tiles, and even solid-surfacing materials in beachy hues. Other manufacturers offer plumbing fixtures that coordinate with the tiles. Use these colors to ground a palette.

3. Make color the focal point by setting it in a mostly white background or by covering the walls in a variety of greens and blues. A blue vessel sink really pops against a white background while a shower lined with blue glass tile makes a dramatic color statement.

Bring in nature

for an inspiring bathroom scheme that delivers quietude and simplicity.

1. Take a walk in the woods to gather colorful textures and tones that can turn any bathroom into a peaceful spa.

2. Shop the market for products. Look for slate look-alike ceramic tiles and real slate tiles. Consider cobblestone glass tiles for a shower base, honed marble for countertops, pulls shaped like bamboo, and accessories that look like river rock.

3. Start building a palette by grouping products on a neutral background. Study the combinations. Begin eliminating pieces until you've settled on one wood, one stone, and one metal. If the palette seems too narrow, slowly add other pieces.

4. Use rich natural materials in abundance. Natural colors and textures are easy to combine and also deliver style when only one material is used on floor and walls.

5. Opt for basic shapes, such as a silver ring to hold a bath towel, and classic elements, such as a teak vanity defined by simple slats.

Uncover the spa

waiting to take shape in any basic builder bathroom. The path to bliss may be challenging, but it's worth the effort.

Before: Blah, blah, blah—that's the only word that can describe the boxy bathroom with orangey oak trim, below.

After: A sophisticated new look builds from the bones of the boring "before" bathroom. The existing white basics—ceramic floor, cabinetry, and countertop—suit the new color scheme of brown, green, and white. Ample floor space makes room for collections, a rustic cabinet, and an iron garden chair, all ingredients that help a bathroom look a little less antiseptic. Check out these makeover ideas.

- **Ban the oak.** Oak woodwork can be beautiful. Here, however, it's applied in thin strips that

Before

Worth noting

Suit the paint to the room and the surface. Mildew-resistant paints work well in high-moisture interior spaces such as bathrooms. For woodwork and cabinets, opt for easy-scrub, durable semigloss paint.

accent the wrong elements: a half-wall and a single window. Paint the oak white to make it disappear.

- **Coat the walls with color,** such as a yummy chocolate brown paint, opposite. Brown is a strong color that warms up this big bathroom and accents the high ceiling. The contrast between white woodwork and brown walls adds design energy.
- **Focus on the sink area.** Rather than remove a large plate-glass mirror above the vanity, use the mirror as a backdrop for a pretty frame, left. Fill some of the counterspace with glass-door cabinets that provide storage for soaps and lotions.
- **Invest in metal.** Think of a quality faucet, brushed-silver knobs, and silver cup pulls as investment decorating. They make everything in the bathroom look richer.
- **Introduce furniture.** A flea market cabinet painted white adds storage and a focal point. Use the shelves to hold collections, and stash extra supplies behind the doors. A pretty metal chair can hold bath gear or provide seating.
- **Bring in collections.** Old-fashioned mirrors add a touch of elegance and suit the scale of the high ceiling. Seashells bring back memories of great vacations.

Bathing space may be closer than you think. In an old house check out the height and square footage of the attic.

Before: Rafters and insulation might seem like a long way from a finished bathroom, above. Sometimes, though, it's easier to start from scratch than it is to rip out existing walls and plumbing.

After: The fresh new bathroom showcases vintage-look materials and smart design choices, including air ducts hidden under the window seat and a layout that preserves maximum headroom.

- **Get the shell right.** The bathroom preserves ample headroom by tucking storage under the low ceiling at the sides of the room and placing the sink and toilet in the center of the space.
- **Welcome daylight.** Centered windows above the window seat pair with a skylight to illuminate the room. Window treatments cover

only the lower half of the windows in the third-floor space.

• **Add traditional details.** Wood planks on the ceiling and paneling on the endwall add period detailing. The arch over the window seat copies architectural elements from the 1920s, when the house was built.

• **Relax with dreamy colors.** The palette of soft blue-gray and cream adds a restful feeling while the dark floor anchors the room. The floor was originally painted white, but the look was too austere. The floor was stripped, leaving a little white paint in the wood, then finished with a three-stain process using dark walnut, red oak, and ebony oil stains.

• **Build in storage.** Stock cabinets line undereave space on both sides of the bathroom. Upper cabinets were used because they're only 12 inches deep, half the depth of lower units.

• **Mix vintage and new fixtures.** The exterior of the old claw-foot tub was painted to freshen the style while the sink and toilet are new from the home center. When mixing old and new, select for style compatibility rather than trying to find an exact match.

Modern luxury

Touchable textures and warm colors give this powder room a handsome look.

Select flooring. Woven sisal flooring adds the right texture and color to ground this warm and natural decorating scheme. Sisal works in a powder room but its scratchy texture wouldn't be a good choice in a barefoot bathroom.

Color the walls and woodwork. Warm red wallpaper with a burnished golden color overlay brings warmth and personality to the room.

Accessorize the sink. A tortoiseshell mirror frame adds oomph to the classic round shape. A brass-and-china knob secured to the wall serves as a towel holder; polished brass faucets with a modern shape adorn the sink.

Dress the window. A Roman shade with a fanciful valance adds a masculine note to the room. The fabric is brown with metallic diamonds.

Add lighting. The wall sconces have an intriguing harlequin motif that echoes the pattern in the Roman shade. The soft light from the candlestick lamp is perfect for a powder room and creates a welcoming mood for guests.

Move in furniture. A traditionally styled embossed leather console balances the chiseled appearance of the stool.

Finish with details. Tortoiseshell and wood elements make a sophisticated statement. The mirror frame, vases, and chest top are all tortoiseshell. Other accessories feature a subtle diagonal wood pattern that's punctuated with bold contrasting stripes.

Classic glamour

Posh and powerful, this powder room builds on a base of fuchsia and crystal.

Select flooring. A handpainted floorcloth mixes white and metallic, a fitting stage for this fancy space.

Color the walls and woodwork. In a 7×7-foot powder room, such as this one, a statement color like fuchsia adds energy. Egg-and-dart molding painted in metallic silver provides a luxe edging to frame the walls.

Accessorize the sink. Fine materials, from the Venetian glass mirror to the crystal faucet handles, add to the glamorous look. A curved crystal finial serves as a towel hook.

Dress the window. An opaque pattern etched onto glass panes mounted in the window frame diffuses light and adds privacy. For an easier option check out vinyl films that cling to any glass surface and are easy to remove.

Add lighting. A trio of crystal pendants in delicate pink creates the effect of a dazzling chandelier. A glass-base lamp on the dresser enhances the mood.

Move in furniture. When space allows move furniture into the bathroom. It's an easy way to add storage and style. The mirrored dresser used here also reflects visual space.

Finish with details. Jeweled items, including a perfume bottle, picture frames, and even a strand of pearls, are glamorous touches that work perfectly to dress up a small space.

Turn the clutter

of bathroom gear into an example of stylish organization with these clever ideas.

1. For by-the-tub ease

Towels are always ready for bath time when rolled and stuffed into an open basket. Use baskets in a variety of sizes for other bathroom supplies, such as toilet paper, hair dryers, and wrapped soaps.

2. For tucked-away toiletries

A double-wide vanity cabinet offers plenty of space for storing toiletries. Even a small bathroom has room for a shallow cabinet like this. Maximize shelf space to ensure enough room for all you need to store.

3. For splash-free reading

A chrome towel rack offers a space-saving solution for magazine storage in the bathroom. Mount a rack on the wall, using anchors to keep the screws from pulling loose. Slip a magazine or two over each rod. The rack takes only inches of space.

4. For undercover towels

A built-in window seat offers a handy bath-time perch and storage for towels. A flip-down door provides access to storage underneath. Substitute a bench with a bottom shelf or baskets underneath for a quick-and-easy solution.

5. For stacking in style

Bath gear can be pretty stacked in piles or corralled in baskets. For even more impact sort the gear into a tall cabinet with doors that allow a peek at the contents through a metal grille. Consider replacing solid door panels with glass or metal mesh.

6. For maximizing space

Simple changes turn an ordinary vanity cabinet into a stylish centerpiece. Removing the cabinet doors and replacing them with a fabric skirt gives the cabinet a new look. Vintage wire baskets provide stand-up storage for bulky towels.

7. For antique appeal

A vintage table adapts to use as a vanity with storage below. The cross supports offer a handy resting spot for a large flat basket. A wood shelf would also work. Keeping well-used items in view simplifies morning grooming routines.

Organizing the bathroom can make your morning routine less hectic. Here are a few ideas.

- **Retrofit cabinetry** with pullout trays and hampers, tilt-out waste cans, and drawer organizers sized to fit the gear you need to store.
- **Create a storage ledge** by adding a narrow shelf above a pedestal sink or along a soaking tub.
- **Use between-stud space** to carve out recessed shelves for toiletries or to install a medicine cabinet.
- **Install hooks for towels** below a window or on the back of the bathroom door. Make space count by installing two or three rows of hooks on a door.
- **Add shelves** above the toilet or over the door to make use of vertical space.
- **Bring in a freestanding storage unit.** Consider an open shelf unit for towels and pretty toiletries, and a closed cabinet to hide other supplies.
- **Squeeze a storage ottoman** into a bathroom corner. It can hold bulky items while serving as seating for grooming routines.
- **Sort grooming supplies** often; discard dated items.

donna hay
today is.
PRESENTATION

Working spaces

for chores and projects

chapter 16

Granted, work happens in every room in your house. In an at-home office or laundry room, though, work is the focus. You'll be spending plenty of time in the space, so why settle for a thrown-together look? Is the laundry or office tucked into a closet or is it spacious and roomy with lots of storage? Is there daylight? The laundry location—first floor or basement—affects the look of the makeover. So does the use of the office. Is it for family budgeting, or do you also do professional work at home? If the budget is tight, paint is your strongest ally on this job. It's time to get started. Your work is waiting.

in this chapter

Turn working at home

into a stylish experience whether you have a room devoted to an office or a mere slice of space in the family room. Adapt some of these ideas to get your time clock ticking.

Left: All work and no style can make an office dull, so bring in a favorite antique desk and crystal sconces. A change in atmosphere will result in a change in attitude. You'll love going to work again. New built-in bookcases create a wall of storage around the desk. For a tidy look consider covering part of each unit with doors.

Below: A handsome table and chair can turn a corner of the living room into a home office. Add a personal touch with vintage tumblers filled with pencils and a bulletin board made by wrapping coarse linen around medium-density fiberboard. Store other items in bins and baskets.

This disappearing desk is hinged at one corner and swings out from a wall of built-in cabinets. A drawer behind the desk keeps files handy. When not in use the desk and drawer slide into the cabinets and out of sight.

Think through your needs.

- **Desktop space.** Plan a desk height of 26 inches for a computer keyboard and 30 inches for a work surface for crafting. If you have room for only one work surface, opt for a pullout keyboard shelf. To keep everything within easy reach, arrange the work area in an efficient L- or U-shape.
- **Storage space.** Standard filing cabinets provide efficient storage. Use a closet with pullout storage bins to organize bulky supplies. Tall cabinets add vertical interest and storage without hogging floor space.
- **Office chair.** Save your back. Use a chair designed with extra support.
- **Internet and telephone.** Consider wireless Internet and a cordless telephone to eliminate the need to rewire the space.
- **Lighting.** Plan for overall general lighting and specialized task lighting. To cut glare on computer monitors, use adjustable desk lamps, general lighting on dimmers, and lamps that bounce light off the ceiling.
- **Bulletin boards/chalkboards.** Organize work with bulletin boards that hold calendars and in-process projects. Chalkboards are easy to create using chalkboard paint.

Left: This family room features a work surface and custom built-ins that hide function behind good looks. Open shelves filled with baskets provide storage that's visible and out of sight.
Below: Open shelves make it easy to find supplies and put things away. Combining them with drawers creates a perfect storage duo. Wicker baskets replace desk drawers. Mixing a vintage metal chair with modern bookshelves adds warmth.
Opposite: A library ladder maximizes storage space in this sophisticated kitchen office. Deep drawers serve as file cabinets. Natural linen covers a bulletin board.

Worth noting

Spend five minutes at the end of each day clearing off your desk. Spend 30 minutes at the end of each month sorting through projects and tossing unneeded items in the trash.

It's ironic. A desk is supposed to be the place for organizing all the details of daily life, yet it's often a mess. Here's how to keep it tidy.

- **Sort it.** Trays come in all shapes, sizes, and materials and can hold almost anything.
- **Stack it.** Think vertically and store boxes and bins on top of each other to maximize space.
- **Post it.** Gather invitations, special dates, and favorite photos on bulletin or magnetic boards.
- **File it.** Accordion files handle papers, fabric samples, bills, and invoices. They're perfect when you need to keep these items handy near your desktop.
- **Store it.** Make room for seldom-used items in easy-to-access containers. Unless you use it daily, pack it up.
- **Shred it.** Protect your identity by shredding papers that include your name, address, Social Security number, or other account numbers.

Imagine a dungeon

of a basement and a nasty "before" photograph becomes unnecessary. No matter how dismal your space appears, consider these makeover tips.

Before: Picture cobwebs and soot as the main occupants of this roomy space. On the bright side, with direct access to the backyard, this laundry room is in a smart location.

After: Unfitted kitchens composed of stand-alone furnishings offer vintage appeal for modern living. That same technique can make a laundry room out of even the most neglected of spaces, and the makeover can be easy on your budget. Check off this laundry list of strategies.

- **Paint it out.** Think of white paint as correction fluid that can eliminate the problems an unfinished basement contains. Empty the room, mask or cover windows, and use a spray gun to coat every surface, including concrete walls and plumbing and heating pipes, opposite. You may need to use several types of white paint to get it to stick to surfaces such as concrete walls and floors, metal pipes, and wood trim. In most cases a primer will be the best way to start.
- **Think about function.** Plan a sink area for hand laundry and stain removal, below left, room for a washer and dryer, below right, folding and stacking space, and an ironing spot.
- **Bring in unfitted pieces.** In this case a bench provides storage under the seat and a temporary holding spot for folded laundry on top. A custom-made rack surrounds the bench and provides a hanging space for just-laundered clothing. Topping the washer and dryer with a cabinet for laundry soaps keeps them right where they're used.
- **Warm it with accessories.** Woven baskets and bowls, indoor plants, metal pendent lights, and soft rugs add character.

Worth noting

Redoing a laundry area? Consider appliances with a government Energy-Star rating. These appliances promise energy savings of up to 30 percent. For rated brands and models, check www.energystar.gov.

Remake a long, slim

space into a laundry room, storage shed, repair workshop, and more. Start with a list of goals: which chores you want to squeeze into the space and how much you need to store. Planning with specific goals in mind ensures a finished space that works efficiently. Divide a narrow room into opposing sides, making one side shallow and the other deep. Use the shallow side for open racks and narrow cabinets and the deep side to house a washer and dryer, which demand at least 26 inches of depth. Pair open and closed storage as well, using open hooks for jackets by the back door and a cabinet with doors to contain clutter.

Left: Front-loading appliances create space for a folding counter. Ticking-stripe fabric hides the washer and dryer between loads. Rustic sconces look good and light the way.

Above and right: Put an old armoire to work by fitting it with containers, hooks, and other organizing items. Look for bins and baskets that reflect your style. Small bins help organize little, easy-to-lose items.

To-do list for a back entry makeover

1. Select a color scheme. A favorite hooked rug adds style oomph to the floor and establishes the country color scheme of gold, cream, black, and muted red.

2. Divide the space into laundry, workshop, and storage. Use freestanding cabinets for closed storage and a counter and skirt to hide the washer and dryer. A narrow wall with hooks can store coats and scarves.

3. Add storage using armoires and cabinets that slip into alcoves or along a long wall.

4. Install task lighting where needed, such as above the counter.

5. Personalize the space by displaying collections, such as a hooked rug and washboards.

Shake up your home office, even if it's in the basement, by applying liberal doses of color and pattern. It's sure to boost your creativity because you'll want to spend every minute in the lively space.

Before: Serviceable but uninspired, this home office features a mishmash of furniture set in a dull world, below.

After: A below-grade space just begs for light, color, and pattern. Here's how to add style to an office.

- **Banish underperformers.** That means the folding party table and storage cubbies have to go.
- **Get the surfaces right.** An easy-to-install white plank ceiling and engineered-wood floor eliminate the basement look of the office. Although the wall color is unchanged, it looks more stylish with fresh companions.
- **Plan for lighting.** Pendent shades on each side of the computer offer task lighting, while an overhead fixture provides general illumination. Depending on your eyesight and the size of the office, consider adding specific task lighting, such as a lamp, for sewing or other crafts projects.
- **Furnish the space.** A stationary desk nudged against the wall and a second table on wheels ensure flexibility for projects. A commercial-quality adjustable desk chair adds comfort for long work hours, and another chair, updated with paint and fabric, provides guest seating. Tall storage units make savvy use of vertical space. Lining upper glass doors with fabric creates out-of-sight storage.
- **Bring in pattern and color.** Nature patterns, featuring leaves, vines, and flowers, bring the outdoors in. Ground the room with a bold patterned rug, use smaller patterns to complement the rug, and repeat the colors and patterns on other fabrics.
- **Add fun accessories.** Colorful bowls corral everything from paper clips to thread. Open-top storage containers in fun patterns handle files and notebooks. Even the dog's bed looks updated with a slipcover of vine fabric.

Before

Worth noting

Shop online for products for a home office. It's a fun way to squeeze play into your workday. To get started type product names into a search engine. Look for general household storage items as well as office supplies.

Turn two nightstands

and a large piece of plywood into a roomy hobby space. Start with unfinished furniture pieces that can be painted and adapted to suit your needs. Take these steps:

1. Buy the nightstands. Look for two similar pieces at an unfinished furniture store. Check that their height plus the tabletop will work for your needs.

2. Cut the tabletop. Decide how deep and wide you want your tabletop, allowing 30 inches for chair space between bases and 6 inches of overhang on the front and each side. Have a home improvement store cut plywood to the desired size.

3. Paint. If your nightstands are unassembled, paint before assembling. If they're already assembled, remove drawers, feet, and knobs to make painting easier. Prime all pieces, including the sides of the plywood tabletop; let dry. Top with two coats of satin-finish latex paint, allowing drying time between coats.

4. Paper. Measure a drawer front and cut wallpaper to cover four drawers, leaving the top drawers out. Apply wallpaper according to manufacturer's directions. Repeat on three other drawers. Replace knobs and place four of the drawers back into nightstand bases.

5. Assemble the desk. Add cleats or small metal brackets to the nightstand tops to screw the top to the bases.

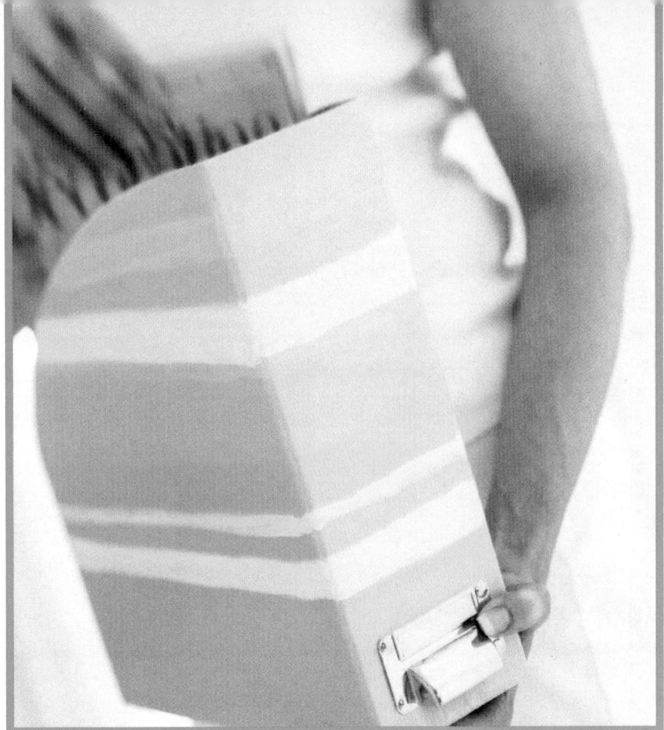

Dress up office gear with a selection of favorite paint colors and a collection of paint brushes from narrow to wide. Use handpainted stripes for an arty look and a rainbow of pastels for fun. Play with the technique; always leave enough solid planes of color for relief. Here's how to start.

1. Prepare the surface. For wood, cardboard, and plastic, rough up the surface with fine-grit sandpaper; wipe with a tack cloth. Prime the surface after ensuring that the primer is suitable for the material; let dry. Wash fabric first to remove sizing; priming is not necessary.

2. Paint stripes. Consider the pattern of stripes you want; use chalk to draw straight lines across the surface. Use the chalklines to keep the painted lines from running downhill. If you like the effect, create random brushed edges so the stripes look handpainted.

3. Seal the painted surface with clear polyurethane. Either spray or brush on the finish.

Kids' rooms

for growing up in style

chapter 17

Designing a room that grows with a child requires compromise and clairvoyance. After all, what's perfect for a newborn might seem too babyish in as little as two years. Take time to think through the options so the room that's perfect now can be modified easily as the child grows. Get started by asking these questions: Will the room be occupied by one child, or will two children use the space? What background colors can anchor the look as the child grows? Does the budget allow for new furniture, or will a collection of hand-me-downs need to be adapted? Are there special storage needs? Is there space for a flurry of childhood activity? Gather your ideas. It's time to play with the possibilities.

in this chapter

Newborn boys soon become growing boys whose rough-and-tumble play may punish bedroom furnishings. Opt for furniture that leaves plenty of floor space for active play. Select soft surfaces that can cushion a fall or muffle the noise. If your child is old enough, include him in the decorating fun. Starting at age 3 or 4, children can help choose wallcoverings, paints, and fabrics. If they pick a color you dislike, compromise by using it in easy-to-change accessories.

Below left: Cars and trucks are a perennial favorite with boys and set the mood in this designed-for-two bedroom. The bold black of the beds adds a crisp note that can grow with the child. Magazine racks provide book storage at each level. A second bed is a smart solution for overnight guests; a bunkbed fits in even the smallest of bedrooms.

Below: Vibrant-color fabric squares offer a modern version of a pieced quilt. The headboard slipcovers are made from T-shirts. If you're short on T-shirts, download copyright-free animal pictures online. Print the images onto photo-transfer paper, and iron them onto white cotton fabric. Band the blocks with colorful cotton fabric.

An alcove bed adds a cozy note to a child's room, frees floor space, and offers storage. Depending on the size of the space, fit the alcove with a crib or twin mattress. A resilient cork floor promises comfort underfoot and style with staying power.

just for kids

Consider these kid-friendly tips.

- **Select the bed first.** It's the largest piece of furniture, and it will be the focal point. Choose twin beds, a trundle bed, or bunkbeds that meet American Society for Testing and Materials standards (www.astm.org). Reserve the top bunk for children older than 6.
- **Outfit the closet** before filling the room with furniture. A well-designed closet might be all the storage that's needed for a toddler or even a teenager. Equip it with hanging racks, pullout bins, and storage baskets.
- **Soften the space with fabrics.** They have a calming effect and often kick off a color palette. Use fabrics that are washable.
- **Provide low storage** for small boys and taller storage boys can grow into. Portable baskets that hold toys make it easier to teach a child to pick up after play.
- **Cushion a hard-surface floor** with a washable oversize rug that provides a softer play surface.
- **Coat walls, woodwork,** and furniture with scrubbable paint.

Give a girl the opportunity to imprint her personality on her bedroom. That means starting with good basics, such as a pastel or neutral wall color and classic furniture, and adding the details that make it perfectly hers. Expect the look to change with her interests: dolls and costumes this year, soccer balls and ballerina shoes the next. If the background remains neutral, it's easy to change colors and patterns.

Above and right: Sweet fabrics and candy colors make this little girl's room feminine and fun. A palette of pink, green, blue, and yellow makes the space interesting, while grown-up fabrics ensure that the look will grow with the child. Paper butterflies hang from the ceiling and add a lighthearted touch. For a quick change a slipcover ties to the headboard and can be removed easily for a simpler look. Lacy-edged pillowcases, a ruffled duvet, and a sheer dust ruffle add girly accents.

A child's favorites dictate this color scheme and design. Crib mattresses, slipcovered and stacked, make a kid-friendly sofa. Other playful touches include a lampshade covered with fabric flowers, a window valance made from hula and ballerina skirts, and a scalloped chalkboard propped against the wall.

Celebrate a baby's arrival by designing a nursery that appeals to the parents and the baby. Infants respond to contrast, bright colors, and patterns. Avoid going overboard; if walls are patterned, for example, select solid-color rugs. Place some of the patterns in the room at crib height, so the baby can see them from the crib. Experiment with a big splash of color and pattern on one wall. It's easy to change as the baby grows.

Left and above: This nursery, a basic 10x12-foot box, had little architectural character. To create a focal point, a painted armoire angles into a corner and displays a stack of decorative hatboxes. The playful mermaid fabric used on the crib bumper pads and curtains is the source of the room's design and color scheme. Numerous pastel paint hues plucked from the fabric play up the walls and storage boxes. The waves and dots painted on the walls form a lively backdrop. Two round chenille rugs overlap on the floor and provide a cushiony spot for play.

Above: Bold and bright, the painted wall grid is a focal point in this nursery. It's a fun solution if selecting a single hue from a handful of well-loved colors proves too difficult. Buy paint by the quart; use painter's tape to create a grid on the wall. Make the grid large—three or four squares for an 8-foot-tall wall. Add fabrics that duplicate the grid colors. The look is gender-neutral so the room can serve as a nursery for a boy or a girl. Adapt the same idea for a grade-school child who loves color and can't pick a favorite.

Right: Washable white fabrics give this baby's room a heavenly attitude. The netting, hung from the ceiling on hook-and-loop tape, provides a cozy surround for a crib that floats in the center of a room. (Remove the netting once the baby can stand.) White offers a perfect option if you choose to decorate one room to serve as the nursery for each new baby. Add soft pastel accessories for a touch of color.

Start planning your nursery purchases using this list of necessities.

- **A crib** that meets current safety standards. Avoid secondhand cribs with chipped paint, missing parts, and shaky construction. Place the crib away from windows and out of reach of window coverings.
- **A standard crib mattress** of $27\frac{1}{2} \times 51\frac{7}{8}$ inches. For safety, no more than two fingers should fit between the mattress and the crib.
- **A rocking chair or glider.** Select one with flat arms for comfort to use while feeding the baby.
- **A double-duty changing table.** Look for one with a high top rail and open shelves to hold diapers now and toys and books later.
- **Adjustable lighting.** Dimmers allow brighter light for changing the baby and softer illumination for feedings.

Opposite: A wall-mounted crafts table is just one of the many features in this underground family playroom. It easily can seat four little artists. A ribbon strung between two flower pegs creates an instant art gallery where masterpieces are hung with clothespins. A secret door to the playhouse is hidden under the table.

Below: Chalkboard paint on the wall transforms one large section into art space for temporary creations. Even the frame of the chalkboard is painted in place.

Adapt a downstairs play space into a room that draws kids as reliably as honey attracts bees. With an infusion of color and pattern, it's easy to perk up a space that makes room for all sorts of play. In fact, in an out-of-the-way location, such as a basement or attic, it's OK to make a kid-friendly statement. This room features raspberry pink carpet, a lime green playhouse, a curvy crafts table, and a checkerboard floor that looks like a giant game board.

Above: This basement playroom is divided into distinct, colorful spaces, including an arts-and-crafts area accented with a checkerboard floor, a pink-carpeted TV area, and a lime green playhouse tucked under the staircase.

simple rules

During the kid years, make choices that simplify rather than complicate.

- **Opt for inexpensive rag rugs** or larger cotton rugs that can be shaken out or tossed in the wash.
- **Paint floors** for a great-looking and practical alternative to wood floors and carpet. It's easy to repaint as wear and stains require.
- **Select sturdy upholstery** that's easy to clean. Washable slipcovers are also a good option. White slipcovers might seem like a bad choice, but they can be bleached to remove grime.
- **Choose durable surfaces** that downplay nicks and scratches and are easy to clean. Laminate makes a tough surface for tables and countertops while painted and distressed pieces look good even as they wear.
- **Forgo valuables** or store them away for a few years. Children can learn to be careful around breakable things, of course; however, it's still wise to protect valuable pieces.
- **Use scrubbable paint finishes.** If you like the look of matte paint, test one of the new, scrubbable matte paints on the market to see if it will hold up in your house.

Think beyond the bed

to create a kids' room that will be a great place to play and learn. Use the bed as a lounging spot or as a surface for holding large crafts projects. Combine the bed with ample storage, a roomy tabletop, and walls that serve as mini art galleries.

Design with kids in mind when you decorate other rooms in your house. A kid-size table gives them their own place in a family room. Small chairs and scootable ottomans let them create furniture groupings that support playtime.

Kid's bedroom

1. **Add a table** to the center of a child's bedroom. It can be used for hobbies and homework.
2. **Use the bed as a sofa;** make it comfy with throw pillows or a long bolster.
3. **Combine a dresser** for clothing with a draped cabinet for creative play and puppet shows.
4. **Suit a child's interests** with an easel for painting, a chalkboard for games, and display space for posters and school projects.
5. **Define spaces** in a large room by using an area rug.

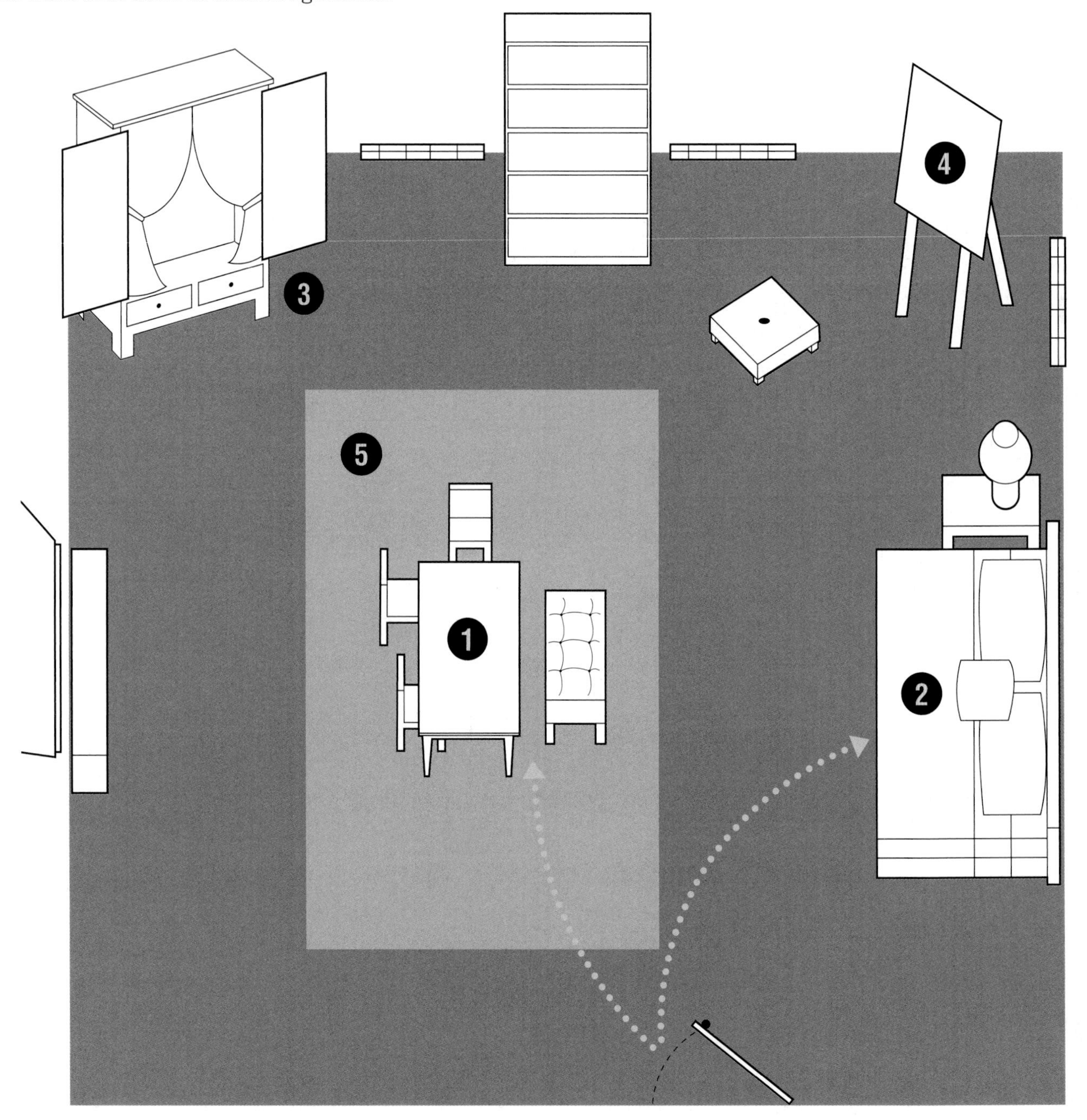

- **Plan for flexibility.** Kids grow fast so keep their current and future size in mind as you plan. Look for furniture that can suit them as they grow. Hang bulletin boards and chalkboards low while they're small and raise them as the kids get taller.
- **Use the bed like a sofa,** lining it with pillows during the day. A small bedroom usually lacks space for other upholstered pieces.
- **Provide project space.** A centered table and a chair or two make room for homework, crafts, and games. Put a washable rug under the table to contain messes; choose a table with a scrubbable finish.
- **Outfit the closet** to take the place of a dresser. This frees up play space in the bedroom and maximizes closet square footage.
- **Keep furniture low.** Although stretching a built-in bookcase to the ceiling makes sense in a family room, it can invite kids to climb in their bedrooms. Screw bookcases to the walls to keep them from toppling.
- **Make room for overnight guests.** Invest in a trundle bed to maximize floor area and provide sleeping quarters for guests.
- **Line the walls.** Wall space adds function to a child's bedroom. Use it to display your child's art. Add rows of shelves or hooks to increase storage. Coat them with bright paint to add personality.

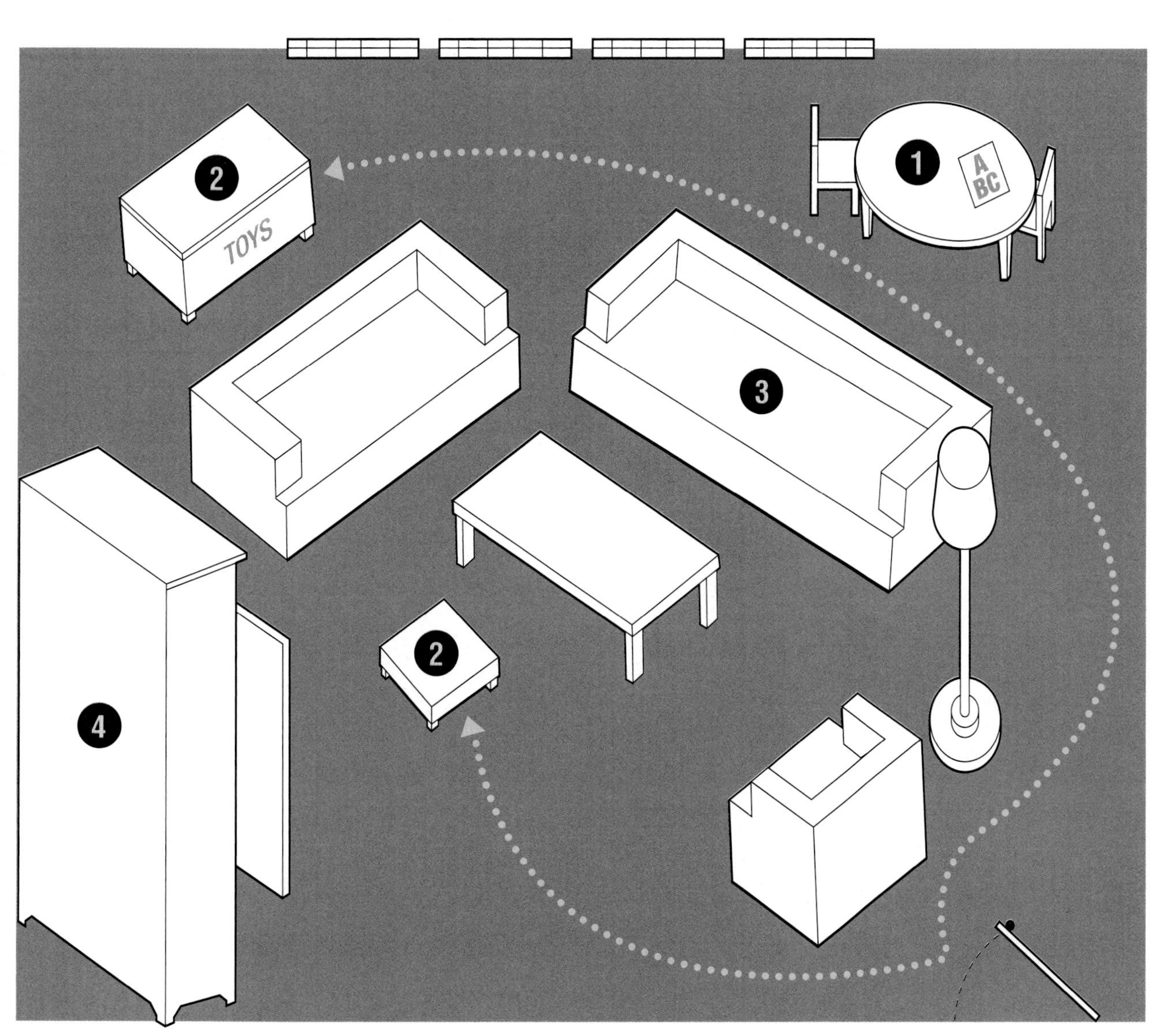

Kid-friendly family room

1. Suit any room to children. Tuck a child-size table behind the sofa. It's a handy spot for snacks and crafts.

2. Look for double-duty furniture that's also handsome. A trunk and an ottoman store toys and provide seating.

3. Minimize furniture, both in number and size, to allow plenty of crawling and exploring space for small children. A sofa and loveseat combo is best.

4. Use large cabinets with doors and drawers to hide all the clutter that comes with kids. Place some storage, such as a trunk, where kids can reach it.

See page 422, "Room Arranging."

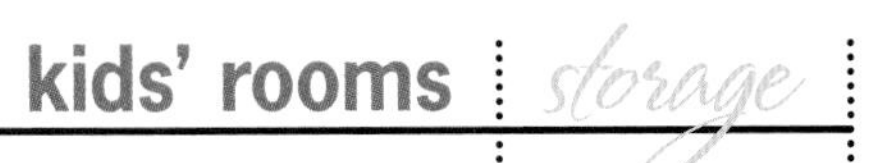

Savvy storage

for kids should be fun and creative as well as handy and easy to reach. So consider these clever ideas for making organization and picking up the best game at your house.

1. For the true-blue kid

Go red, white, and blue in this patriotic storage cubby. Cut ½-inch-thick medium-density fiberboard to fit the back of each cube. Lay the squares on a protected floor in the correct pattern. Paint four squares with dark blue paint; let dry. Then stamp white stars on top. Paint the remaining squares white; let dry. Use painter's tape to mask off stripes, paint them red, and let dry. Glue a square to the back of each cubby.

2. For the little organizer

An unfinished seven-drawer chest makes the perfect day-by-day wardrobe organizer for a kid. Paint the chest inside and out with scrubbable paint. Label the drawers with the days of the week, using lettering decals available at a crafts store. It's a fun way to teach a child to plan ahead and organize what to wear for the week. Add double hooks on the chest sides to hold a favorite sweatshirt where it's easy to grab.

3. For the cars-and-blocks set

Tab-top storage bags made of oilcloth provide the perfect containers for storing blocks and cars. Place one bag on the floor and unzip it to provide a flat playing surface. When playtime is over scoot the toys to the center of the bag and zip them inside. Hanging rods attached to the outside of a closet door offer easy-to-use storage.

4. For a curious toddler

A closet in a toddler's room features plenty of open shelving that gives parents quick access to frequently used items. Fabric-lined metal bins corral socks and small items to keep them tidy. Low, open cubbies give a toddler easy access to toys. Secure the shelving units to the wall to keep them from tipping.

5. For a family of kids

An entry closet outfitted with shelves and hooks provides lots of easy-to-use storage space. Remove the door so things get put away rather than thrown on the floor in a back entry. Small clipboards with hooks provide handy spots for each child to keep a schoolbag and notes for parents.

6. For a school-age collector

Roll-up shades hung side by side soften a wall of built-in shelves and provide hidden storage on top and display space for a nautical collection below. The fabric was adhered to boards, which then were mounted to the shelves. The fabric is attached to the boards with hook-and-loop tape so it can be removed for cleaning.

Big bags, little bags, mesh bags, oilcloth bags, floor bags, wall bags—think of bags as the kids' version of file drawers and closet organizers. Use them to organize everything from toys to school papers. Here are a few ideas.

- **Stuff sports gear in mesh bags** and hang them in the back entry where they're easy to gather on the way to weekly practice.
- **Use mesh cosmetics bags** to store toothbrushes and combs. Add labels; hang the bags on a towel bar.
- **Turn a pillowcase into a bag** by stitching a narrow casing in the top and threading cord through the pocket. Fill it with toys and hang it below a bedroom window.
- **Transform tote bags** into laundry hampers, toy boxes, or clutter catchalls. Label the bags using fusible lettering.
- **Buy colored plastic bags** with zip tops to use for organizing small toys. Select a separate color for each child. Look for colorful bags at crafts stores.

Get clever with projects for kids' rooms. Pick one of these or create your own.

1. Create an art center.

A plate rack provides smart storage for children's art supplies right by the kitchen table and reverts to a plate rack when the kids grow up. Add hooks to hold art supplies in buckets, and use the slots to store original artworks. Turn wainscoting into gallery display by coating the wood with magnetic paint and using clip magnets to hold the latest creation within easy view.

2. Frame doll clothes.

Showcase favorite doll outfits in shadow box frames, then hang them above a dresser for a playful accessory. Hang the frames close to the dresser so they create a visual link with the furniture. To set up the shadow boxes, line the back of each frame with colored paper or fabric; stitch through the back and into the outfit to hold it in place. Slip the finished piece back into the frame and secure.

1

2

3. Build a play table.

Turn playtime into a picnic with this fun table. Buy two sets of metal sawhorse brackets. Cut lumber for legs to the desired height. Build a frame that will sit on the sawhorses and provide support for a desktop. Create a desktop from ¾-inch-thick medium-density fiberboard (MDF) or plywood; nail to the frame. Instead of a chair substitute a picnic table bench painted to match the table.

4. Map out a dresser.

Color copies of pages from an old world atlas transform these dresser drawers. The copies were glued and sealed using a decoupage medium. To start, prime and paint an unfinished dresser, including the drawers. To create a patchwork effect, buy a number of inexpensive maps, and overlap them for a random pattern on the drawer fronts. Seal the paper surfaces using decoupage medium.

Bedrooms

for round-the-clock living

Dream bedrooms are more than a place to catch a few zzzs. If your bedroom puts you to sleep, start making it better by considering how it suits your lifestyle. Consider, too, whether it needs a complete style makeover or just a yearly tune-up. What little luxury would make the space a haven? Will the room be used as a part-time office or sitting area? Is there space for a television, or is this a no-TV zone? What size bed fits the floor space? Study closet space to determine if it meets your needs. Is it possible to remove a piece of furniture and organize closets to work harder? Start now to claim your space.

in this section

Pair simple lines with bold colors

for a look that's cool and contemporary. Furnishings in classic shapes surrounded by plenty of white space make a room feel restful. To create this look in a cluttered bedroom, start by removing everything but the bed. Update a dated headboard with a simple slipcover of solid fabric. Layer on new bed linens, then move a dresser, nightstands, and lamps back in place. Live in the room for a few days before adding more accessories. Backtrack if the cluttered feeling returns.

Above: Vibrant color works its style magic on the walls of a small bathroom. White accents create a crisp look.

Left: One dynamite fabric pattern is a smart investment for a bedroom makeover. Use the piece in a prominent place, such as the front-and-center pillow on a bed. To harness the design power of repetition, use the fabric colors at least two more times in the room.

Above: Geometry plays a starring role in this bedroom. Diamonds show up on the box-spring cover while colorful rectangles appear on the floor, window, and bed.

Suite steps to a changeable haven

1. Paint ceiling and furniture in a snowy white.

2. Create a bold color palette by collecting linens in solid colors.

3. Find a signature fabric in a graphic pattern to give the room pizzazz.

4. Soften the floor and add contrast with throw rugs that wrap three sides of the bed.

5. Gather a few accessories in graphic patterns and shapes that support the color scheme.

Worth noting

Contrast counts in decorating. It can be the noticeable difference between strong colors or the subtle variation from rough to smooth textures. Even old and new items offer contrast.

Left: A new bed is distressed to look like old iron with chipping paint. The taupe wallpaper feels like suede.
Below: A French-style chair and a tasseled, striped silk balloon shade dress up the room.
Below right: A crackle-finish wallpaper with a pattern of classical urns complements the marble tile floor in the bathroom.

Add dressy details to romance

a boxy bedroom and bath. Sconces dripping with glass prisms, elegant fringe on a curtain, and a curvy iron bed offer feminine charms. Pairing these soft elements with a neutral palette of taupes, creams, and khaki ensures that the spaces—bedroom and bathroom—have a masculine side as well. Comfort is key to the design: The chair and ottoman in the bedroom function like a chaise longue, and an upholstered chair stands ready near the bathtub.

Divide an open bedroom suite

by using furniture to separate the space into its functional parts: a cannonball bed to define the sleeping alcove, a love seat and coffee table for the seating area, and a desk tucked into an office corner. Create a gender-neutral oasis by using black furnishings as a counterpoint to the soft lavender and green palette and by selecting fabrics in stripes, solids, and plaids to offset flowery prints. Chunky furnishings also keep the space from feeling too sweet.

Above: A window seat with drawers adds bonus bathroom storage. The cushion topper makes it a soft spot for lounging. The shower curtain repeats the color scheme by combining a tan linen band with green.
Left: An antique oak sideboard, now painted black, was retrofitted to make space for the sink. The extra height of the sideboard brings the sink to a more comfortable level for grooming. For durability on the vanity top, use an alkyd paint, or coat latex paint with polyurethane.
Right: A bold black bed adds a strong masculine note that's softened by the choice of lavender bedcoverings and pillows. A cushioned ottoman at the foot of the bed provides handsome storage for bedding.

make your bed

Pile on bedtime comfort with soft fabrics and cushy fillings for pillows, duvets, and comforters. Here's a shopper's guide:

- **Sheets:** Balance thread count—threads per square inch—and thread quality when buying bed linens. Test for softness by rubbing the fabrics on your cheek. Sheets made of pima or Egyptian cotton (200-count) will feel softer than 280-count sheets with poor thread quality. For a no-wrinkle alternative, consider sheets made using nanotechnology that draws sweat away from skin and delivers a super-soft feel.
- **Duvets and comforters:** Note fill power (number of cubic inches an ounce of down occupies). The higher the number (300 to 700), the more ability the comforter has to trap air and provide warmth. The best fill is white goose or duck down.
- **Pillows:** Buy pillows that suit sleeping preferences: all down for soft; half down and half feathers for medium firm; and all feathers for firm. Purchase downlike polyester pillows for allergy sufferers.

Welcome guests with a

room that feels like the best room in a favorite bed-and-breakfast getaway. Borrow some ideas from charming retreats where you've stayed. Remember, it all starts with the perfect bed or two. The style of a bed anchors a bedroom in the same way a table defines a dining room. Choose cottage-style twin beds for a country getaway, a contemporary headboard for a streamlined urban space, and a daybed for a room that functions for sitting and sleeping. Just before guests arrive add fresh flowers and ice-filled water carafes. To gather memories place a journal in the bedroom so guests can write notes about their visit and let you know how they liked staying in the room.

A pair of classic white-painted headboards stands out in graphic relief against walls painted bright blue. The effect is at once calming and energizing. To keep guests content layer on enough pillows so that one combination is sure to suit. A swing-arm lamp by each bed ensures adequate lighting for reading while a large dresser provides storage space for extra linens.

Outfit a guest room as a haven for visitors, then give the room a trial run to discover what's missing. Here are some amenities to consider:

- **A chair or bench** to hold a suitcase and other gear.
- **A nightstand** with a reading lamp.
- **Extra blankets** and pillows.
- **A full-length mirror.**
- **Closet space** with empty hangers.
- **A telephone** so calls can be private; also include a local telephone book.

Fluff the room with these extras before guests arrive:

- **Local maps,** brochures featuring local sites, and books on the area.
- **Daily newspapers,** complete with the week's weather report.
- **Snacks** for late-night eating or to take along on an outing.
- **Small coffeemaker** and an assortment of coffees, teas, and hot chocolate as well as pretty mugs.
- **Single-use cameras.**
- **Spare toiletries** in case guests forget something.
- **A basket of soaps,** shampoo, and body and hand lotions.
- **A basket with note cards,** stamps, and pens.

Opposite: A contemporary quilt provides all the design surprise a guest room needs. To preserve the quilt turn down the bed each night and lay the quilt over the basket at the foot of the bed.
Above: Full beds snuggle into undereave space, creating comfortable nooks for guests of any age. A bench at the foot of one bed is the perfect size to serve as a suitcase rack. A swing-arm lamp lights each alcove while saving floor space.

Above right: A classic poster bed looks fresh and updated, thanks to a fabric combination of prints, stripes, and plaids. The canopy fabric is attached to the frame with hook-and-loop tape so it can be easily removed for cleaning. A pair of Ming-style rosewood chairs at the foot of the bed provides convenient seating in a small space.

Right: A tailored daybed upholstered in a raffia fabric and topped with a faux-fur coverlet is the perfect double-duty furniture for a room that serves part-time as a guest bedroom. Plumped with orange and fuchsia pillows, it converts to comfortable sleeping quarters. An adjustable floor lamp and a small bedside stand can be pulled into place before guests arrive.

Choose a classic blue wall hue

as a restful backdrop for a collection of bedroom linens and furniture in analogous colors. A palette including blue, blue-green, green, and yellow-green illustrates how neighbors on the color wheel work together.

1. For a soothing analogous color scheme, pick a favorite hue, then use its neighbors on the color wheel as palette partners.

2. Practice restraint. Use three or more adjacent hues but no more than half the colors on the wheel. Pairing warm and cool colors adds energy.

3. Choose fabrics first, then find paint to match. Pick paints that are slightly brighter versions of the fabric colors.

4. Make 2-foot-square test patches of paint on foam-core board. Check the colors against the fabrics at different times of the day and in a variety of locations in the room.

5. Use color contrast to make an analogous scheme come to life. The kiwi-color nightstand pictured here illustrates the effect.

6. Boost the oomph of a blue space with bright neighboring accents, or add a complement, such as apricot. To vary the look use complementary colors to surprise and analogous ones to blend.

Add color to a white bedroom

by using bedspreads, pillows, and sheets in favorite hues such as pink and green, which are opposites on the color wheel. Select several shades of white to add interest to the background.

1. Complementary colors such as pink and green create an energizing duo that's tamed a bit because they're tinted with white. Look to nature for other inspiring palettes.

2. When using complementary hues let one color be the star. If complements struggle for attention, they neutralize each other. Because the pink and green scheme uses only two hues, it's easy to implement.

3. Choose a major fabric piece, such as a handmade quilt, that uses both colors but lets one dominate. That will set the tone for introducing other pieces into the palette.

4. Add fabrics that mix and match green with white, grass green with yellow-green, and peony pink with raspberry. Always compare fabric against fabric while making choices.

5. Strengthen the power of all colors by placing them against a background of white: headboard, floor, walls, and furniture. White always adds a crisp note to a palette.

6. For a visual pop add accessories in stronger hues of pink and green. Optimum contrast shakes up a color scheme.

Bedroom 1

1. Use the bedroom night and day by incorporating some foldaway features, such as a crafts armoire. The tabletop folds out when needed and closes up to hide the mess.

2. To save space, use a single nightstand. Another choice: Add a sconce on the other side.

3. Line a wall with low storage units to contain crafts supplies as well as clothing.

4. Create flexibility with a lightweight chair that can be moved as needed when the table is folded out of the cabinet.

5. Consider using the bed as a large surface for laying out patterns or organizing projects. Create a plan that makes it easy to change the room from a daytime crafts center to a nighttime sleeping space.

6. Group a chair, side table, and floor lamp to create a sewing or reading nook.

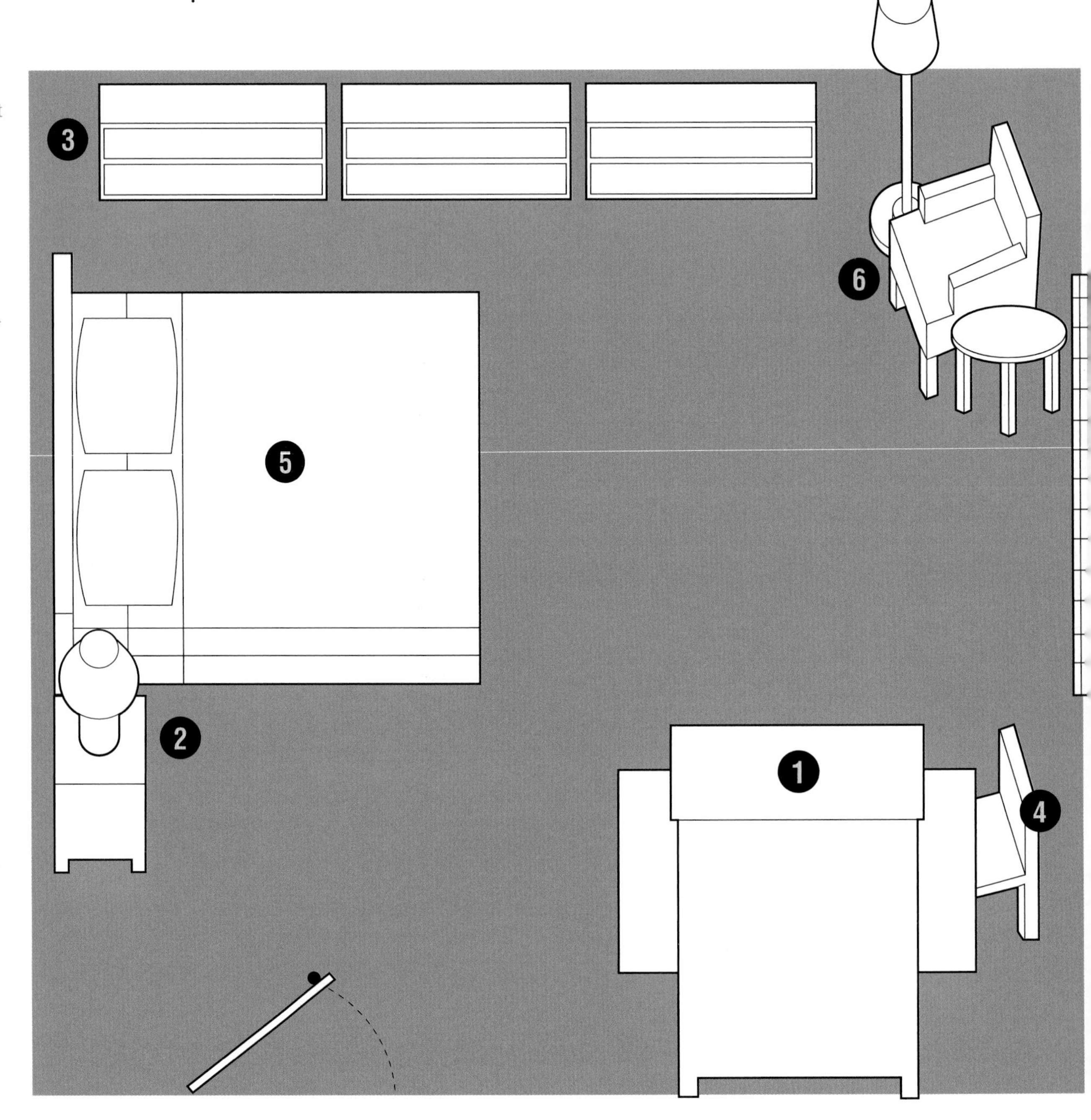

Place the bed first. The bed is the center of attention in any bedroom, and it should have the best view. Options might be limited if the bedroom has only one large wall; if you're creative though, you could open up a view of a great piece of furniture or a wall arrangement. Even a painted finish or wallpaper can create the view. In a space-starved room, use every inch of the closet to create room for folded and hanging clothing. This eliminates the need for bulky dressers or armoires.

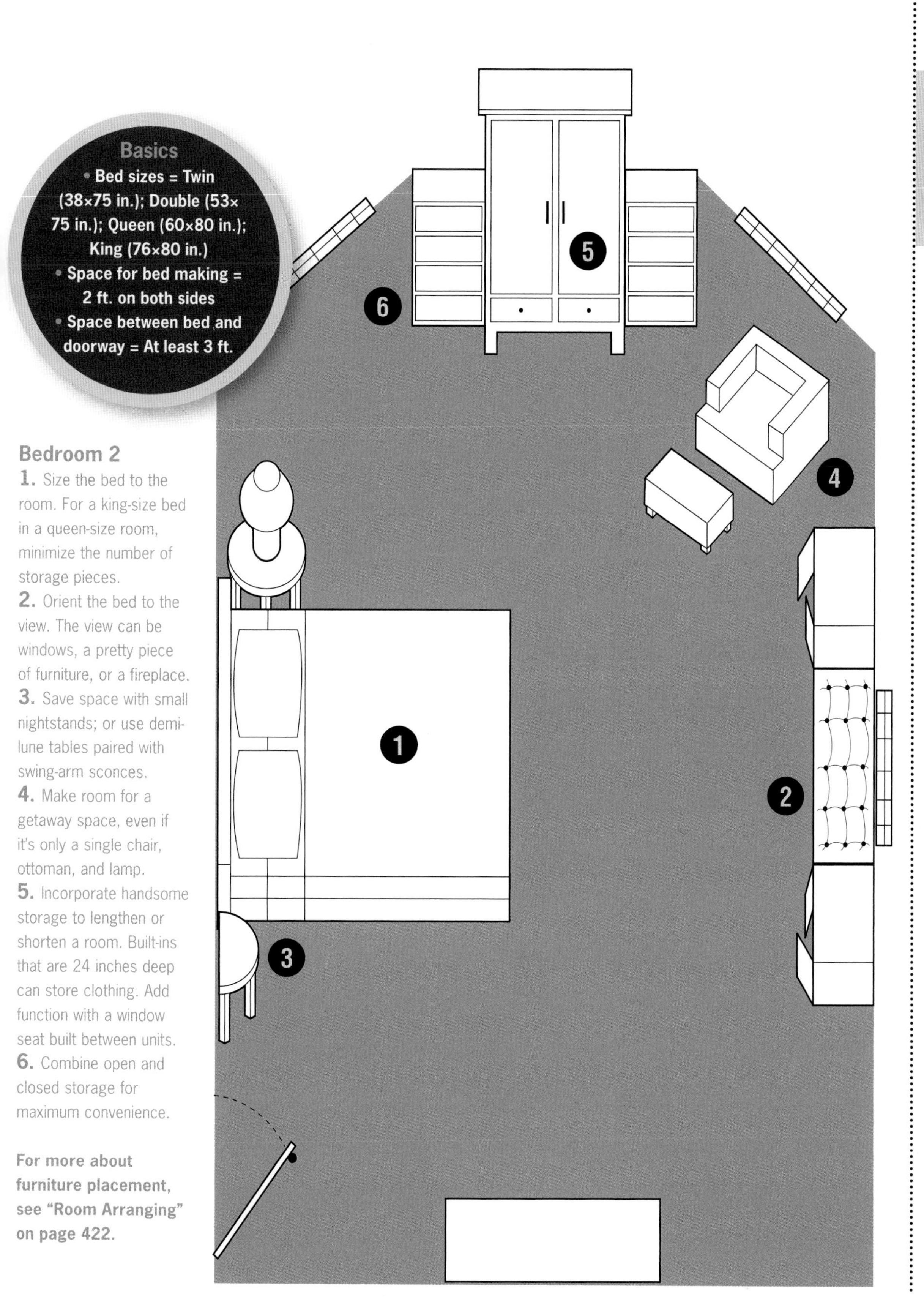

Bedroom 2

1. Size the bed to the room. For a king-size bed in a queen-size room, minimize the number of storage pieces.

2. Orient the bed to the view. The view can be windows, a pretty piece of furniture, or a fireplace.

3. Save space with small nightstands; or use demi-lune tables paired with swing-arm sconces.

4. Make room for a getaway space, even if it's only a single chair, ottoman, and lamp.

5. Incorporate handsome storage to lengthen or shorten a room. Built-ins that are 24 inches deep can store clothing. Add function with a window seat built between units.

6. Combine open and closed storage for maximum convenience.

For more about furniture placement, see "Room Arranging" on page 422.

• **Consider the size of the bed.** It's possible to use a larger bed if you don't need a lot of storage furniture. Keep scale in mind too. Apparent size of a bed is more than a matter of its dimensions. A scroll-like metal headboard consumes less visual space than a tall wooden headboard.

• **Create easy access.** See if you can easily navigate around the bed. Allow at least 2 feet on both sides of the bed for bed making. Avoid placing the bed within 3 feet of the door; otherwise the bed becomes a roadblock.

• **Plan for use.** Allow 3 feet of dressing space in front of a closet and 36 to 40 inches in front of dressers for drawer pullout space.

• **Adjust for size.** In a small bedroom use fewer pieces of a slightly larger scale to maximize floor space. Keep major furniture pieces parallel or perpendicular to walls. Opt for tall storage pieces that add volume on a smaller footprint.

• **Add comfort.** Place a seating piece, such as a bench, at the foot of the bed, or tuck a small-scale chair and ottoman near a window.

Fall into comfort

A bedroom designed to change with the seasons relies on basics that stay, reversible pieces that flip from crisp to cozy and accessories that slip in and out of storage. Here's how it works for fall.

Darken it: The fall palette picks up an earthy feeling from the warm glow of gold, olive, and red added to yellow. With minimal pattern on display, the bedroom peacefully snuggles in.

Keep it: The headboard upholstered in faux suede, bedside lamps, mismatched nightstands, white sheets, striped rug, and rattan blinds suit both seasons.

Flip it: In fall the duvet flips to its all-gold side and pulls up to the pillows. The draperies slip off their rods and switch to their darker side.

Replace it: New pieces, including faux-cashmere draperies surrounding the headboard, a patterned lampshade, fringed throw, velvet pillows, and earthy accessories, add warmth.

Flip to spring

Spring arrives accompanied by an urge to fling open the windows and lighten up inside. It only takes a few changes to make a bedroom feel spring-fresh again.

Lighten it: Kiwi, yellow, and hot pink brighten the palette while white sheets and shams make every color feel lighter and brighter.

Keep it: The gold tones of the headboard go partially undercover with a flowery throw draped over the front.

Flip it: The duvet flips to its kiwi and yellow side and folds in thirds to pile on the foot of the bed in anticipation of some still-cool nights. The draperies show off their lighter flip side with a band of yellow. Even the bolster slips out of its darker fall cover.

Replace it: Voile sheers lighten up the head of the bed and add a subtle touch of pattern. A knit blanket, instead of a dark comforter, signals a return to warmer nights.

Start fresh.

Strip dated wallpaper and remove worn-out window coverings to turn a bedroom nightmare into a dream.

Before: With stained flowery wallpaper and worn-out window coverings, this bedroom needs help.

After: Sometimes common materials, such as yards of linen and quarts of paint, may be all the raw materials a makeover requires. Start by removing all vestiges of the old room. To create a similar look, use these ideas.

- **Start with a neutral backdrop,** such as walls upholstered in off-white linen. For the most economical way to reproduce this look, find yards of bargain linen at a discount fabric retailer; look in the business directory or on the Internet to find one. Seam floor-to-ceiling lengths of fabric to create one piece large enough to cover one wall. You'll need two people and a little patience to accomplish this. Staple the top edge of the fabric to the back of a 1×2 cut to wall width; holding the fabric out of the way, nail the board to the top of the wall. Stretch the fabric to a 1×2 nailed just above the base molding; fold fabric under the 1×2 and staple along the front edge. Wrap excess fabric 3 inches beyond one corner; fold the adjacent corner piece under and staple into the corner.
- **Paint a focal point.** The chalkboard headboard may appear hefty but it's simply thin plywood coated with black chalkboard paint and edged with molding. Metallic paint gives the plastic molding a sophisticated finish.
- **Dress the windows with romantic coverings** made from the same linen that's used on the walls. Roman shades descend in soft folds within the window frames, while generous draperies hang on each side from the ceiling to the floor.
- **Update vintage furniture** with a paint treatment that looks old. Use multiple layers of paint in tones from warm yellow to steely gray, thinned half and half with glazing medium. Update brassy hardware with silver metallic spray paint.
- **Make the bed to suit the space.** A shiny quilt reflects silver tones, and a raspberry red throw adds changeable color.

Below: Classic furniture looks fresh with a soft paint finish that combines a variety of neutral tones. **Opposite:** Walls upholstered in white linen create a comfort cocoon in this bedroom, while a new headboard made from plywood and molding adds drama. The headboard was painted with blackboard paint for a muted look. A shiny bedspread adds a touch of glamour.

Before

Add personal

style to an unfinished Bombay chest. It's a fun way to outfit a bedroom to suit. A small chest like this makes a perfect bedside table, a pretty accent piece for a narrow wall, and even added storage in a large bathroom.

Paint it pretty

Stenciled patterns add elegant detailing to this simply painted chest. To create this look combine leaf and fan stencils with scriptlike initials. Trade out the hardware that comes on the chest for pulls that duplicate the fan motif. For a durable finish cover the chest with two coats of polyurethane.

Paper it country

A pretty bird wallpaper creates the look of an artist-painted chest without all the muss and fuss. A coordinating striped wallpaper gives the top a custom finish. Choose patterns carefully for the prettiest effect. Paint the chest first, sanding between coats for a smooth finish. Use repositionable adhesive on the back of the paper to experiment with the design. Once the piece is cut to fit, remove it from the chest, apply permanent adhesive, and secure the paper to the chest.

1

Say "good night"

to outdated rules about selecting nightstands. Instead pick the bedside table that suits your style and works hard. Here are some to consider.

1. For the romantic

A contemporary parsons table at bedside doubles as a useful desk and provides a surprising design counterpoint to the wispy bed curtains, rustic stool, and antique ladderback chair.

2. For the nature lover

The rustic textures of sisal and reed pair with organic leaf shapes in this woodsy bedroom. The bedside dresser offers storage space for clothing and an earth-friendly attitude.

3. For the purist

The simple lines and elegant finish of a Chinese bureau blend into the serene design of this room. The bureau top is larger than most nightstands and offers lots of drawers for keeping bedside gear out of sight.

4. For the collector

A glass-door cabinet on top, a flip-down desk, and deep drawers below offer display as well as storage space. Desks of this vintage can be found at flea markets in original finishes. Lighten them with paint.

5. For the list maker

A small bedroom calls for a space-saving nightstand that can function as a part-time desk. The diminutive chair is covered in a powder blue gros point fabric that's also used on the headboard.

6. For the glamour fan

A mirrored nightstand adds a note of sophistication to this bedroom. When a nightstand is small opt for a lamp with a clear acrylic base to preserve visual space.

7. For the reader

An extra-roomy wicker top and a lower shelf offer plenty of stacking space for books. Consider an oversize table, even in a smaller room, for the extra style and display space it delivers.

Craft an easy custom headboard

using one of these inventive ideas. It's an inexpensive way to create the focal point of a bedroom. These basic techniques can serve as a springboard for your personal style. Change the colors or shapes to create a headboard that suits your haven to perfection.

1. Linen-wrapped panels

Wraparound comfort starts with plywood panels cut to create a continuous curve behind the bed. To upholster each panel wrap it with a layer or two of polyester batting; staple the batting to the panel back. Place the batting-wrapped panel facedown on the wrong side of a piece of linen, stretch the linen around to the back of the panel, and staple in place. (For a smooth finish, pull the fabric taut and staple at the center of each side and the center of the top and bottom to start the process.) Add hinges between the panels.

2. Fabric-wrapped canvas stretchers

A geometric fabric collage above the bed serves as a dramatic focal point in this master bedroom. To create the color blocks, wrap coordinating fabrics of different textures around canvas stretchers; staple the fabrics to the back of the stretchers. Screw panels together to make one large wallhanging. Although the headboard is large, it's lightweight and easy to hang using metal picture hangers.

3. Cut and painted fiberboard

Graceful curves cut from a ½-inch-thick piece of medium-density fiberboard (MDF) give this headboard its cottage style. Create the template for the headboard by drawing the pattern on kraft paper and cutting it out. Use a saber saw to cut the MDF. To give the headboard a soft sheen, use two coats of primer and two coats of off-white paint. A freehand leaf border was applied using watered-down black paint. Consider using a stencil for a similar effect. Two finials spray-painted gray add the final touch.

4. Collected and hung letters

Vintage aluminum, wood, and plexiglass letters and numerals gather to make a statement of personal style. Plan the layout before you begin: Mark the desired headboard height and width on the floor and arrange the pieces until you like the look. To attach the pieces to the wall, use predrilled holes and screws if possible or use double-sided tape for lightweight letters and heavy-duty hook-and-loop tape for heavier pieces.

4

Outdoor living

for the love of fresh air

chapter 19

It's no wonder Americans are so in love with the idea of extending living space to the great outdoors. Spending time on the porch or patio without sacrificing comfort and style gives the feeling of a favorite getaway. To get started transforming spaces outside your house, consider these questions: Which activities—eating, reading, napping—do you want to include? Is the space a front porch, a kitchen patio, or a deck? As you plan, consider the best way to block wind, sun, or noise. Do you want soft seating and elegant lighting, or are you looking for a rustic feeling that ties in with a lakeside or wooded lot? Start making a to-do list right now and you'll soon be vacationing outdoors at home.

in this section

Draw inspiration

from this elegant outdoor living spots, then revamp the ideas to suit a leaner budget. Beauty, comfort, and practicality share starring roles.

To create this look, start here.

- **Get the structure right.** Use fences or the walls of your house to provide the feeling of a room. For a sense of enclosure, use at least two "walls."
- **Create a "roof,"** especially if the patio is next to a two-story house that seems to loom overhead. The roof could be the overhang of a tree; installing an overhead trellis might create the same effect. A trellis makes a handy space for hanging a candle chandelier. Two or more market umbrellas also can add the "ceiling" an outdoor living area lacks.
- **Pave the floor.** A mix of outdoor paving materials, such as stone and brick, adds a designed-over-time look that brings richness to the setting.
- **Turn one wall into the focal point.** If your budget doesn't include a fireplace, add a long shelf to duplicate the feeling of a mantel. Then decorate it with a mirror and candlesticks.
- **Decide on a color scheme.** The house color certainly dictates the palette. Enhance it with colorful accessories and furniture.
- **Bring in weather-resistant furniture.** A pair of settees or four chairs can anchor a seating group while a table-and-chair set provides space for dining.
- **Add fire.** Consider using a portable fireplace or a collection of votives on the table.

Above: Sophisticated seating suits this refined patio. Keep the style of the space in mind as you shop for outdoor furniture.

Opposite: Cushions and pillows soften any outdoor space. Use weather-resistant fabrics and pillow forms for outdoor locations.

1

Seize the warm seasons

by decorating the porch—any open-air space with overhead protection. The porch might be small, with barely room for a single chair or large, with an old-fashioned wraparound porch. No matter the size, design the space to reflect the style of your home. Then draw friends and family outside to enjoy sunlit days and balmy evenings. Plan for privacy, especially on a front porch. Consider folding screens, container plants, and even draperies and roll-down shades.

1. Chaise longues with a view offer supreme comfort for lazy summer days. Choose materials that will stand up to the conditions of your area. Even if outdoor furniture is protected from rain, it's subject to moisture damage. Outdoor ceiling fans increase the livability of a porch. Select the right fan—rated damp or wet—for the conditions.

2. On this large porch space is divided according to function. Seating occupies the larger and wider area and a hammock hangs in a narrow alcove. For minimum upkeep consider vintage rattan furniture. It resists moisture and looks porch-perfect with a coat of white paint. Many old porches are divided by a central door. Use half of the porch for sitting and the other half for dining. For balance anchor each half with a large piece of furniture, and link the two halves with a center rug.

3. A roof overhead and a tiled surface underneath give this space all the comfort of a family room. To suit the outdoor location, select antique garden chairs and benches for seating, add a potted garden that can be freshened when plants start to fade, and hang overhead lanterns to keep the room open even after the sun goes down. Allow space to move around, generally a minimum of 3 feet for a walkway.

4. With the great outdoors for color, it's OK to create a porch setting using a solid neutral fabric and black-painted furniture. Floral-print pillows and vases of just-picked flowers add color. For a wicker look without high maintenance, check out weatherproof wicker furniture that's made of highly UV-resistant vinyl wrapped around powder-coated aluminum frames. Easy-care tables made using powder-coated aluminum can also be found.

Step outside into a garden room with blue sky above and a solid footing of stone or brick. A patio can be small and cozy along one side of your house or open to a large expanse of grassy backyard. Wherever it is, treat it with style. With outdoor kitchens and family rooms gaining favor, especially in warm climates, consider building a wall or two around your patio and adding a fireplace, kitchen counters, and handsome storage. This space may become the most-used "room" in your house.

Above: A tiny side yard provides space for a table for four. Canyon-stone pavers are softened by a planting of grass. When choosing a dining spot, take advantage of any shade the house provides. If that's not possible, use a market umbrella for bistro charm. For flexibility use an umbrella stand that does not require a table for support.

Left: A flagstone fireplace is a dramatic focal point in this alfresco dining room. Fabric lanterns add a party effect but won't withstand permanent use outdoors. Random-laid stone plays off the angular lines of the trellis, fireplace, and table. For a fireplace on a smaller budget, consider a chiminea, a portable outdoor fireplace, or a fire pit.

A mirror works its magic in a garden setting by duplicating views and turning a plain house wall into a dramatic focal point. This piece is an old window frame outfitted with a mirror. Vintage finds—a metal table, wood trough, and iron grates—look good in the garden and can withstand the elements. The trough holds plants on a daily basis. It also can be topped with a rustic board for use as a buffet for entertaining. Stone pavers add interest underfoot; consider painting stone shapes on an aged concrete patio. Combining old metal, rustic wood, and worn stone delivers cohesive style. The trellis overhead defines the space.

1. **Build "rooms"** in the garden using plants as architecture, letting their shapes form walls and ceilings. The sense of enclosure makes spaces feel cozy.
2. **Plant with a color scheme** in mind. Choose flower colors that complement the colors of outdoor furniture and accessories.
3. **Introduce a focal point,** such as an urn, statue, or water feature.
4. **Create seating** and dining areas. Rocks and bricks can be laid in rug shapes to anchor these areas.
5. **Bring indoor furniture out** to the porch. In a sheltered space use wood pieces; first coat them on all sides and ends with marine varnish.
6. **Weather-resistant fabrics** and polypropylene rugs bring a soft touch and shot of color to outdoor spaces.
7. **Plant pots and urns** as permanent flower arrangements you can enjoy throughout the growing season. Fill with evergreens in winter.
8. **Light up the night.** Consider a chandelier or candles in hurricanes.
9. **Play with texture.** Start with garden-friendly materials, such as brick, stone, metal, and wood.
10. **Use collections,** including ironstone pitchers for flowers and vintage rakes as sculpture.

Play with garden hues that feel as fresh as a just-picked bouquet.

1. Start with a cool background. A white-painted floor, dry-brushed with a blue top coat, supports the color scheme. The walls and ceiling sport a cool gray-blue shade of paint. This soothing blue backdrop creates a relaxing attitude for hot summer days.

2. Add furniture that grounds the palette. A daybed and wicker chairs feature a coat of steely gray. This dark color adds visual weight and keeps the blue from seeming too sweet.

3. Layer on color and pattern with fabrics and a room-brightening rug. Vintage fabrics step in as pillows on the daybed and a flouncy cover for an ottoman. Bold ruffles add bright spots of color on the pillows. Dark velvet trim and thick cushions give the new wicker chairs vintage appeal.

4. Support the color scheme with accessories. The best accessory is a bouquet of roses in colors ranging from yellow to red.

Embrace the neutral side of the outdoors with a color palette that starts with stained cedar shakes.

1. Build on natural materials. The warm cedar walls and natural mahogany decking provide texture and tone that start this porch on its way to style.

2. Vary the neutrals. When using neutrals combine them in a variety of tones, from warm to cool and light to dark. This technique adds visual interest. Note the urn-shape metal lamp bases that look almost black and the drop-leaf coffee table in a rich, warm brown.

3. Cool down with crisp white. Summertime whites keep a porch feeling cool and fresh even when the temperature soars. They also complement the seaside architecture of this classically styled screen porch.

4. Use artwork to convey a palette. The porch makes use of only a few of the colors in the painting, and that's OK. A bouquet of flowers, plants in urns, and a pitcher of lemonade reflect other colors from the art.

Transform a run-of-the-mill screen porch with clever ideas and some surprises.

Before: Basic and dull, this screen porch had little to recommend it except that it's generally bug-free. The homeowners call it the "neglected room."

After: Hardly a trace of the "before" version remains in this romantic space. Dividing the room into lounging and eating areas capitalizes on floor space. Here's how to start creating your own summer getaway.

- **Update with paint.** Keep the walls neutral. Splash a fun color, such as sage, on the ceiling.
- **Soften the floor with an indoor/outdoor rug.** It's a quick way to ground an outdoor room with comfort.
- **Create a wall of fabric for privacy** or to hide a view. Line one wall of a screen porch with cotton panels hung from hooks at ceiling height. For durability and easy care, use an indoor/outdoor fabric for the panels.
- **Suit furniture to the space.** Even chaise longues are available in a variety of sizes. Create templates of the furniture and check that the pieces will fit with ample space for traffic.
- **Choose furniture for function.** A sideboard adds storage and a serving counter. Fabric panels on the sideboard hide two shelves of storage. A large table works perfectly for dinner or summertime projects.
- **Select a color and pattern scheme** that's a surprising departure from florals and bright colors, typical porch fare. This brown and white scheme, with a touch of sage, adds sophistication, while classic patterns inject French style.
- **Bring in shine using glittery chandeliers** hung in pairs over the table. Add glass vases filled with sand and use them as candleholders.
- **Add topiaries and miniature rose bushes** to bring the garden to the porch.
- **Make it personal with collections.** China, pottery, metal, and glass offer weather-resistant finishes.

Before

Right: A table and chairs fill one side of the porch. A pair of amber chandeliers accent the long, narrow table and provide romantic nighttime lighting.
Far right: A sideboard provides much-needed storage, hidden by stylish patterned fabric.

A pair of chaise longues offers serious relaxation space. Nesting tables can slip together to save floor space.

Relax in style

on a three-season porch. Outfit it as a sitting area, or flip the look and the furniture to turn it into a dining room.

Sitting easy

- **Keep it.** The basics that stay for both looks include white woodwork and car siding, a blue-painted ceiling and rafters, and a checkered floor of blue and taupe under a sisal rug.
- **Furnish it.** A sitting space needs a sofa and chairs. Vintage wicker pieces give this room a classic look while a tile-top outdoor table, used as a coffee table, adds an unexpected twist. Good task lighting and an end table large enough to hold a beverage perfect the space.
- **Color it.** The blue and blue-green of the ceiling and floor inspired an analogous color scheme that includes shades of blue and green played against white. The cool colors and analogous scheme create a serene and relaxing effect.
- **Soften it.** Patterned fabrics add interest while supporting the color scheme. A bold stripe mixes with an overscale damask-style print for a graphic combination.
- **Accessorize it.** Collections add a personal story to a room. In this case shells and ironstone illustrate two of the homeowner's favorites. A wreath hung from a ribbon creates a focal point in the window without blocking the view.

Dining in color

• **Keep it.** The solid basics stay put.

• **Furnish it.** Sofa and chairs exit to make room for a wicker table and four contemporary laminate chairs. The combination of cottage and modern styles works well in a porch setting.

• **Color it.** The blue and blue-green of the ceiling and floor serve as counterpoint to a complementary color scheme featuring orange, orange-red, and yellow. The colors appear in a striped rug, a table runner, and oversize napkins draped over the chair backs. A complementary scheme is energetic and playful.

• **Soften it.** The sisal rug provides a base for a softer striped rug and a table runner stretches across the wicker table. Ruffles on the edges of the runner add even more softness. Double-layered napkins help relax the laminate chairs.

• **Accessorize it.** In a boldly colored space, accessories need visual oomph or scale. A large lantern feels right above the table. Oranges give a clear glass bowl a color makeover.

Go ahead and buy that classic, standard-looking outdoor bench at the going-out-of-season sale. Its good bones make it worth revamping. In most cases benches like this are built of pine which doesn't last outdoors without intervention. Since the finish needs beefing up, consider painting it Monet blue so it stands out in a sea of foliage. Here's how to make it a keeper.

- **Prime every surface,** including the ends of all boards, the bottom of the feet, and the underside of the seat. Use a good-quality exterior primer. It's crucial to protect the wood from moisture. If the primer doesn't cover completely, brush on a second coat.
- **Use a good-quality exterior paint.** Here again paint all surfaces and edges. For durability paint at least two top coats.
- **To care for the painted bench,** set it in the garden during the growing season and store it covered the rest of the year. Periodically check the surface for signs of moisture penetration.

Right: Two benches are better than one for an outdoor dining area. Look for a table that matches the benches inch for inch, or add a custom-made wood top to a vintage base to build a better outdoor table.

Before

buy smart

Outdoor furniture can be as big an investment as indoor pieces, so use these tips to choose wisely.

- **Aluminum** is lightweight, durable, and rustproof. It comes in wrought or cast forms with a baked-on enamel or textured finish.
- **Iron** is heavier and less expensive than aluminum. However, it rusts and may need more upkeep.
- **Wicker** needs a home out of the weather unless it's a synthetic, all-weather variety. On all-weather wicker look for aluminum frames and baked-on polyester finishes. Update old wicker with a stain-blocking primer and exterior spray paint; use it under cover.
- **Wood** requires a lot of maintenance and needs to be protected from moisture. Select exterior paints with an enamel finish or industrial paints that contain more binders to adhere paint to surfaces. Woods such as teak, cedar, and redwood last longer than pine.
- **Plastic** lasts for years and can be freshened using spray paints specifically designed for plastic.

Serve a crowd

with an outdoor dining area that's supersized. It's easy and quick to pull indoor furniture outdoors if you're inviting all the neighbors for a barbecue. For permanent dining space embrace the season with charm, romance, or character. Not sure what you want? Let the interior of your home inspire the look.

Below: Sheer curtain panels suspended from a porch overhang enclose a poolside party table. Dining outdoors makes it easy to have a table with a great view. Dress the table for the occasion, using fine china, cloth napkins, and handpicked flowers.

Right: Rustic farm tables and benches brought outside turn space under an arbor into a casual dining hall. Straw strewn underfoot adds to the relaxed feeling. Consider using straw to camouflage a concrete patio during a party. A second table makes a bountiful buffet. Set the table with pottery and linen napkins, gather lavender for an aromatic centerpiece, and scatter votives down the table for after-dark dining.

Left: A courtyard garden offers perfect seclusion for everyday dining. Rough stone pavers, a stacked-stone wall, and lush plantings create the backdrop for an elegant tile-top table. Curvy metal chairs and table legs contrast with the linear stones. A chandelier revamped into a candle fixture provides romantic lighting for evening meals.

Below: An assortment of mismatched chairs and a fabric-draped table create a heavenly dining area in one corner of the garden. Old porch posts and cedar boards create the framework for a simple garden gazebo. A flea market chandelier painted white hangs above the table. Using indoor elements such as a lacy tablecloth adds romance to the outdoor location.

Cushions add comfort to any seating, and they're especially important in places meant for relaxing. Whether the cushions can stand up to weather or need to come in from the rain, include them on benches, swings, and wicker chairs. It's worth the effort and it's a perfect way to pair comfort with style.

Left: A collection of vintage fabrics adds style to a metal daybed. Red connects the geometric and floral designs. Varying the shapes and sizes of the pillows creates a collected-over-time look that adds to the appeal. Fabrics made for indoor use need to come in out of the rain and sun so use them on a sheltered patio or porch.

Above: Handsome striped ticking covers the wing chair in the indoor dining room and the cushy settee on the adjacent porch, blurring the line between indoors and out. Tailored fabrics such as solids and stripes make smart choices for the porch because they mix well with the other patterns.

Left and below: A collection of colorful, printed fabrics warms up a porch swing that's been painted a cheery hot pink. The one-piece cushion pairs with throw pillows that can be arranged for sitting or napping. "Blossoms" on each end of a bolster pillow are made of fabric gathered and secured with a tie. Leaf-shape fabric cutouts add dressmaker's detailing to the ties. Grass bouquets sprout from Mason jars hung in rows above the swing. To duplicate this look wrap wire around each jar rim, loop it at the back, and hang it from a nail.

House Tours

Top-to-bottom style, quick tips, ideas to copy

Visit houses of every size and style, fall in love with ideas that suit your own home, and learn how to translate big ideas into real makeovers.

Builder Style made better

Learn how minor tweaks transformed a basic builder house into the best-looking home on the new block. While houses like this one may be purely plain vanilla at the start, they offer affordable square footage and a canvas for personal style. Use the great ideas shown here to transform any house that needs a style facelift. Here's how to get started.

- **Evaluate the house.** Take note of features worth showing off and those needing to be disguised or removed. A classic fireplace surround or a vaulted ceiling could become focal points, while low-quality materials might need to be replaced. Boxy spaces are perfect candidates for treatments using molding, paint, or wallpaper. These add-ons pump up the visual interest and character of a room.
- **Create a wish list** and a budget list side by side. Deciding what to change and what can wait becomes a balancing act. For example, it might make sense to use paint for children's rooms and pour more money, time, and materials into the kitchen, living room, and dining room. Paint can be an affordable change while wallpaper might be on the future to-do list.
- **Forget room labels.** Instead consider how square footage is used. This home had a combination living-dining room with a family room off the kitchen. The homeowners instead use the living/dining room for lounging and the family room with a fireplace as a dining room that suits their love of entertaining. Customizing rooms to suit your needs makes every room into a well-lived space.

Built as a living/dining room in the original plan, this space now serves as a lounging area with two sofas, a beefy sideboard, and occasional tables. Two tables take the place of one massive coffee table and offer the flexibility of moving right where they're needed. White slipcovers and bold pillows and throws make strong color statements that can change with the seasons.

Worth noting

Diagonal furniture layouts offer a no-cost fix in rooms with too many windows and doors. Place matching sofas on the diagonal to create a seating island, or float a bed diagonally from the corner in a small bedroom.

- **Ban off-white paint,** the "as is" color that comes standard. Instead use paint in deep tones to accent spaces such as the kitchen or soothing earth tones to define walls in the living room. If the house is small, pick a palette of colors and use them throughout the house to improve flow and harmony.
- **Fearlessly change things that don't work.** Builder-grade kitchen cabinets in oak got a style upgrade from white paint. The owners also extended the peninsula and added open shelves below because they didn't want a breakfast counter with stools. Other changes worth considering in a builder's special include redesigning the fireplace surround, replacing floor coverings, and adding window seats.
- **Upgrade for style.** That might mean adding plantation shutters on windows, replacing laminate countertops with stone, and ditching builder-grade light fixtures for vintage ones. Accessories, such as original artwork rather than reproduction pieces, also can lift the look from basic builder to custom.
- **If a room lacks architectural interest,** outfit it with a focal point piece. A vintage stove adds charm to the kitchen while an estate sale chair re-covered in red fabric creates a cozy reading spot in the living room.

Opposite: Bright upholstery on an occasional chair adds color to the living room. Using the color in several places adds balance. **Left:** A sideboard provides storage space and the perfect surface for setting up a bar for entertaining. Black paint on the sideboard repeats the black found in other furniture pieces and accessories. This lends a cohesive look to the room design.

Above right: This family room serves as a dining room. Its location near the kitchen is convenient, and the existing fireplace adds charm. The room easily accommodates a large table and comfortable seating. For an unexpected touch mix a bench with woven chairs.
Below right: Oak cabinets painted white give this bathroom a fresh new look. Other upgrades include a porcelain-handle faucet and ceramic tile floor and countertop. New knobs complement the metal of the faucet.
Far right: A vintage stove is the centerpiece of the once-boring kitchen. The oak builder's cabinets look classy with white paint and new crown molding. Slate gray paint on the walls accents the cabinetry. For character and extra storage the owners lengthened the peninsula and added shelving beneath the overhang.

MALVOISIME
AU VIN BLANC
LYONS

Family friendly

In one old Chicago house, a young family proves that stylish decorating, kids, and easy living can coexist. The secret? Mix short- and long-term purchases, bleach the whites, and relax. The choice is to either decorate to suit your lifestyle stage or to spend lots of time worrying about dings and stains. For the easy life with kids, start with these tips.

- **Design the house to suit family activities.** That might mean creating lots of spots where family members can sit and read—together or alone. It also can mean a computer desk everyone shares, a table dedicated to games, or a back entry with room for sports equipment. It also might mean using a formal dining room as a family hobby/computer center.
- **Invest in elements that last,** such as built-ins and wood furnishings. Deep built-in cabinets add architectural distinction and plenty of critical storage for items such as a television and other media gear. New and vintage wood pieces add an anchor of richness and color.
- **Look for bargains for everything else.** Shop in a variety of places—outlet stores, thrift shops, and big-box retailers—and buy items based on form and function. An inexpensive laminate coffee table can be perfect while kids are small and easy to replace after hard wear. Pillows and lampshades in trendy colors and patterns can update a scheme for pennies.
- **Keep the background clutter-free** to manage the inevitable landslide of kids' things. Whites and neutrals compose

Build a family-friendly scheme around classic furniture pieces. These pieces are still the homeowners' favorites after eight years. A white cotton duck slipcover relaxes the sofa. To change the look, pop on a few colorful pillows and throws. Because the decorating is restrained, it's easy to breeze through for a quick pickup when company is coming.

A classic pedestal table anchors the dining room. This investment piece is out of the way of everyday kid routines, a smart place to start incorporating good pieces. The slipcovered chairs are ample enough for comfort and match the scale of the table. The painted cabinet was chosen because it did not match the table, a trick to use when buying furniture a piece at a time.

the color scheme in this house, from woodwork to slipcovers. White is the chameleon of the decorating world. It reflects the character of any style, changes with the seasons, and allows pieces to move from room to room.

• **Whitewash everything.** Then you'll know when things are dirty. Slipcovers pop off for a quick wash. Walls and built-ins are coated with scrubbable paint that wipes down easily.

• **Stock up on white** tableware and linens for ultimate flexibility. It's easy to add pieces as the budget allows. A variety of shades of white can intermingle for a heavenly look so matching is unnecessary.

• **Consider other kid-smart strategies.** To mask the color of smudges, paint lower kitchen cabinets taupe. To camouflage muddy footprints, stain floors dark and add washable rugs. To hide clutter consider baskets, dressers, and cabinets with hidden storage. To create a place for messy art projects, add a washable metal-top kitchen table. Either buy a table with a metal top or have a sheet-metal contractor wrap an old tabletop in stainless steel.

• **Devise a system to manage school stuff.** When projects come home, showcase some on a bulletin board and store the rest in baskets. At the end of the year, frame one or two pieces and transfer the rest to long-term storage.

Above left: Built-in shelves wrap the doorway to the family room and provide plenty of book storage. Shelves set in a permanent grid soothe the eye because they're more orderly than a flexible shelf system. **Above:** The entry is the first spot visitors see and the perfect place to introduce personal style and color statements. With limited space for furniture, use a rug to soften the space and to add color.

Worth noting

Books provide affordable, framable artwork. Look for books filled with photographs or illustrations printed on quality paper. Buy with the intent of cutting the books apart and framing some of the pages.

Above: Framed photographs of water towers torn from a photography book make an arresting, affordable arrangement above the table. Matching white frames emphasize the artwork. Chairs painted in shiny white are easy to keep clean. The stainless-steel tabletop stands up to everyday fork dings and offers the side benefit of easy cleanup. Hooks hung under the window frame are the perfect height for kids and adults and a smart use of space.
Right: The lower cabinets are painted taupe to hide fingerprints. The countertops are granite, honed to look like the desired appearance of marble. Granite offers more stain resistance than marble, so it's a wise choice for a kid-friendly kitchen. A partial wall between the eating area and the kitchen keeps the family together and apart.

Collected by design

Matching furnishings to the style of a house makes good design sense. This 1949 ranch house in Miami is filled with contemporary pieces from the same era. The revolutionary designs produced in the middle of the 20th century feature clean-line spaces, furniture, and accessories. Take these steps to create a home that's modern at heart, not a museum of modern art.

- **Become an expert on the era.** Study so you can recognize good pieces and accurate reproductions. This means reading books on the era, surfing the Internet for information, talking to dealers who specialize in modern pieces, and shopping in stores and catalogs catering to contemporary style. Several manufacturers feature reproductions of midcentury pieces.
- **Build a modern look based on key pieces of the past.** That might mean selecting favorite designers and incorporating one or more of their pieces into the house, even if the pieces are affordable reproductions rather than originals. The influences on the design of furniture and accessories in this

The lime-green walls of the sunroom provide a light-filled transitional space between the interior and the outdoors. Terrazzo floors are a hallmark of modern style and the perfect stage for a pair of Eames-inspired clamshell chairs. The mobile is inspired by the work of Alexander Calder, who combined arching lines and geometric shapes in a famous mobile first made as an avant-garde art piece. A monolithic mirror, clad in aluminum flashing from a home center, adds drama.

The Barcelona chair by Mies van der Rohe is the epitome of modern design. Mies defined the modern movement with his statement, "Less is more." A gridded sideboard provides the perfect foil for the sweeping curves of the chair.

house read like a Who's Who of the modern movement: Mies van der Rohe, Jacobsen, Eames, and Noguchi.

- **Look for designs done in the spirit of the modern movement,** such as the playful mobile or a new cabinet designed to hold CDs. They reflect the simplicity of midcentury modern style, while blending with a contemporary look 21st century look.
- **Mix freeform and geometric shapes** to add tempo and balance to a house done in one style. The pairing of a Noguchi glass coffee table and a striped rug shows one way to mix it up. Experiment with other ideas, such as pairing oval-pattern bed linens with a sleek rectangular headboard.
- **Create a color palette** based on the trendy hues of 1940 to 1960. Because the furniture is simple and the look is spare, color can be the best way to warm up the space. Choose hues that add a surprising jolt of style, such as lime green or orange. Most paint manufacturers offer a collection of historic hues, including those popular in the middle of the 20th century.
- **Include plenty of storage** to keep clutter under wraps. Opt for furniture pieces with storage behind solid wood doors or add built-ins outfitted with doors. Open bookcases, in general, will distract from the clean lines and finishes of modern design.

Above: An Isamu Noguchi freeform coffee table contrasts with the geometric pattern of the area rug by fashion designer Gene Meyer. And the boxy sofa contrasts with the organic coffee table.
Right: A pair of Arne Jacobsen-inspired chairs and a new cabinet sit beneath a 1930s Spanish portrait. Jacobsen, a Danish architect and designer, is best known for his simple, functional furniture.

Below: A fabric-wrapped panel serves as art above the platform bed. The fabric is by designer Maija Isola, who is noted for working primarily in vibrant colors and bold geometric shapes. Neutral linens on the bed let the artwork dominate the space.

Right: Forget the ubiquitous plastic lawn chair. This molded polypropylene club sofa by Philippe Starck is a new piece inspired by the era. It provides all-weather poolside seating and a big dose of style. Other weatherproof furnishings include outdoor lighting, rugs, fabrics, and cushions that deliver indoor style outdoors.

Worth noting

Introducing a few modern pieces into a room of mostly traditional furniture and accessories is like taking a deep breath—the clean lines and minimalist shapes relax the space and lighten the style attitude.

Spare the details

Collecting might seem like a hobby that invites clutter. That's not the case with the collectors who own this home. Instead they ruthlessly edit their possessions to create a home that's cozy and simple. They refer to the look as farmhouse modern. Follow these suggestions to begin decorating their way.

- **Edit possessions,** especially large pieces of furniture. For a room that's already furnished, clear out the clutter and leave only a few pieces of furniture. In a living room that might mean a sofa and two side chairs. Experiment with furniture placement by moving the pieces around until the arrangement feels comfortable. That's crucial in creating a cozy feeling in a room with minimal furnishings.
- **Incorporate materials that reflect both styles** to create the farmhouse-modern look. That's the strategy behind juxtaposing features such as beaded-board and raised-panel cabinetry with stainless-steel countertops and terrazzo floors.

Left: The strong unadorned lines of the brick house hint at the style inside.

A single garage is now home to a family room/eating area, conveniently located by the kitchen. A fireplace creates a focal point; lining up the bookcase tops with the mantel creates a strong horizontal line. Neutrals give the room a classic look.

In this kitchen expensive basics, such as cabinetry, countertops, and flooring, are kept in neutral tones; color and pattern are added with accessories. The floor is terrazzo with thin aluminum divider strips in a diagonal checked pattern.

Above: The island is both new and old. The base was built to fit the vintage wood top, which was originally a farmhouse table. The counter overhang provides space to tuck simple metal stools underneath.
Left: Vintage locker doors and a slate chalkboard add old-world charm to this new space.

- **Build a neutral color palette** that's anchored by the liberal use of white paint. White feels more modern than taupe and provides crisp contrast to pale shades. Pairing white woodwork with taupe walls creates a fresh look and feeling. For style punch add bold notes of color, such as a green pie safe in the eating area.
- **Use texture and contrast to create interest,** especially when working with a neutral color palette. Go-together texture choices include rattan chairs, zinc tabletops, cotton duck, old metals, vintage pottery, and wood paneling. Each layer of texture—nubby, woven, smooth, sleek, and worn—adds interest.
- **Introduce pattern with restraint.** In this home a geometric pattern adds interest on the kitchen floors, while bold stripes call attention to the pillows in the eating area. A soft floral shows up on the master bedroom duvet.
- **Leave windows mostly bare** except where privacy or light control is an issue. Rattan blinds, roll-up window shades, and Roman shades provide effective solutions because they pull up and out of view during the day and cover windows at night.

- **Incorporate old pieces** to keep the look from feeling too new. That's the strategy behind setting a new zinc top on a vintage base to create a dining room table, and building a pantry using old locker doors.
- **Mix it up.** The farmhouse chairs in the dining room share a similar silhouette yet were collected one or two at a time. The owner left them in their original finishes, some white and some brown.
- **Plan for plenty of storage** so it's easy to maintain a simple look. Built-in bookcases, closed cabinetry, and baskets can house miscellaneous items. A new back entry filled with a wall of storage makes room for back door gear. Metal baskets and screw-top jars keep everything handy and organized inside the cabinets.
- **Add collectibles.** A fun collection can add personality to a room that's mainly neutral. This home includes collections of sports trophies, old photos, dog prints, McCoy pottery, schoolhouse light fixtures, and dog statuary. The collections share neutral tones and soft shades so they're easy to incorporate into the rooms. Look for collections you can put to use: vases to fill with flowers, old photographs to frame and hang on the walls, and vintage baskets to use for storage in every room.

Opposite: The collection of framed photographs on the stairway wall features sports teams from the 1920s through the 1940s. The vintage Minnesota map is also a favorite. Some of the owners' McCoy pottery pieces stand in as a centerpiece on the zinc-top dining room table. **Left:** Pendent school lights add vintage charm over the dining room table. The cabinet in the room was painted white and combined with a collection of brown and white transferware plates hung on the wall.

Left: Nestled between two small built-in closets, the stained beaded-board cabinet gives the bedroom a not-so-new look. Although the cabinet was probably built for a kitchen or utility area, it also works well in a bedroom and greatly expands storage space.

Above: A vintage kitchen sink found a new home in the master bathroom. The sink is large enough for two people to use it at the same time. The sink drainboard is used as a dressing table.

Mastering the mix

This 1930s Houston cottage showcases a masterful blend of Mexican, French, and Italian furnishings united by a serenely simple palette. The casual combination belies the real talent of the homeowners for collecting interesting objects and combining them in surprising ways. Here's how to get started creating a similar look for your house.

- **Build a collected look.** Even before you move into your dream house, start collecting the perfect objects to fill it. That's the only way to amass a collection that fills an entire house with style and character. Many of the pieces in this house are vintage, and finding them involved a bit of sleuthing. Searching can be fun and rewarding.
- **Develop a relaxed attitude** toward decorating a home. Consider installing open shelves on kitchen walls, placing a rustic pine table alongside a formal French chair, or plumping a daybed with pillows for midday naps.
- **Mix it up to add interest.** That's the strategy behind using a modern cube softened with a linen slipcover as a coffee table. The straight lines of the cube contrast with the curvy French sofa. Other unexpected pairings include an intricate Mexican mirror hung above a French dresser and a crystal candelabra next to a woven rattan chair.

An open archway joins the kitchen and living room. To keep the look consistent, use the same color of paint in both rooms. Incorporate similar accessories as well to dress up the kitchen and relax the living room.

Vermont soapstone countertops contrast with classic white cabinets in the remodeled kitchen. A vintage butcher-block table adds character and convenience in the center of the room. Minimizing upper cabinetry helps the kitchen blend with the nearby living room.

• **Use texture** to support a neutral color scheme. The textures of linen and silk combine with carved wood, woven wicker, worn metal, shiny glass, and coral to create an interesting partnership. Color subtlety—white, cream, brown, and tan—balances with textures that invite a closer look.

• **Opt for comfort.** Neutral schemes feel immediately comfortable and casual. You might not kick off your shoes and settle in for a nap, yet the attitude of the space indicates that it's OK to make yourself at home. Tactile comfort includes cushions filled with down, worn wood tables and chairs rather than new, and washed linen and cotton for slipcovers and pillows.

• **Magnify the light.** Interior windows maintain a porch-like ambience and flood the master bedroom and sitting room in sunlight. Mirrors, crystals on light fixtures, and clear glass pieces reflect light around the spaces. Minimizing window treatments ensures that light flows into rooms unhampered.

• **Bring the spirit of the garden inside.** Views of the garden can add a relaxing note to any space. Consider planting an outdoor look inside using garden elements such as rattan, wrought iron, and fresh-picked blooms. Maximize the connection between house and garden; consider adding French doors. Cover windows only as needed for privacy.

Above left: Open shelves put beautiful cookware on display, transforming everyday objects into works of art.

Above: Extend your decorating to include simple elements. Here showcasing a wheel of cheese on a covered cake stand adds a party feeling to a basic appetizer.

This page: Worn finishes add texture and character to a room. To protect fine fabrics coat flaking finishes with clear polyurethane to freeze them in time.
Right: As you decorate be open to chance opportunities and alternative possibilities. For this room, the homeowner was looking for a pair of chairs for the bedroom sitting area, but she fell in love with this French daybed. It provides a luxurious nesting spot by the window.

Above right: Although the Mexican mirror is new, its gently aged tin surface helps it blend with antiques spread throughout the house.
Below right: A turtle print suspended between two pieces of glass looks vintage and modern at the same time.
Far right: A cozy arrangement of three chairs and a sofa makes this room conversation central. A centered ottoman serves as a coffee table and footrest.

Worth noting

Even if you love antiques, not all pieces are up to everyday wear. Consider repurposing unsafe items—ones with wobbly joints or dangerous splinters. A rickety chair can be adapted as an easel for a painting.

Romantic notions

As a high school student in France, the owner of this house fell in love with French style. What she brought home is her own interpretation of that style. She calls it "French country meets California beach cottage." Here's how to copy it.

- **Start with a subdued palette** that wraps a home in the soft light so important to French style. When the owners bought this house, the wood-paneled walls were stained a dark wood tone. Washing them in soft creamy yellow paint and coating the trim in white banished the cave feeling. Gray-green, red, deep pink, and lots of white keep the palette fresh.
- **Mix old with new** to create a collected-over-time look. That's the basis for French decorating and a good rule to follow when duplicating any European style. It's easy to find reproduction pieces if the real thing costs too much. Changing the finish on new pieces can add age: Tea-stain fabric to soften tones, rub a stain-wash over painted furniture, and abrade new hardware with steel wool.

The ample rooms of this 1960s ranch shelter a decorating scheme that is feminine and family-friendly. Revisions include lightening dark wood paneling and adding character with molding and trims.

A floating arrangement of soft furnishings relaxes the room. The pedestal table and armchair combine to balance the large overstuffed chair. The color scheme of soft yellow and green gets palette punctuation with red. Red repeats in trim and flowers, adding rhythm to the space.

Opposite: The walls in the living room were once stained dark. A soft buttery yellow lightens the look and provides a fresh background for a collection of French furnishings. The wicker chairs are new; the cushions are made from vintage French fabric. **Left:** Vintage fabrics add personality to the front entry. Hanging curtain panels romance the door, and French ticking adds a spot of color on a reproduction bench. **Below:** Baskets of shells relax the formal attitude of the living room.

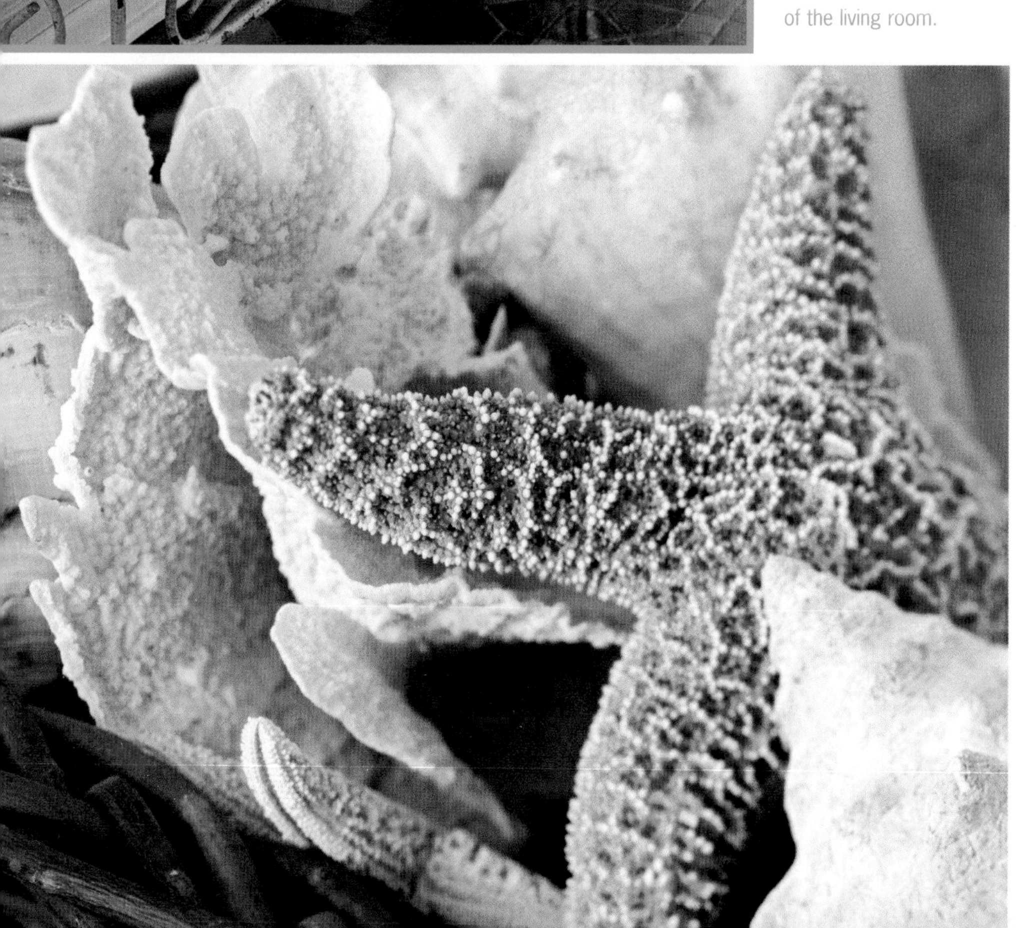

- **Add romance to every room,** including the kitchen and bathroom. Top a kitchen light fixture with toile-covered shades, dress a bathroom sink with a fabric skirt, and separate the living and dining room with a sweep of fabric hung above the doorway and pulled to each side.
- **Incorporate pretty elements,** such as curvy chairs, full draperies, soft rugs, and gilt-frame mirrors. Search out fabrics in florals and toiles. Look for ribbons and upholstery trims to add to pillow and curtain edges.
- **Mix and match patterns.** For inspiration check out fabric and wallpaper collections featuring French style or study books filled with images of vintage French homes. Rather than copying these houses exactly, look for inspiration, and adapt the ideas to suit your lifestyle. Note the mix of stripes, florals, and toiles in French interiors as you decorate your house.
- **Scale for lushness.** Opt for these elements: mirrors that stretch to the ceiling with thick handcarved frames, lined and trimmed window coverings, table linens, upholstered pieces that

Below left: A kitchen corner provides a cozy space for a family of four. The collection of bench, wing chair, and farmhouse chair adds an unexpected twist.
Below right: New white paint on cabinetry and French Country yellow paint on the walls freshens the working end of the kitchen. Baskets, a hooked rug, and flower prints add personality.

Opposite: From the curtained doorway to the draped table, the dining room is designed for special occasions. The table is plywood covered with damask and layered with vintage tablecloths. Slipcovers dress up the chairs; ruffles add a fun and flirty detail.

are roomy and large, and overscale accessories such as a silver punch bowl used as a vase. Hang curtains and bed canopies as high as possible.

- **Relax the formality of French style** by adding slipcovers to a curvy sofa and chairs. The white slipcovers bring a bit of beachy attitude to the more formal lines of the trumeau-style mirror hung on the living room wall. Baskets of shells relax the space even more.
- **Use a strong hue as a color thread** that weaves through the house. Choose red, for example, and repeat it as muted red on dining room chairs and a bold block of intense red on the entry bench. Then edge pillows with a red line and pop armloads of red flowers in a dining room punch bowl.
- **Decorate to hide architectural problems.** A window centered on the master bedroom wall disappears behind a floor-to-ceiling bed canopy. This simple move made a new floor plan possible, creating a more comfortable spot for showcasing the bed.

Worth noting

Decorating involves a little yin/yang: Relax a formal look with informal pieces. Pair gilt-edged mirrors and baskets of shells, or frameless oil paintings and ornate mantel clocks.

Opposite: A window stood in the way of the plan to divide the master bedroom into two areas—half for sleeping and half for relaxing. The solution? Hang a rug over the window, add bed hangings and a cornice, and turn what could have been a problem into an elegant focal point. The seating area includes an overstuffed sofa and a wing chair for comfort. Touches of red show up in this room as well. **Above:** Although a nine-year-old occupies this bedroom, it's designed to grow with her. With only a few changes, the style can remain unchanged through her high school years. And it fits with the style of the home. Roman shades, altered into bed bonnets, top new iron beds. The fabric hung behind the beds matches the dining room chairs. **Right:** Instead of fighting the grey and dark red bathroom tile colors, an alternative approach embraces them. A toile fabric in dark red and cream appears as a sink skirt and a Roman shade.

A change of address

Moving is always stressful, and when you're downsizing from a large family home to an empty-nester condo, moving can be fraught with emotion. Even if you ruthlessly sort keepers from giveaways, a few favorite things will probably fail to make the cut. One empty nester who made the move adopted the brand-new style you see here. Love the look? Here's how to make the right moves.

- **Downsize before you move.** Start by editing possessions and reducing them to a chosen few. Make your selections before the move. Get rid of excess now. It might mean that very few large pieces of furniture survive the cut. If the job seems overwhelming, ask a friend whose taste you trust to help you sort. Keep your favorite meaningful pieces. If you're not sure that the move will be permanent, rent a storage unit and put a few decisions on hold.
- **Create a neutral palette** with variations in shades and tones. Ignore the list of hot colors and instead choose ones that appeal to you. Most people find that neutrals create a serene environment, flow from room to room with ease, and expand the feeling of space. Subtle color shifts—two or three whites, taupes, and grays—add interest without creating visual clutter.
- **Consider all rooms as one** if the house has open spaces and large doorways. Views into other spaces demand a coordinated look. To keep it interesting combine paint shades separated by at least one color on a paint chip card. Use a darker tone in a dark room for a rich look. Duplicate silhouettes, patterns, and sheens from room to room.

This end of the living room draws in sunlight and passes it around, thanks to a light color palette, glass objects, mirrors, and shiny painted surfaces. Soft neutrals create a serene environment that reflects the relaxed attitude of the beach painting.

A silver-edge mirror leans against the wall, reflects the staircase, and repeats the materials of the X-base side table. Always position a mirror to reflect something of interest.

Left: Tucked behind the sofa, the dining area is defined by a graceful chandelier suspended over a glass-top table. The lightness of both pieces keeps the space from feeling claustrophobic. A French armoire creates a wealth of vertical storage. **Below:** In the kitchen deep gray walls contrast with white cabinetry to create a sophisticated attitude. Armchairs and an upholstered love seat offer comfortable seating around the glass-top kitchen table. A vintage sign and collectible wood eggs add charm.

- **Add dressy touches** such as mirrors and silk draperies that evoke the feeling of a ball gown. Paired with neutrals and textures, they feel comfortable for everyday living and add a dressed-up attitude that's perfect for entertaining. That versatility is essential in a home that lacks an informal family room.
- **Incorporate classy comfort** with beautiful touchable fabrics and sink-in seating. Soften the noise of condo living with floor-to-ceiling draperies in a sound-absorbing fabric.
- **To make a smaller home feel large,** use space-defying tricks such as glass tabletops and mirrors to expand views and light. Always check to see if the view in the mirror is pleasing. If you're after more light, place the mirror opposite a window so it reflects the maximum amount.
- **Search for statement lighting.** A graceful chandelier hung over a dining table in a combination living/dining room decorates both ends of the room as do table lamps by the sofa. Opt for oversize lamps for added impact.
- **Be selective about accessories.** Constantly tweak a room by adding objects or taking some away. The challenge is to edit possessions so rooms always feel composed and comfortable and never cluttered.

Opposite: A handpainted dresser provides the color palette for the bedroom. A metal sconce on a dimmer provides soft illumination or light for reading. The all-white bedding adds a luxurious feeling to the poster bed, whose small scale is appropriate for this home. **Left:** Elegant wood pieces offer style and storage in any room. A mirror hung above the dresser reflects light from outside and balances the visual weight of the fireplace (not shown) on the opposite wall. A mandarin-inspired lampshade adds an unexpected element.

Style Solutions

Clever spacesavers and easy style shortcuts.

Live big in a small house, clear the clutter from every room, add style to pint-size spaces, arrange furniture like a pro, and freshen up in no time.

Small houses
for style that lives big

chapter 20

A small house can be a dream home or a temporary stop on the way to better housing. Either way it's important to give it style that measures up. Before getting started ask these questions: Is there one larger open area or are all the rooms small? Do openings between rooms expand space or can you enlarge openings? Do windows and doors connect to a yard, deck, or patio that can supplement living space? Is there enough built-in storage? Check if your budget can accommodate custom built-ins, furniture scaled to the square footage, or room-expanding pieces. Working with a small space delivers challenges, bonuses, and endless choices. What will you make of your small house?

in this section

Sweet simplicity

Transform a small house into a country cottage that honors simplicity by contrasting rustic and refined elements—all in neutral shades. A no-fuss plan like this requires design discipline. Here's how to decorate with restraint.

- **Work with the house you have.** While it would be difficult to turn a tiny farmhouse into a modern space, a small rustic home serves as the perfect starting point for a cottage look.
- **Repeat materials and finishes.** Floors painted in semigloss white, walls painted in a white satin finish, and furniture treated to white matte paint illustrate how the same paint color can vary depending on its sheen. Floors throughout are made from ½-inch sanded plywood, cut into 8-inch-wide planks, and nailed to the floor. The planks are spaced the width of a quarter apart for an old-fashioned effect.
- **Plan for comfort.** Wraparound wicker chairs encourage diners to linger at the table while a slipcovered sofa and chairs invite long conversations in the living room. Small rolled arms create a silhouette of comfort without hogging space. The dining room chairs can move to the living room to accommodate after-dinner guests.
- **Create a neutral palette.** Fabrics range from natural linen to pure white cotton. Colors—off-white, white, cream, and khaki—blend. A touch of black adds accent. Accessories in clear glass and white china support the palette.

A sisal rug anchors the all-white scheme with texture and subtle color. The matching sofa and chairs add comfort while the centered coffee table eliminates the need for a table by each seat.

Worth noting

Embrace the concept of less can be more. A small house requires fewer pieces of furniture and simpler accessories. It also takes less time to clean.

• **Embrace the light.** White paint and fabrics, bare windows, and shiny surfaces spread sunshine around. Lamps, sconces, and ceiling lights brighten the night.

• **Save money by uniting a mishmash** of flea market furniture with white paint and neutral fabrics. Even the headboard sports a slipcover of linen gauze.

• **Build storage into every room.** It's the real secret behind livable small houses. For starters look for spaces to adapt for storage, such as the area under a staircase or an alcove in a room.

• **Accessorize in moderation.** Opt for accessories that are clear or in tune with the color palette. Add only a few pieces in a contrasting hue.

• **Look for furniture** with interesting details and pieces that work overtime. A French-style coffee table has just enough curves to look smart dressed in white. Benches work perfectly for sitting or for stacking items. An old table can be a desk or a nightstand.

• **Add playful touches.** A paper lantern over the kitchen island, glass canisters, and ball fringe on a bathroom shelf establish decorating focal points.

Opposite: Open shelves and a minimum of cabinetry keep the kitchen open and bright. An island separates the kitchen from the traffic flow and triples the counterspace. The dining room, now open to the kitchen, creates the biggest room in this bright little house.

Left: Open shelves store white dinnerware and clear glass containers. Colored objects would destroy the simplicity of this look. On the lower cabinets shelves are outfitted with metal bins that echo the tones of the stainless-steel appliances.

Face space shortages with a plan.

- **Clear clutter** before decorating. That will help you see the space.
- **Evaluate light quality.** A brighter space will feel larger, so opt for window coverings that can be pulled out of the way, colors that spread light, and light fixtures with dimmers.
- **Develop color palettes** that flow from room to room. This space-expanding strategy will yield a cohesive look. Use the same materials, such as wood floors and window shutters, to ease transitions between rooms.
- **Plan for storage** and choose mostly closed storage to minimize clutter and maintain a calm look. Consider hanging draperies a foot out from a wall and tucking floor-to-ceiling bookcases behind them. Snuggle storage boxes under a window for an instant window seat.
- **Arrange furniture** to take in views and expand visual space.
- **Keep traffic flowing.** Arrange furniture so traffic can move through a room in a variety of ways. Draw a floor plan to take along when you shop for furniture. It will help you avoid costly mistakes.

Opposite: A see-through gauze slipcover and a matching dust ruffle freshen and lighten the bed. A corner cabinet offers storage without blocking traffic flow. **Right:** An open bookcase keeps bathroom supplies handy while fabric panels tacked to the shelves provide hidden storage.

Above: A linen skirt gives the original sink a soft, updated look. The shelf is trimmed with ball fringe for a flirty detail, and a large mirror reflects space and light.

Shipshape style

Draw inspiration from a small house that's as tidy and shipshape as a cabin cruiser. Small-space tricks make it as livable as it is handsome while affordable materials spare the checkbook. Here's how it rides the waves.

- **Build on neutrals.** Birch and Baltic birch plywood set the color scheme of warm neutrals played against lots of white with touches of orange, yellow, and green. The colors flow through every room in the house, a smart strategy that helps small rooms suit up for the same team.
- **Watch the budget.** A clever use of materials suits a tight budget, often a component of redoing a small house. This house includes kitchen and dining-area flooring made from pine plywood cut into squares, laid in alternating grain directions for a subtle checkerboard effect, and whitewashed. The tongue-and-groove wainscoting on the living room walls is medium-density fiberboard with horizontal grooves routed every 8 inches. The frosted-glass doors of the kitchen cabinets are acrylic plastic roughed up with sandpaper. In the bath pine lattice strips installed horizontally on the tub wall give the feeling of an outdoor shower. And plywood is the budget-wise material used for cabinetry and furniture.
- **Rethink spaces.** Having four small bedrooms in this tiny house made little sense. Removing a wall opened up one of the bedrooms to the kitchen and made way for a dining area.

Above: An entry console occupies only a slice of space and provides a handy surface for setting packages. Closed storage below takes pressure off the entry closet.

Opposite: Color adds a surprising pop to the neutral scheme. Painting the ductwork bright green contributes to the young attitude of the space. The walls are covered in medium-density fiberboard (MDF), routed every 8 inches to create strong horizontal lines.

Left: Cubbies and cabinet doors inset with acrylic plastic panels give the kitchen cabinets sleek style. Keeping countertops and cabinetry in the same neutral material maintains an open and bright feeling. A tower of grooved fiberboard corrals the refrigerator.

- **Scale furniture to the room size.** The two-column entry table occupies only a slice of space, while the media cabinet comes in three pieces that can be assembled to suit a variety of uses. Thin legs on side tables and chairs preserve visual space. Bookcases and closets tuck back into stud spaces.
- **Seek out storage spaces.** A sideboard includes open cubbies for dishes near the table. Side tables, nightstands, and the coffee table include handy shelves for storing gear.
- **Make outdoor areas into fair-weather living space.** It might be as simple as hanging fabric panels to create "walls" on a front porch and furnishing the area with seating and dining pieces. For ample seating consider lining a deck with wraparound benches. One or two small tables can cater to guests when the weather is good.
- **Dress windows in matching treatments.** Tab-top curtains pair with narrow blinds for sun control that's tailored and effective.

Above: Once a fourth bedroom, this dining area opens to the kitchen. Birch plywood covers the tabletop and frames favorite photos on the wall. In a small space, opt for slender legs on tables and chairs to preserve space.
Right: The sideboard in the dining area offers graceful curves and a shelf for storing dishes.

Worth noting

Separating rooms with French doors magnifies light and makes both rooms seem bigger. Using a French door between inside and out blurs the connection and makes a small house live larger.

Left: Pine lattice strips installed horizontally over oriented strand board and coated in marine-quality paint add texture and style to the tub area.

Above: Birch doors make the bedroom closet look like a fine piece of furniture. The back of the closet bumps into the adjoining room to preserve a comfortable walkway in the small bedroom.

Opposite: The slatted headboard slopes slightly for reading in bed. Soft tones of yellow, green, and orange repeat the colors in the living room. Tab-top curtains and blinds soften the windows.

Here's how the pros use design elements in small spaces.

- **Limit pattern.** Too much pattern can make a room feel frantic. Select patterns in a two- or three-color palette to keep the look cohesive. For a calming effect select patterns in neutral tones. Use texture instead of pattern to add interest.
- **Experiment with palettes.** Light colors can make a space feel open and airy. Dark colors can blur the sharp corners of a room and give the illusion of more space. Choose whichever look you like.
- **Think big.** A single oversize object, such as a four-poster bed in a small bedroom, can make a room feel grand. Too many pieces of small furniture can make a room feel small.
- **Mix scale.** Pair an oversize sofa with petite chairs, for example, to help a space feel larger.
- **Reflect the glow.** Consider reflective finishes, such as metals and glossy paint, to spread light.
- **Build volume** to make up for a lack of square footage. Add apparent height by using crown molding or hanging window treatments at the top of the walls. Avoid drop ceilings.

Above: Built in 1910, this worker's cottage features two rooms up and two rooms down.
Left: No entry closet? Make a stylish one in the small space at the bottom of the steps by hanging hooks in a row.

living Large

Eliminate room labels and style constraints to expand the livability of a small house. By building on a cohesive color theme and adding dressy details to every room, even the kitchen, you'll soon be living it up. Here's how.

- **Select a color plan.** Two rooms up and two rooms down requires color consistency. The top floor features a cool gray, while the downstairs is painted warm gray. Using the same wall colors helps a small house feel and live larger.
- **Inject dashes of color.** The upstairs bathroom is an eye-popping shade of yellow, a memorable choice that adds a fun note. The same color repeats on the bed linens. A green love seat in the den, a red table in the living room, and blue draperies in the kitchen add more color. Mixing up the colors of furniture and accessories keeps design boredom at bay and opens the way for quick, easy changes.
- **Make a statement.** Swaths of bold-patterned curtains accentuate the 9-foot ceilings while a bust of Diana takes center stage in front of the nonworking fireplace.

Painting a square of light gray above the fireplace mantel accents the wall and calls attention to the intricate mirror. A pair of coffee tables can be used together or pulled to other spots in the room.

Opposite: Bold patterns in brown and white add interest to the living room. The overscale Moorish rug pattern repeats the same hues. A clear side table is a small-space knockout that delivers style without hogging visual space.
Left: A sofa with modern lines and sink-in comfort anchors the living room. A small table of dining table height can be called into use when a party expands beyond the kitchen table.
Below: Simple molding on the edges of the kitchen shelves adds a dressy note.

- **Blend vintage and new.** The classic shapes of French-style chairs and ornate mirrors blend with cube-shape plastic tables and modern chairs. The combinations feel grounded in design history, but they embrace the trend of mixing vintage and modern.
- **Rethink room labels.** In a house without a formal dining room, the kitchen has to dress up for entertaining. Here, going dressy means painting cabinetry to match the walls, topping one section of cabinetry with honed black granite, adding open shelves to mimic the look of a handsome hutch, draping the window from floor to ceiling in a polished-cotton print, snuggling a Victorian cabinet near the table, and hanging an ornate mirror over a counter.
- **Be inventive to spare the budget.** Cotton bedspreads cut in half and secured with clip rings serve as living room draperies. Electrical conduit and threaded rods replace expensive drapery hardware. Furniture from big box stores mingles with vintage finds.

Below left: The kitchen dining area is dressy enough for company and stylish for everyday use—perfect for a home that lacks a formal dining space. Leaves expand the table to cozily seat up to 10.

Below right: Style and function meet head-on in the kitchen, where an upholstered French chair contrasts with walls of cabinetry.

Opposite: Painting kitchen cabinetry the same color as the walls helps it blend into the background during dinner parties, when the pendent fixture softly glows. Eliminating some upper cabinetry and adding an ornate mirror amplifies the style of the space.

- **Showcase collections.** Edit collections and combine them to create character-filled rooms. A selection of black and white prints creates a vertical focal point in the bedroom, while silver, ironstone, sea shells, and wood stack up on the kitchen shelves.
- **Mix it up with lighting.** A metal shade from a trouble-light serves as a kitchen light fixture in front of the mirror. A pair of desk lamps provides lighting by the range. Vintage crystal chandeliers light the bedroom and the landing at the top of the stairs, while a modern plastic shade adds style punch to the bathroom. The light fixtures repeat the same blend of vintage and new that reflects the style of the house.
- **Decorate with mirrors.** Mirrors expand light and views and add immediate style. Note the ornate rectangular mirror hanging over the kitchen countertop and the circular mirror centered above the fireplace.

Worth noting

Light is as much a decorating material as color and texture, and in a small house it delivers the illusion of extra square footage. Mirrors, metal, glass, glossy paint, and ceramic tile all reflect light.

Decorate with an eye toward size.

- **Balance size and function.** When selecting furniture consider armless chairs, slim sofas, nesting tables, and drop-leaf tables.
- **Use transparent furniture.** A glass-top table, for example, adds function that's almost invisible. Lamps with glass bases and glass cabinet doors visually expand space.
- **Show a little leg.** Unskirted furniture adds the illusion of depth and expands apparent floor space.
- **Incorporate mirrors** to double pretty views and sunlight. Consider a floor-to-ceiling model in a dining room and a collection on a hallway wall.
- **Add double-duty furniture.** Scootable ottomans offer seating and storage. A sofa table can work as a desk or serve up a buffet.
- **Use shallow wall shelves** for art display and to hold keys and sunglasses by the door. A row of hooks can become an instant closet.
- **Trade in oversize electronics** for a slim television and a digital music player.
- **Choose art strategically.** Consider a landscape painting with a definite horizon line that gives an illusion of depth.

Opposite: A 3-yard piece of decorator fabric purchased at a discount fabric store showcases one way to gain big style with a small splurge. The fabric wraps around the mattress and tucks under the duvet. White draperies edged in black twill tape soften the windows. Lined in room-darkening fabric, they also control light.

Above: Curves and rectangles offer pleasing contrast above a buffet that now serves as a dresser.

Right: Bathroom style can be as simple as painting walls a bright color, adding shelves to hold cosmetics, and draping towels from a row of hooks.

Small-Scale dining

Many homes have rooms that measure only 9×9 feet. A tiny space can be more than a child's bedroom. Here's how to adapt a small, boxy room for dining or working.

- **Opt for a color scheme** that's built on the use of white plus one dynamite shade, such as this sunny yellow. Touches of its complement—magenta—add energy without overpowering.
- **Paint horizontal stripes** encircling the room. Position an extra-wide white stripe around the center of the room to make the space feel bigger.
- **Scale furniture to fit.** Classic chairs scaled to fit snuggle up to a fabric-covered table. Either drape a table or cut plywood to the perfect tabletop size before draping it with fabric.
- **Simplify window treatments.** Wood shutters set within the window frame preserve room space. Curtain panels add a soft layer of color and texture.
- **Edit accessories to a chosen few.** Colored glassware holds a few blooms rather than full bouquets.

Worth noting

Window treatments do more than cover windows; they can expand their apparent size. Leave as much window exposed as possible and install curtains so they hang over adjacent walls instead of over the glass.

Organize for homework

- **Go neutral.** Neutrals blend with ease and settle into the background to make a space feel larger.
- **Get cozy.** A toile fabric with plenty of white space drapes the window and wraps all the walls. Blurring the edges of the room makes it seem larger while the draped fabric hides the boxiness.
- **Plan the space.** Built-in cabinets stretch from wall to wall and from the windowsill to the floor. A new parsons-style desk butts against the cabinet, making space for two students. The cabinet top supports two desk lamps. Custom furniture is a worthwhile investment in a small room because it can be designed to use every inch of space.
- **Create storage.** A clutter-free desktop makes a room feel larger, so plan space for built-ins or a closet where office extras can hide until they're needed.

Viola

Storage
for cleaned-up style

chapter 21

Storage space is like money—most people want more. However, more space may not be the answer; keeping clutter in its place might be as simple as customizing an existing closet or gathering all the media equipment into one spot. Solving storage problems and organizing your stuff frees time for activities that enrich your life. Is clutter driving you crazy? Are you always asking, “Where does this go?” Do you need to sort out and reduce your possessions? Do you have an underused closet or cabinet that can store more? Are your DVDs, toys, or clothing spread all around the house? The challenges are apparent. Now it’s time to sort through your options.

in this section

Confront the "big black eye"

by considering how you want to store the television. For some that may mean placing the TV in view on a rolling cabinet or on a built-in bookcase. Others may want to hide it. Whichever option you choose, you'll need storage nearby for media gear. Before shopping measure your TV; not all storage units are deep enough to hold big TVs.

1. For show-and-tell

New streamlined televisions and sleek audio and video components beg to be displayed rather than hidden away. Opt for a low and modern cabinet to keep almost everything within view. Use covered boxes for hidden storage.

2. For media under wraps

Create a hideaway spot for a television to maintain the serenity of a bedroom. This built-in bumps out above the fireplace and features paneled doors that swing open.

3. For art that works

In a family room the television hides behind a piece of art that splits down the middle into two doors. Molding applied to the wall frames the painting and provides support for hinges attached to the artwork doors. Birch plywood offers an easy-to-paint surface and strength for use as doors.

4. For thinking outside the box

Mixing open and closed storage makes sense when it's time to build an entertainment center. Colorful rectangles create a stylish grid that keeps the television within view and includes closed storage only inches away for stacks of DVDs and CDs.

5. For a focal point

Big-screen TV has replaced the hearth as a focal point, and it needs cabinetry to suit its status. Shelves surround the screen, glass-front doors protect electronics, and drawers hide clutter.

6. For vintage appeal

Craftsman-style cabinetry offers a classic hideaway for media gear. Choose cabinetry—stock, semicustom, and custom—with solid doors and drawers that allow you to quickly clear clutter and keep it hidden.

3
5

4
PHOTOREALISM

6
NEW CITY HOME
ALSACE
POLAND

Revamp unfinished furniture

into storage that suits your style. These unfinished armoires—one designed for clothing and the other intended as a computer cabinet—offer tons of storage space and strong construction. Pieces from a thrift store also can be adapted for storage using some of these clever ideas.

Hobby haven

Packed with art and sewing supplies, this double-wide armoire satisfies a passion for projects.

- **Dress up the exterior**

The exterior update includes a sunny shade of yellow paint over the frame and sides. Embossed wallpaper adds texture to the recessed door panels; blue paint gives it a refreshing finish. New silver knobs replace the dull brass ones that came with the armoire.

- **Make the interior work harder**

The interior, which features a pullout desk area, drawers, and cubbies, suits its new use as a crafts and sewing cabinet. Painted in the same sunny yellow, it provides a bright spot for crafting. To customize it even further, add covered plastic jars, mesh bins, and plastic containers to keep supplies handy and neat. The doors offer lots of square footage for supplies. Outfit them with curtain rods and brackets to hold ribbons. Add metal panels that hold magnetic clips and install corkboard squares outfitted with cup hooks for holding supplies.

Before

After

Before

After

Potting shed

An armoire built for storing clothing becomes a gardener's potting shed.

• Dress up the exterior

Exterior alterations hint at the new job this piece has taken. The top panel on each door has given way to wire fencing that is stapled in place. A wood shelf for baskets replaces the top drawer. The finish includes a base coat of apple red paint and a top coat of spring green. Sanding the edges gives the armoire a pleasing weathered look and lets a bit of the red paint show through. New metal pulls that look like miniature garden tools replace standard wood knobs.

• Make the interior work harder

The inner part of the top area is lined with perforated hardboard and wears the same paint finish as the exterior. A new stainless-steel shelf provides a potting surface. Loop-style hooks inserted into the perforated hardboard provide flexible tool storage. A canvas shoe holder, revamped with hooks, offers handy storage for garden tools. The bottom section lifts off its hooks and can be tied around the waist to easily transport tools to the garden. Metal bins hold soil mixes, and paper towels are handy above the potting shelf.

Dressy enough for the living room, this cabinet, below, adds flavor to kitchen storage. Neatness counts when storage is in full view, so organize copper pots, rattan baskets, and extra foods in a handsome cabinet. Because the doors slide it's an ideal piece for a kitchen hall or dining area with no room for a swinging door. The honey-tone finish provides a background with minimal contrast to the contents. To include some hidden storage, consider applying a frosted or patterned window film on the lower doors. These films are available in adhesive-back or static-cling versions. Look for them using an online search engine.

A long and lean cabinet, below, slips into a sliver of space and bulks up on storage. Consider the design of a potential storage piece to determine its best use. The open top of this classic cabinet showcases a collection of barware while the lower shelves, just out of view, provide storage for bar supplies. Adjust shelves to add function. Here, one shelf allows enough vertical space for a basket filled with bottles. The black interior provides a dramatic backdrop for sparkling crystal stemware and tumblers.

Use these storage ideas.

- **Skirt a table** to make hidden storage underneath. This strategy works for a dressing table or dining table. Add casters to the bottom of baskets and slide them in and out with ease.
- **Tuck a storage piece** in the space underneath a staircase. If you have extra room, add storage components that stack to mimic the shape of the stairs.
- **Build up.** Stretch shelves above a desk or install a long shelf at door height in an entry corridor.
- **Raise the bed and tuck** built-in or ready-made storage underneath. Look for premade bed risers at bed-and-bath superstores.
- **Place a screen** in the corner of a room and stack clearly marked boxes behind it. Screens also make rooms feel cozy.
- **Stack oversize books** to make a side table and free some bookcase space at the same time.

A closet is a closet, right?

Think again. It can be an office, a china closet, or even a special space that turns a bedroom into a guest room. Put preconceived notions aside, consider your storage needs, and face that standard storage space with imagination. Here are a few ideas to fuel a redo.

Below: Wood bifold doors transform a standard closet into one fit for fine china. To dress up ordinary doors, use this technique: Glue and nail willow branches and pinecones to the doors. Use garden shears to snip the branches and a crafts knife to angle them to fit at the joints. New shelves painted white provide storage and display space inside the closet.

Above: A once dark and dreary closet works like new thanks to a fresh color scheme and some thoughtful features, such as a towel rack and message board that are perfect for guests. The chocolate brown and white scheme started with the dressy wallpaper. Storage boxes hold extra towels and blankets. New vintage-style leather pulls look like handles from an old trunk.

Opposite: Painted mint green, this freestanding storage closet serves as a handy baking center. The closet interior and shelves are lined with oilcloth for wipe-clean ease—a must for smart food storage. Magnetic strips and clips display recipe cards and shopping lists to inspire the cook and keep favorite recipes hidden in plain sight. Cup hooks can hold a measuring cup or utensils. Jars store baking staples, and large bags of sugar and flour hide inside lidded cans on the bottom shelf.

Worth noting

Storage space works best if you regularly sort through your belongings. Schedule an annual "sort-save-donate-pitch day" to reduce clutter. Refrain from adding space to store items you no longer use or want.

made to measure

Use these standard measurements to help configure clothing storage.

- **Blouses**—30 to 36 inches long/hanging
- **Shirts**—34 to 40 inches long/hanging
- **Dresses**—48 to 66 inches long/hanging
- **Skirts**—34 to 44 inches long/hanging
- **Pants**—28 to 32 inches long/folded for hanging
- **Suit jacket**—32 to 48 inches long/hanging
- **Coats**—48 to 66 inches long/hanging
- **Rod space per item**—1 inch for blouses, 2 inches for suits, 3 inches for coats
- **Shelves for shoes**—7 inches of width for a pair of women's shoes and 9 inches for men's
- **Shelves for folded clothing**—vertical space of 12 inches
- **Shelves for clothing storage boxes**—at least 14 inches deep with varying widths

Add a little personality

to a plain bookcase to make it work in one of three ways. Here's how to sort out the options.

1. Board-and-batten shutters with diamond cutouts offer hideaway storage that's perfect in any room. The shutters are attached to the bookcase with cabinetry hinges. Tan paint inside and out provides a soothing finish. For easy care use semigloss paint, sanding lightly between coats.

Before

2. A linen roller shade looks handsome when pulled only partway down, but it springs into action to completely cover the bookcase when shelves are messy. Order the shade custom-made to fit the opening. Ebony gel stain lends a modern look and contrasts with the linen shade. Polyurethane protects the finish.

Worth noting

Check that freestanding storage is securely installed to prevent tipping. For a unit on a shallow base, screw through the back of the unit and into wall studs to anchor it in place. Store heavy objects below shoulder height.

3. A coat of cream paint and a pretty wallpaper in eggshell and blue soften the basic lines of the "before" bookcase. The shelves on top provide display space for books and collections. A linen curtain hanging on a tension rod conceals storage in the bottom of the unit.

Style shortcuts

for fuss-free changes

chapter 22

Even when time is tight, style can squeeze into your everyday lifestyle. Learn how to make quick and easy changes to welcome guests or to change your home with the seasons. Before you get started, ask these questions: What skills do you have? Can you sew, saw, or draw? Do you have a garden filled with flowers? Would you spend a day making seasonal changes or only work for an hour or two? Can you spare a few dollars to buy flowers or trims? Now make a list of the projects you'd like to do. Consider your skills and budget as you decide which project to tackle first. Then jump in and be creative.

in this section

Plucked from

a store shelf, ready-made curtains, dishes, and frames provide the raw material for a quick makeover.

1. For a fast frame-up

Note cards make supersimple mats for photos. Use a crafts knife and straightedge to cut the center out of the note card; then tape a photo inside the mat opening. Slip into a purchased frame.

2. For party fare

Duplicate a favorite pattern to make temporary designs on basic white dishes. Peel-and-stick sign-making vinyl from a sign-making or office-supply store provides the colorful material. Transfer the design to the vinyl, cut it out, peel off the backing, dip the decal in water, "float" the design into place, and rub with a soft cloth to secure. The dishes can be handwashed while the vinyl is in place. When the party is over, peel and toss the design.

3. For having a ball

Glue wooden balls in one or two sizes (from ½ inch to 1½ inches in diameter) around a mirror frame. Working from the inside out, attach the balls using adhesive suited for wood and the frame material. Spray the completed frame with several coats of paint.

4. For a dressy chandelier

Freshen a chandelier with new lampshades. Use a lampshade kit that includes a fabric template and an adhesive-coated shade. Add ball or bead fringe.

5. For pillow personality

Enhance a store-bought pillow by stitching beads on a starburst design. Or apply a running stitch in a random pattern using embroidery floss. Finding the right pillow to embellish will be the most time-consuming part.

6. For a one-of-a-kind table

Dress up a plain tablecloth with a painted stencil. Thin acrylic paint with textile medium. Dab the paint over the stencil; remove. Use a metallic paint pen to create squiggles around the flower centers. Follow care instructions on the paint for washing and ironing.

1

2

3

4

5

Experiment with these ideas for personalizing store-bought items.

- **Tack or stitch contrasting braid** in a curlicue or letter design on the center of a pillow.
- **Turn a pillowcase into a sham** by stitching ribbon ties to the open end.
- **Edge the cuff of a top sheet** or pillowcase with a row of buttons, ribbon bows, or beads.
- **Punctuate a plain pillow top** with two special buttons that dent the center, front and back.
- **Create a reversible place mat** by stitching buttons and two mats together at the corners.
- **Stitch or glue ribbon** to a center spot on a napkin, where it can be used as a permanent napkin tie.
- **Adhere fusible appliqués** to napkins, tablecloths, or place mats.
- **Make a runner** from several place mats connected in a line with ribbon strips or buttons and loops.

Company's coming

Use time before guests' arrival to create a special welcome.

1. Set the table

An outdoor location provides the perfect atmosphere for a leisurely breakfast. Find a spot under a backyard tree or on the front porch. Make it special by moving indoor furniture out and suspending candle lanterns over the length of the table. Gather alliums from the garden for a centerpiece.

2. Accent the front door

Oversize numbers have been popping up everywhere. Bring that playful attitude to your house number with this fair-weather idea. Use outdoor crafts paint to create big numbers on purchased throw pillows; toss them on the bench next to your front door. Your guests will know they have arrived.

3. Dress the bed

Layers of bedding and stacks of pillows provide all the comfort a guest could desire. If you assemble pretty combinations, guests can decide how many layers they need for warmth and how many pillows they want for sleeping or lounging. Colorful pairings make the bed the center of attention.

4. Get ready for breakfast

A breakfast tray is the ultimate luxury when it's filled with a simple breakfast and a great cup of coffee. If your guests aren't interested in breakfast in bed, use the same idea to create a snack tray for late-night noshing.

5. Perk up the bathroom

Organize bathroom supplies so it's easy for guests to find what they need. Trays and compotes can serve up towels and toiletries. Play up a black-and-white color scheme, or add accents of hot pink and orange.

2

3

1

4

Add guest-pleasing extras.

- **Fill a basket** with a collection of books. Tuck notes in the books so guests can read your reviews.
- **Match a vase** to the color scheme of the room by stretching grosgrain ribbon around the vase and taping it in place on the back.
- **Celebrate the seasons** with nature's bounty. In winter fill a basket with pinecones. Replace the pinecones with shells in summer, leaves in fall, and tulips in spring.
- **Incorporate a bench** that can hold an open suitcase or a lounging guest.
- **Customize lighting** by plugging lamps into an in-line dimmer. It takes only seconds to complete this task.

Wardrobes change with the seasons. Why not make seasonal changes to a favorite room as well? For inspiration check out the fun ideas that give this dining room four distinct seasonal looks.

Spring

A just-washed window and bouquets of spring-blooming peonies give this dining room a bright outlook. Other fresh fix-ups include adding a pastel wreath to the front door and replacing entry seating with a garden bench.

Summer

Warm weather arrives with a party attitude. Fill a bucket with sand and stick Chinese lanterns in the bucket. The color palette warms up with red flowers. Consider rolling up area rugs and storing them under the bed, moving furniture to take advantage of garden views, and removing window coverings except where needed for privacy.

spring

summer

Fall

Cool weather signals a return to the hearth and candlelight. Woodsy textures and warm earthtones fill the table. Candlelight offers a golden glow. To get ready for fall, gather seating pieces around the hearth, create instant glow with glass votives nestled among logs in the fireplace, and gather colorful leaves on branches to fill a rustic container.

Winter

Winter blows in on a cold wind and leaves behind frosty glass and a snow-inspired table covering. Candles add warmth until the temperature takes another plunge. Then it's time to tuck throws around upholstered furniture as quick and cozy slipcovers. Layer two rugs on the floor, and while you're at it, throw another blanket, quilt, or duvet on the bed.

Cut blooms

and grasses instantly decorate any room. Use a few affordable blooms rather than buying an expensive armful. Look for inexpensive blooms at the grocery store or in your backyard.

1. Supermarket flowers

Dyed daisies and mums fill the bins at most grocery stores. To give them style cut only a few blooms and place them in a random pattern in sake cups. The plastic platter picks up the tones of the flowers. If the flower is playful, make the composition fun as well.

2. White roses

A narrow shelf showcases a stylish way to display three, four, or more white roses in inkwells. Stretching a dozen roses along a wall-hung shelf creates a more dramatic effect than one big vase of roses.

3. Fresh-picked grass

Creating a centerpiece for an outdoor meal is as simple as clipping a few strands of grass from along the fence. Long blades of grass fill glass vases while other strands wrap around the napkins to create a fresh table setting.

4. Gladiolus bouquets

Several small vases filled with gladiolus stocks illustrate the impact of displaying one type of flower in one color. The dramatic red blooms contrast with the white vases. White gladioli in white vases would create a dramatic but different effect.

5. Trio of poppies

Poppies clipped from a garden bed add a pop of color that coordinates with the vase.

6. Hosta leaves

Bold and bountiful, hosta leaves fill a vase with lush green. These leaves also look good as a collar around colorful blooms.

7. Agapanthus blooms

Delicate and strong, agapanthus blooms look almost architectural gathered in a modern vase. These blooms last longer than many cut flowers and single blooms can be displayed for powerful effect.

7

Small projects offer smart solutions while you're building up cash reserves for a big project. Start changing the state of your house now with one of these ideas.

1. Stencil a pattern

Embellish like an artist by dabbing paint over precut stencils. For an easy project create a vertical striped design to highlight a wall. With oversize stencils and a foam roller, a project like this can be completed in less than 30 minutes.

2. Add color with glass

Give a room a shot of seasonal color by massing a collection of glass on a table or windowsill. Take a shopping trip through your house with color or shape in mind. Bring all the pieces to one location to make a design statement.

3. Define an area with paint

A surprising mix of color calls attention to the architecture around the front door and to the door itself. Using unexpected colors in a small entry adds to its importance. Consider other ways to define with paint: creating blocks of color in a long, narrow room, visually raising a ceiling by painting a border around the ceiling/wall edge, and shortening a too-tall room with a wainscot painted darker than the upper walls.

4. Build a stylish bar

A trunk and a colorful tray provide the basis for a portable bar. Use vintage bottles and decanters for character, a throw for color, and a mirror as a reflective backdrop.

Save money and add style using these ideas.

- **Splurge.** If you can't afford fabulous fabrics on everything, splurge on a small amount of silk or cut velvet for wonderful pillows.
- **Gather.** Use large groupings of candles to add fabulous light quality.
- **Collect.** Search for vintage blankets in less than perfect condition and use them to create pillows, curtains, or chair slipcovers.
- **Play.** Add utility and beauty with little tables. They're easy to move to wherever you need them and come in a variety of styles from ceramic to modern metal.
- **Celebrate.** Bring out the good china for occasional everyday meals.
- **Invent.** Consider new uses for everyday objects. Turn small stools into plant stands, stack books into side tables, and turn deep platters into vases for floating flowers.
- **Rearrange.** Move the sofa table to the foot of a bed, gather a series of benches for seating in the back entry, flip the living room furniture to the diagonal, and move a favorite chair so it cozies up to the fireplace.

Deciding what piece of furniture goes where

can leave anyone bewildered. The good news is that more than one furniture arrangement works in most rooms. So settle in and learn the basic principles before starting to move those heavy pieces.

Here are some tips to keep in mind:

- **Focus on the focal point.** The goal of any room arrangement is to create a simple grouping of furniture pieces that work toward the room's purposes—dining, sleeping, working, eating, and relaxing. Each room should have an architectural feature or dominant piece of furniture that creates the main focus around which all other pieces are oriented.
- **Direct traffic.** Pay attention to how people move through the room—and how you want them to move through the room. Eliminate traffic blockades by getting rid of extra furniture pieces that stand in the way. Create an easy path through the room without interrupting a conversation grouping or television viewing with traffic.
- **Make islands of comfort.** Tighten furniture into islands that serve well-defined purposes and carve out areas within a room. For example place a console table behind a sofa that sits at a right angle to a doorway, creating a back "wall" for a conversation group. An area rug also defines a furniture island. Or place a seating piece at the foot of the bed for extended bedroom comfort.
- **Think big.** Choose one or two significant pieces for each room to avoid the dollhouse look of too many small pieces. These pieces, along with strong architectural features such as a fireplace or a bank of windows, anchor a room.
- **Avoid whole room sets of furniture.** You'll be stuck with their stiff, inflexible arrangements. Acquire furniture one piece at a time, keeping it compatible in style with other furnishings in the house. Then you can move pieces from room to room as your decorating whims change.

Wall symbols + sofas, beds, and chairs

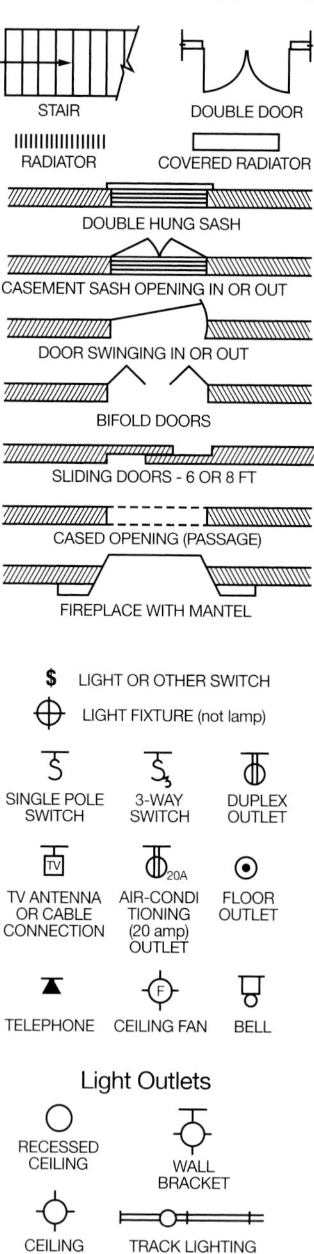

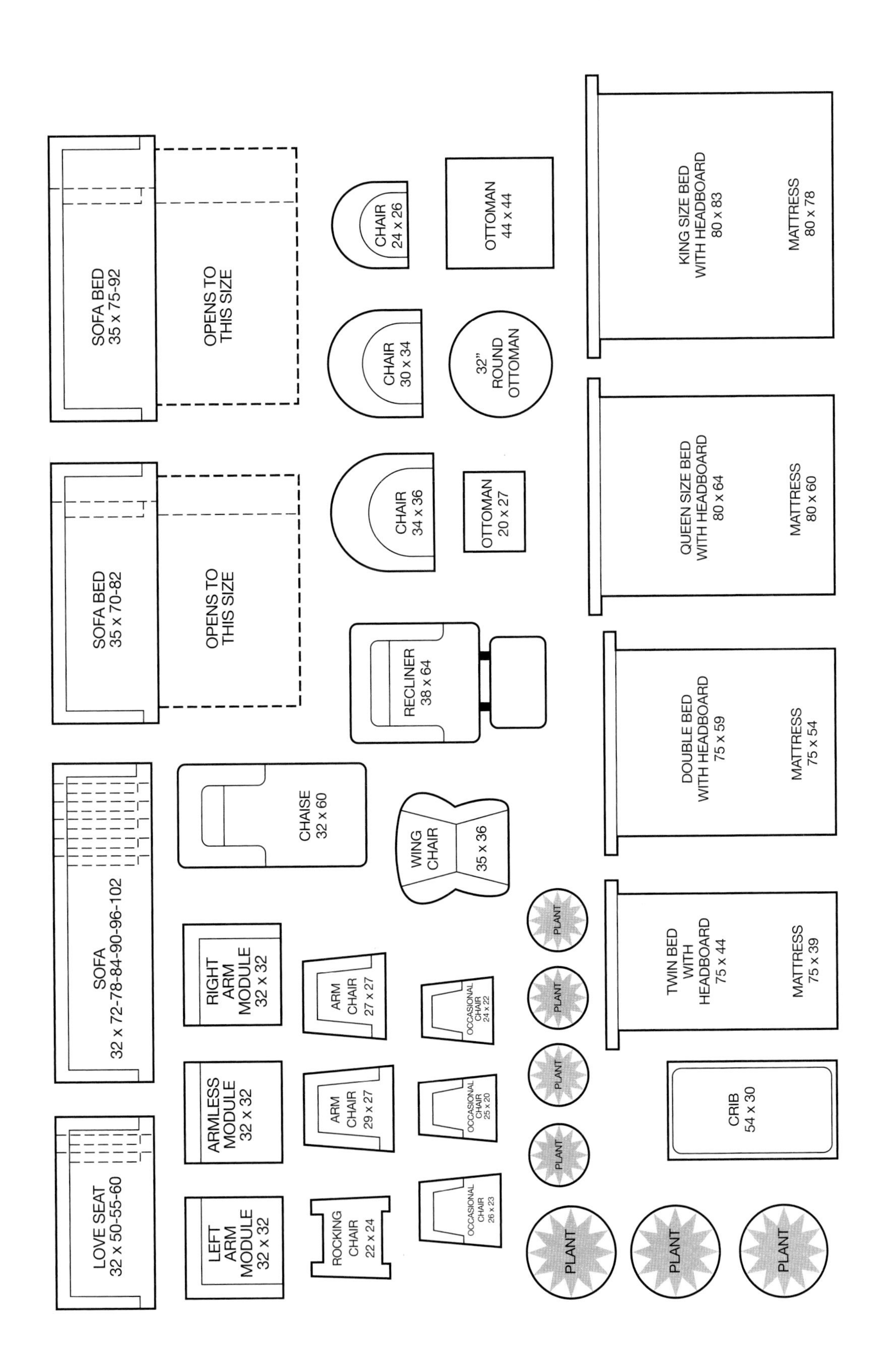

To start follow these steps.

1. Pull out the room floor plans you created earlier. (See Chapter 2).

2. Measure each furniture piece you plan to use. Photocopy the corresponding templates; cut out.

3. Find a focal point. Some are built-in, such as a fireplace or wall of windows. If your room doesn't have one, create it using a dramatic piece, such as an armoire.

4. Direct traffic. Use furniture to funnel traffic around conversation areas. Make sure traffic paths are at least 3 feet wide.

5. Use space creatively. Let furniture determine function. Flop the living area and dining space in an open floor plan, or use a dining area by the kitchen as a family room.

6. Add convenience. Make sure there are tables within reach of chairs, storage for electronic gear, and a place to sit in a bedroom.

7. Cozy up a big room. Break up space by splitting a large room.

8. Maximize a small room. Include a large-scale piece, such as an armoire, to create a focal point. Use built-in storage in tight spaces.

9. Disguise ceiling height. Raise a ceiling with tall furniture and lower too-high ceilings with a colorful rug.

Bookcases and cabinets + tables and chairs

There are plenty of options for furniture pieces in the templates, right. To provide even more flexibility, use the pieces with sizes and no labels to fill in on your floor plans. For example, if the bookcase or table sizes you want to use are not included as a labeled template, create your own using one of the sized boxes. Customize the cutout to match the shape of your piece if, for example, it has a curved or angled front. Or make your own template using the graph paper on page 427.

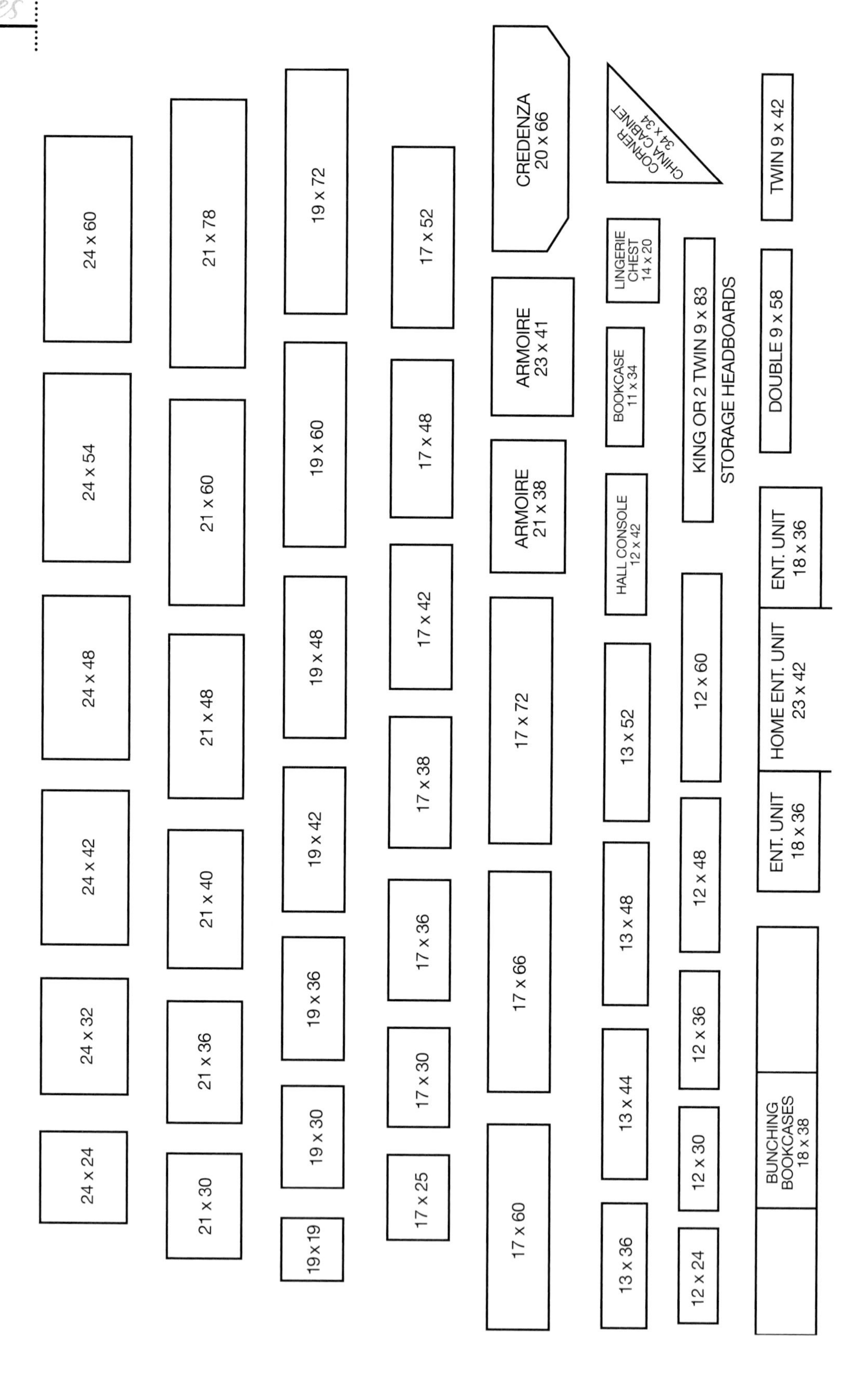

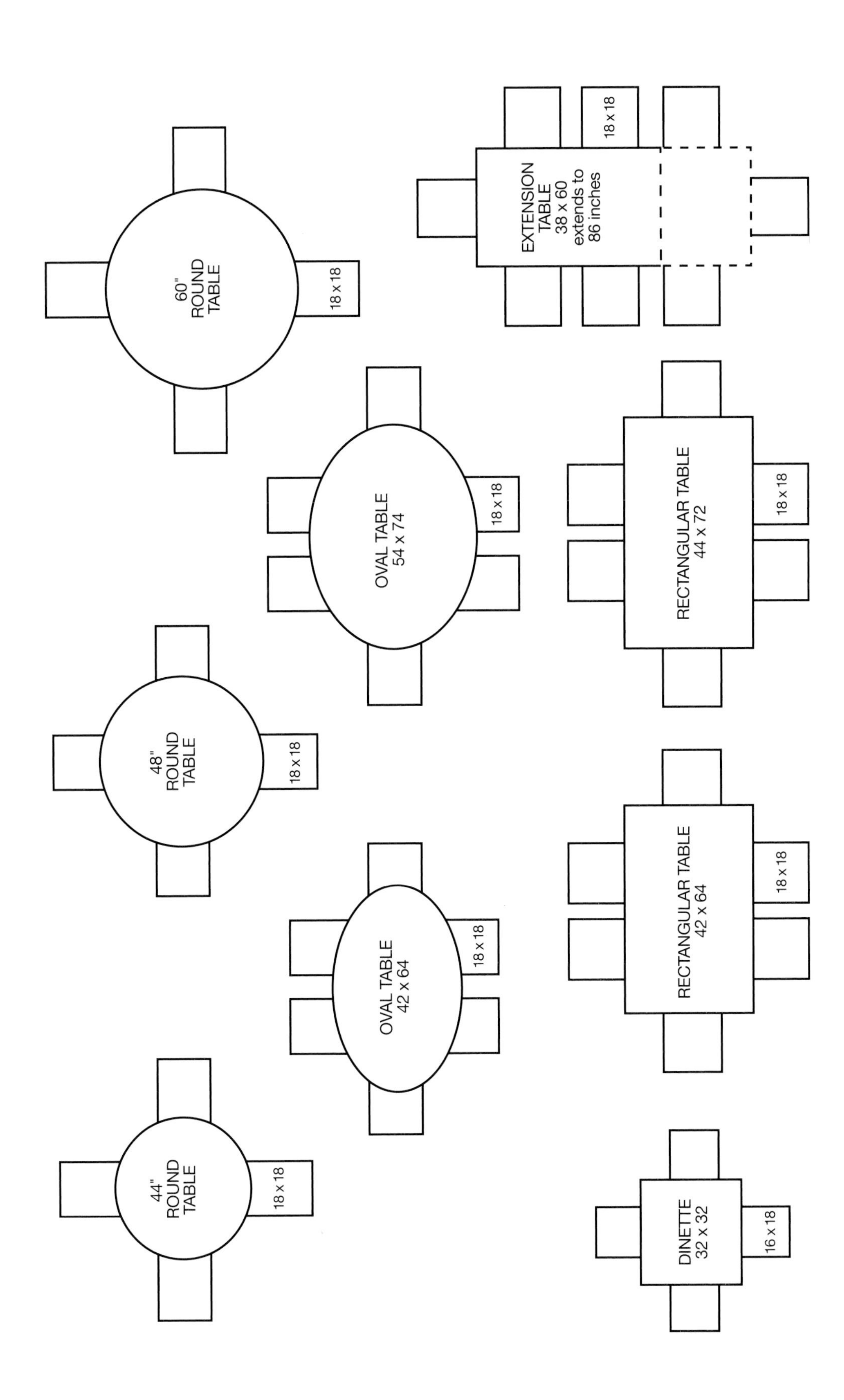

Not all rooms are created equal. Some come with built-in problems. Here are a few solutions.

- **Tunnel.** Dual-purpose living rooms and family rooms with single entrances can seem like tunnels. To give them a wide and spacious look, break up the length of the room with blocks of furniture. Place chairs and tables at angles, set a sofa crosswise, and use tables with curves for navigating ease.
- **Open plan.** One big open space may seem inviting until it's time to move furniture. Start by listing the ways you plan to use the room, then eliminate furniture pieces that aren't needed. Work the plan out on paper, creating separate areas in the space.
- **Corridor.** Directing foot traffic through the room is the main function of furniture arranging. Make sure traffic flows around—not through—conversation areas. Group chairs and sofas, guiding people to walk behind and along the area.
- **L-shape.** Homes built in the 1970s often include an L-shape plan that wraps around the kitchen. The open space can look too busy if small pieces fill the room. Keep furniture pieces at a minimum for a peaceful, relaxed look; leave pathways open.

Occasional pieces + graph paper

Graph paper and templates are the basic tools you'll need to create floor plans. Photocopy the graph paper, opposite, to use for your floor plans. It's crucial to use graph paper and templates that are created using the same size grid. If you want to use graph paper with a larger grid, enlarge the templates and the graph paper to the same scale by using a photocopier.

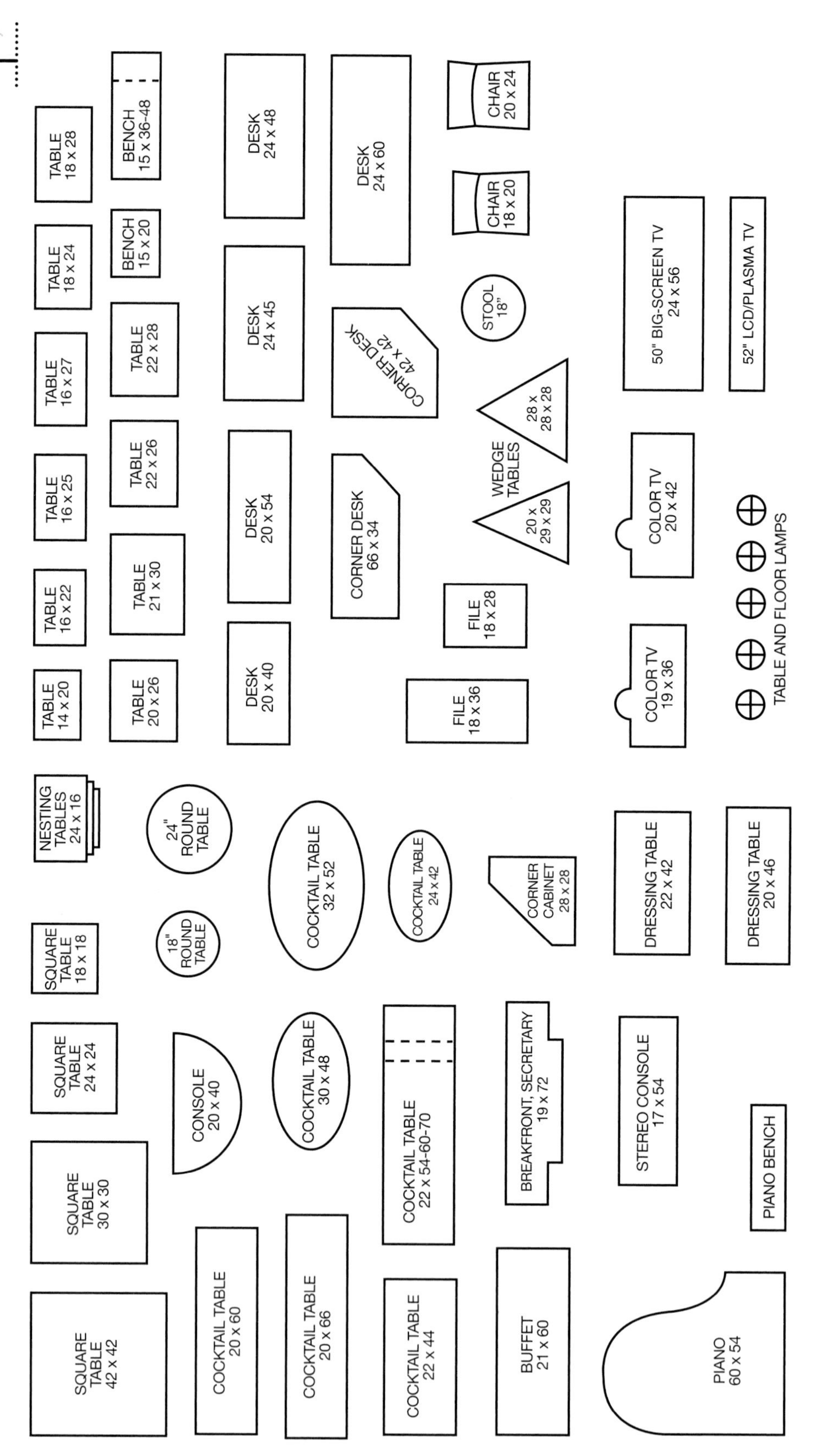

Index

Index